DOING THEOLOGY
IN A
DIVIDED WORLD

DOING THEOLOGY
IN A
DIVIDED WORLD

Papers from
the Sixth International Conference
of the Ecumenical Association of Third World Theologians,
January 5–13, 1983, Geneva, Switzerland

Edited by
Virginia Fabella and Sergio Torres

ORBIS BOOKS

Maryknoll, New York 10545

The Catholic Foreign Mission Society of America (Maryknoll) recruits and trains people for overseas missionary service. Through Orbis Books Maryknoll aims to foster the international dialogue that is essential to mission. The books published, however, reflect the opinions of their authors and are not meant to represent the official position of the society.

Manuscript Editor: William E. Jerman

Library of Congress Cataloging in Publication Data

Ecumenical Association of Third World Theologians.
   International Conference (6th : 1983 : Geneva,
   Switzerland)
   Doing theology in a divided world.

   Includes bibliographies.
   1. Theology—Methodology—Congresses.   I. Fabella,
Virginia.   II. Torres, Sergio.   III. Title.
BR118.E27   1983   230   84-14712
ISBN 0-88344-197-7 (pbk.)

Contents

PART III
ANALYSIS:
THE INTERRELATEDNESS OF OPPRESSION
AND EFFORTS FOR LIBERATION

PART IV
HISTORY OF THEOLOGY

PART V
REFORMULATION OF THE METHODOLOGY
AND CONTENT OF THEOLOGY

Sergio Torres

Preface

Orbis Books introduces this volume presenting the theological content of the Sixth International Conference of the Ecumenical Association of Third World Theologians (EATWOT). This conference was held in Geneva from January 5 to 13, 1983, and its title, "Doing Theology in a Divided World," recalls the difficult task of Christians to be witnesses of unity and reconciliation in a world where there are so many divisions.

The Geneva conference consisted of a dialogue between EATWOT members and First World theologians from Europe, the United States, and Canada. EATWOT had been working for many years in the development of contextual theologies relevant to the needs and concerns of Third World peoples. It had organized five intercontinental conferences where theologians from the Third World dialogued among themselves. In the fifth conference, in New Delhi in 1981, they examined the common trends of Third World theologies and felt it was time to share their discoveries with other theologians. They decided to initiate a dialogue with First World theologians. Subsequently EATWOT convened and organized the Geneva meeting that is reported in this volume.

THIRD WORLD THEOLOGIES AND WESTERN THEOLOGY

In the first conference of Third World theologians held in Dar es Salaam in 1976, the participants were compelled to define their relationship to the traditional theology they had received from Europe and North America, usually referred to as Western theology.

The general conclusion was that Western theology is inadequate for the Third World and irrelevant as the Christian interpretation of the gospel message for the peoples of underdeveloped countries. Through the years this conclusion has been confirmed. In the New Delhi conference, it was stated that Western theology "for the Third World . . . has been alienated and alienating. It has not provided the motivations for opposing the evils of racism, sexism, capitalism, colonialism, and neocolonialism. It has failed to understand our religions, indigenous cultures, and traditions, and to relate to them in a respectful way."[1]

The reason for this rejection of Western theology comes from an interpretation of theology as a "talking about God" in "context." Thus EATWOT members have stated: "Indeed we must, in order to be faithful to the Gospel and to our people, reflect on the realities of our own situations and interpret the Word of God in relation to these realities."[2] Because it takes the Third World context seriously, this theology addresses the needs and aspirations of the poor who struggle for integral liberation. In this struggle, Third World theologians discern the action of the liberating God of the Exodus and the liberating presence of Jesus. The faith experience of the people struggling against the forces of domination is a place where God can be better understood, celebrated, and proclaimed. It is a new locus of theology.

Third World theologies have a dialectical relationship with Western theology. On the one hand, there is continuity with Western theology because both theologies read the same scriptures and confess the same God of Jesus Christ. On the other hand, there is real discontinuity with that traditional theology in the way theology has been understood and formulated. In the first gathering of Third World theologians, in Dar es Salaam, the main difference was stated as follows: "We reject as irrelevant an academic type of theology that is divorced from action. We are prepared for a radical break in epistemology which makes commitment the first act of theology and engages in critical reflection on the praxis of the reality of the Third World."[3]

This difference between First and Third World theologies can be interpreted as resulting from the different contexts and challenges to which theologians have been forced to respond from the Enlightenment to modern times. These challenges have been presented in waves of new forms of thought that have overthrown the dogmatism and authoritarianism of the Middle Ages and have questioned the basis of the theological understanding of society and history. Science and philosophy have presented new options to human reason, and dialogue between faith and science has become very difficult.

After the long period of Christendom, theology was forced to enter into dialogue with a new partner, the person without faith. Almost every effort in the theology of European and North American countries has been directed toward attempting to prove that faith and science are compatible. As a result, theology has been based on philosophy and, therefore, has become academic and intellectual.

In the Third World, the challenge to theology has come from a different quarter. Without denying the existence of small westernized groups dealing with the question of faith and science, the majority of people have been struggling with the problem of survival. National elites backed by international forces of domination have been largely responsible for the heightened poverty, malnutrition, violation of human rights, and repression. Christians and theologians have been forced to dialogue with this challenge arising from the suffering and despair of people struggling to overcome these evils. They have been obliged to discern the presence and absence of God not in the arguments and objections of a priviliged minority, but in the poverty of millions who cannot live as persons—as sons and daughters of God.

Gustavo Gutiérrez, a leading Third World theologian, has expressed the concern of Third World theology:

> The question is not how we are to talk about God in a world come of age, but how we are to tell people who are scarcely human that God is love, and that God's love makes us one family. The interlocutors of liberation theology are the nonpersons, the humans who are not considered human by the dominant social order, the poor, the exploited classes, the marginalized races, all the despised cultures. Liberation theology categorizes people not as believers and unbelievers, but as oppressors and oppressed.[4]

THE PARTNERS IN THE GENEVA DIALOGUE

In Geneva there were about eighty participants, half of them from the Third World and half from the First World. The participants from the Third World were chosen by EATWOT. This was relatively easy because the Third World theologians had been working together for several years. It was more difficult to choose the First World theologians who would be the partners in the dialogue. This was one of the most demanding tasks for the organizing committee, composed of First and Third World members, who were faced with several choices and alternatives.

First World theologians are not a homogeneous group. Among them is found a variety of theological positions. An Irish theologian classified First World theologians according to their position as follows: The first group consists of those who still talk about God and salvation in the abstract and who provide an ideologico-theological legitimation for the existing world order. They attack Third World theologies as purely ideological. The second group is composed of those who devote themselves to academic theology with not enough concern with the present imbalanced world order and the historical responsibility of the West for much of the unjust situation. They are not hostile to the emerging theologies in the Third World, but do not consider them significant enough. In the third group are the liberal theologians who consider themselves nonconformists in the social system in their countries. They are concerned about specific issues in their affluent societies and are very critical of their churches. However, they seem to be more concerned about their own academic freedom than about the complicity of their countries with the massive denial of freedom in the world. The fourth group is a small minority of "theologians" in active opposition to the existing global injustices and to the complicity of the churches and universities in relation to these. The "theologians" are not only those academically trained as such but also the nonprofessionals who reflect upon their own involvement in the light of their biblical faith.

The organizing committee chose most of the First World theologians who were to dialogue with EATWOT in Geneva from this fourth group. However, many conference delegates were surprised by the results of this process of selection. As Letty Russell, a theologian from the United States, admits in her article assessing the conference: "A surprise of the Geneva dialogue was the makeup of the group gathered from the First World, representing a wide range of grassroots communities of struggle."[5] This choice of such interlocutors was a risk, and at several moments during its development the Geneva conference was close to being a failure because of the different expectations about this dialogue.

On the one hand some Third World theologians were disappointed because they thought that after years of dialogue and reflection on their part they were ready to confront their traditional teachers, who were, however, not present at the conference. Others expressed their frustration that this First World group, considered to be commited to liberation theology in their countries, seemed unclear about the analysis of their societies and were not ready to denounce the structures of oppression.

On the other hand, some First World theologians were disappointed with the constituency of the conference both from the Third and First Worlds. They realized that some Third World theologians were not really liberationist and that only a handful were from grassroots communities. They also felt uneasy when they discovered that in the delegation from the First World there were some who were not degreed theologians and whose names were not known in academic circles. At the same time there were some nonacademic First World participants who felt out of place in the academic discussions.

The participants from the Third World were not a homogeneous group either, although they had been working together for the past six years. In the first intercontinental conference in 1976, the dialogue was very difficult and the differences were almost impossible to overcome. Through the years those theologians have come to know each other, to understand their divergent backgrounds, and to work together despite their differences. Tissa Balasuriya, one of the participants who has attended all the EATWOT dialogues from Dar es Salaam to Geneva, writes about his experience: "When we met in Geneva in 1983 the Third World group had converged to the extent of being sensitive to each others' positions. The differences of background were always there, but the tricontinental dialogue had had its impact."[6]

The dialogue had many tensions and difficulties. One of the participants reports both on the tensions and on the progress of the dialogue. He says:

Although we shared a common commitment to interpret and to respond faithfully to God's message in a divided world, we confronted real difficulties in our effort to do theology together. . . . At some moments it appeared that we would be unable to overcome these obstacles;

the differences were too great. At other moments, however, we experienced genuine dialogue as we listened to one another, told our stories, and sought a more comprehensive framework in which to interpret together our different experiences.[7]

Following this initial overview, we turn now to the actual content and process of the conference. The organizing committee gave special emphasis to the methodology to be used. It was decided that the conference would be developed in three stages—storytelling, social analysis, and the reformulation of the methodology and content of theology. These three parts of the process are reflected in the papers collected in this book. We want to introduce the readers to some of those discussions and developments.

STORYTELLING

The theme of the conference was expressed in the title: "Doing Theology in a Divided World." Using the experiences of the participants as a basis, the gathering had as its main purpose to examine what it means to do theology in our world and then to propose a new methodology for doing theology that starts from commitment.

Sharing the experiences was the starting point of our theological dialogue. All participants had been asked to write in advance their personal stories of involvement in a particular struggle for liberation. Their stories covered a wide range of experiences and involvements. Five different case histories of struggle are presented in Part II of this book, namely, those of a woman pastor in Holland, a theologian involved with Christian communities in Nicaragua, an Anglican bishop from Sri Lanka, a union leader from Sweden, and a woman from Canada involved in solidarity work with Latin America.

Not all the participants were satisfied with this starting point of the conference as opposed to a more academic type of structure with long talks and reports. One First World theologian remarked that "quite a number of participants, especially those from a more academic background, tended to slip back into a more impersonal and abstract style of discussion; so the attempt to root the dialogue in personal case stories was only partly successful." However he was careful to add that "the split between the two different styles of doing theology did not coincide with the division between participants into those from the First World and those from the Third World."[8]

A MORE COMPREHENSIVE SOCIAL ANALYSIS

Social analysis has been a preoccupation of EATWOT from the beginning of its work. The final statement of its first dialogue already pointed to the need for an analysis of the social, economic, political, cultural, racial, and psychological contexts of theology and stressed the socio-economic and political.[9] Participants at Geneva were asked to work in small groups and start the process of analyzing their experiences and looking for the causes of oppression. This was followed by a plenary presentation of three short papers, each of which analyzed oppression based on race or sex or the international economy, and each of which also addressed the interrelatedness of those factors. These papers, included in Part III of this book, were written by Rosemary Radford Ruether, Bonganjalo Boga, and Julio de Santa Ana, respectively.

After hearing these analyses there was a widespread sense of dissatisfaction among participants, not with the speakers but with the fragmentary character of the analysis. The Africans and Asians as well as the women asked for a more comprehensive analysis that would take into consideration the cultural and religious aspects involved in the process of oppression and liberation.

This was a turning point in the conference. It became necessary to rearrange the schedule of the program to allow more time to include the cultural dimension of analysis. Special participants were called upon to address this subject.

The Africans underlined their opposition to Western anthropology which is imposed on Third World peoples and cultures and which embodies a concept of human nature based on individualism, competition, and consumerism. They claimed that in African theology the starting point of liberation is the struggle against what they call "anthropological poverty": "This is a serious form of oppression that despoils human beings not only of what they materially have but of everything that constitutes their being and essence."[10]

Asians pointed out that

> while admitting the disastrous effects of capitalism, imperialism, and neocolonialism . . . they have suffered from internal domination long before the coming of the West. One prime example is the cultural oppression brought about by the caste system in India. Poverty and oppression in Asia thus cannot be understood simply in economic or political terms.[11]

The input of the unscheduled speakers helped the whole group to grow in understanding of the complexity and interlinking system of oppression. One participant said that "the functioning of this system cannot be understood merely in economic, political or even military terms. It involves a whole way of life. . . . A more comprehensive analysis requires recognition of the cultural and even spiritual dimensions of this global system."[12]

All the participants were enriched by the more encompassing analysis. James Cone, in his presentation on black theology included in Part V of this book, made several references to the religio-cultural aspect of the analysis as a complement to the socio-economic aspect of it. He said that "in our use of the critical tools of the social sciences, as well as religio-cultural analyses, black and Third World theologians have been attempting to construct theologies of liberation rather than theologies of domestication." He also affirms that "through a political commitment that is informed by social and cultural analyses, a new hermeneutical situation is created."[13]

EUROPEAN THEOLOGY

From the start of their development, Third World theologies have related to European theology through evaluation, criticism, confrontation, and opposition. European theology is considered the theology of the affluent as opposed to Third World theology, considered the theology of the poor.

In Geneva the evaluation and analysis of European theology were done mainly by two speakers from West Germany: Dorothee Sölle, from a Protestant position, and J. B. Metz, from a Catholic. Sölle compared European theology to the position of Christians in South Africa: "Our own First World theology is tainted by our living in apartheid: we do not allow our brothers and sisters from the Third World to enter our thoughts and feelings, our singing and praying, our reading of scripture, and our theologizing."[14]

Sölle suggested that the only possible response for Christians, theologians, and churches in the First World is one that "emerges from a different vision of life." The name of this response is resistance: " 'Trust in God and resist' is becoming the new imperative."[15]

J. B. Metz, a well-known Catholic theologian, offered a hypothesis and presented six theses to confirm it. His hypothesis was: "We are standing at the end of the European-centered era of Christianity." He foresees a new stage in history of the Catholic Church that is "changing from a culturally monocentric church (Europe and North America) to a culturally polycentric world church."[16]

It was exciting to hear the attempts of First World theologians to renew traditional theology. Several of these attempts oppose the old claim of identifying European theology as universal theology. The final statement names some of these efforts: "feminist theology, theology of resistance, European theology of liberation, theology of conversion, theology of crisis, political theology, and radical evangelical theology."[17]

THE POWER OF WOMEN THEOLOGIANS

EATWOT has been attempting to transform itself into an association in which men and women work together as equals. This has been very difficult because of the patriarchal structures of societies and cultures of the Third World and because Third World theologians, who are progressive in political and social issues, are very often insensitive to the plight of women who are oppressed in their own societies and churches. Geneva was a step forward in this effort. The number and quality of women theologians made the dialogue a real challenge to the sexist interpretation of traditional theology and forced men, both from the Third and the First Worlds, to consider sexism not only as a women's problem but as a men's issue as well.

It was clear from the very beginning that several women from Europe and the U.S.A. came prepared to confront Third World male theologians. They said that they had read and benefited from Third World theology, written almost entirely by men, but at the same time they expressed their dissatisfaction with its sexist language and patriarchal perspective.

One of the most exciting factors of the conference was the real impact of women theologians. This came as a result of the encounter of First World and Third World women. It was easy to start the dialogue between women from the Third and First Worlds as they had a lot to share about common oppression in different contexts. But it was not equally easy to forge a common agenda behind which they could unite to challenge the men's interpretation of theology. It was necessary to hold several meetings before coming to a provisional agreement. The women from the Third World refused to have others set their agenda. The final statement declares:

> The oppression of women is a stark reality in the Third World where many cultures are strongly patriarchal. But to what extent this is an issue for Third World women is to be determined by the Third World women themselves. Neither Third World men nor First World women can determine the Third World women's agenda. Third World women maintain that sexism must not be addressed in isolation, but within the context of the total struggle for liberation in their countries.[18]

After women from the Third and First Worlds resolved their differences, they became a strong group in the conference and made an important contribution to the self-understanding of all the participants and to a new methodology of theology, free of sexist language and male domination, and more sensitive to the quality of life.

RECONCEIVING THEOLOGY

This was the title of one of the most appreciated presentations at the conference. It was given by Samuel Rayan, a theologian from India. Even though he spoke only of theology in Asia, he made an important contribution to the main purpose of the Geneva conference, that is, to reconstruct theological methodology in general. Part V of the present book is devoted to the reformulation of methodology.

Rayan strongly asked for a theology at the service of the people. He said:

> We want theology to be a service to life and to human wholeness. It should be a service to life at all levels—from the tiny blade of grass to the singing bird, to the growing baby, to the heights of rigorous thought and warm friendships, to the depths of mystic joy and divine dark-

ness. We want a theology that will be at the service of life with its many needs and spiraling possibilities as well as its transcendence and its endlessly expanding quest and onward thrust. Our theology will be at the service of those who work, suffer, and hope, those who struggle for justice and human dignity for all women and men.[19]

Other speakers brought out further aspects of a new methodology. James Cone, a noted black theologian, underlined the historical character of theology when he spoke of black theology and its relationship to Third World theologies. He pointed out that one of the key elements of this methodology is its starting point in the concrete history of people and events.

We do not begin our theology with a reflection on divine revelation as if the God of our faith is separate from the suffering of our peoples. We do not believe that revelation is a deposit of fixed doctrines or an objective word of God that is then applied to the human situation. On the contrary, we contend that there is no truth outside or beyond the concrete historical events in which persons are engaged as agents. Truth is found in the histories, cultures, and religions of our peoples.[20]

A French Protestant theologian, Georges Casalis, made a presentation entitled "Methodology for a West European Theology of Liberation." For him, this methodological approach starts with a criticism of the conditions of production of the classic theological discourse and with the critique of the sociopolitical role of traditions, theologies, and theologians. He said that European theology has to spring from the faith experience of Europeans involved in the struggles against capitalism and militarism. He condemned the legitimation of the present system by the churches and called for a rereading of the Bible and a hermeneutic of risk and promise.

Mercy Amba Oduyoye, an African theologian, was asked to present a synthesis of the discussions of the small groups on the theme "Who is the subject of theology?" The incisive question was: Who does theology? The discussions led to the answer that, as restated in the final document, "the fundamental subject of theology is the Christian community in its witnessing to the restless presence of God in the history and culture of the oppressed."[21]

THE NEW FACE OF GOD OR CHRISTIAN SPIRITUALITY

Third World theologies sometimes have been misunderstood when stressing the need for social analysis, praxis of liberation, and relations with the poor and the oppressed. That has never meant leaving aside the spiritual quest, the search for God. What it means is the need to be committed to a praxis similar to that of the prophets in the Old Testament and to that of Jesus in the New Testament, who always linked true worship with justice.

Spirituality was not the topic of any one talk at the Geneva conference.

However, it was the focus of a working group as part of the task of theological reformulation. There is a demand for the articulation of emerging spiritualities—for they are the foundation of the emerging theologies—yet the work of formulation is not easy because spirituality is intimately linked to the way we live our life. It is one way of responding to the invitation of Jesus to the life in abundance for ourselves and all humanity and therefore informs all levels of our struggles for liberation and our effort toward unity and reconciliation in this divided world. Though Jim Wallis's article, included in Part V, summarizes the group's discussion on the topic, the criteria for a new form of spirituality were discernible at different moments of the conference. Among the criteria are:

1) The spirituality influenced by the ideology of capitalism, which fosters individualism, competition, and hostility to the earth, differs vastly from the spirituality rooted in the person of Jesus which celebrates cooperation, social responsibility, and integral development and asceticism.

2) Spirituality cannot be divorced from the struggle for justice and liberation, genuine peace and reconciliation.

3) Personal conversion is an essential element of the task of social transformation.

4) The spirituality of justice and liberation is rooted in the Bible. Women at the conference contested the use of the Bible as a weapon of male domination. They were joined by South African blacks who denounced the whites in their country who support apartheid by using selective verses of the Bible.

The liturgies of the conference were an excellent expression of the new ways people are responding to the inspiration of the Holy Spirit and of the solidarity and friendship we aspire for despite the divisions in the world. Part VI gives the flavor of the liturgical elaborations during the conference, the climax of which was the final liturgy, presided over by seven women, which gives "a foretaste of the new church where men and women are equal according to God's plan and where power and authority are at the service of the people."[22] These words, which appear in the conclusion of the final statement, resound the tone of hope with which the Geneva conference ended.

CONCLUSION

The Geneva dialogue was the sixth and final conference in the first stage of the life and work of EATWOT. This new ecumenical organization has been working steadily, since its beginning in 1976, at the contextualization of theology in different cultures and socio-economic realities. Its efforts have been positive, effective, and helpful to the liberation of Third World peoples. At the end of this stage of EATWOT's work, we want to express our gratitude to the many friends, persons and organizations, too numerous to name, that have supported EATWOT's efforts. We do want specifically to mention, however, Orbis Books, the company which has published all our books and has helped considerably to acquaint readers with our thought.[23]

As our initial work concludes with the conference summarized in this book, we realize that we are only at the beginning of an enormous task. Specifically, our continued commitment is to make the gospel of Jesus more relevant to the needs and aspirations of Third World peoples. We ask for God's guidance and strength as we move into the future.

We invite our readers to enter into this book, a synthesis of our most recent efforts and a small sign of hope for a divided world.

NOTES

1. Virginia Fabella and Sergio Torres, eds., *Irruption of the Third World: Challenge to Theology* (Maryknoll, N.Y.: Orbis Books, 1983), p. 197.

2. Torres and Fabella, eds., *The Emergent Gospel* (Maryknoll, N.Y.: Orbis, 1978), p. 209.

3. Ibid.

4. Ibid., p. 241.

5. See below, p. 208.

6. See below, p. 198.

7. Lee Cormie, "Reporting on EATWOT Conference," *The Ecumenist* 21, no. 4/5 (1983), pp. 73–80.

8. Donal Dorr, "Dialogue between Third World and First World Theologians (evaluation presented to Trocaire, an agency of the Catholic bishops of Ireland, mimeographed), p. 3.

9. Torres and Fabella, *The Emergent Gospel,* pp. 259–64.

10. See below, p. 185.

11. See below, p. 185.

12. Cormie, "Report on EATWOT," p. 76.

13. See below, p. 102.

14. See below, p. 82.

15. See below, p. 83.

16. See below, pp. 85 and 89.

17. See below, pp. 192–93.

18. See below, p. 186.

19. See below, p. 124.

20. See below, p. 99.

21. See below, p. 189.

22. See below, p. 193.

23. Torres and Fabella, eds., *The Emergent Gospel*; Kofi Appiah-Kubi and Torres, eds., *African Theology en Route* (Maryknoll, N.Y.: Orbis Books, 1979); Fabella, ed., *Asia's Struggle for Full Humanity* (Orbis, 1980); Torres and John Eagleson, eds., *The Challenge of Basic Christian Communities* (Orbis, 1981); Fabella and Torres, *Irruption of the Third World.*

PART I

INTRODUCTION

1

Nicole Fischer

Welcome to Geneva

Many conferences are held in Geneva, but few of their participants leave their international enclave to pay a visit to "local" Geneva. And yet this is what the organizers of this EATWOT conference, in dialogue here with their colleagues of Europe and North America, have sought to arrange. And we, representatives of the Catholic and Protestant churches of Geneva, have been pleased to invite you to our parishes this Sunday, and to our communities of life and action next week.

In preparing to receive you, we reflected on the theme of this conference, "Doing Theology in a Divided World." This world is divided not only along its north-south axis, but also at the heart of what may appear to you as a small, homogeneous community—Geneva. Everything in Europe bears the rich and heavy weight of history. Our redoubtable task is to know that history well, lest we fall into the traps of its limitations. For traditional churches such as ours, the challenge entails a constant alertness to the distinction between a tradition to be preserved because it is an integral part of the Christian message, and traditional practices that not only are no integral part of that message, but actually mask it.

We have also come to realize how deprived we are in the area of a theological reflection that might respond to the challenge of our time and our precise situation today—in Geneva, this densely populated, affluent city, where material values often take precedence over the gospel summons!—this city where evident wealth has a hard time hiding all the human distress, the loneliness, the *Lebensangst*, of great urban centers.

This is a Western city, where Christians are watching the image of a church of prestige and power disappear. Some entertain nostalgia for the times of past grandeur—but was it true grandeur? There are, however, others (and

3

they include ourselves) who think that our difficulties are leading our churches to greater daring, and greater concert as well, in the proclamation of the good news for all.

For eight years, the Protestant and Catholic churches of Geneva have been making a particular effort in the area of the theological formation of the laity. We have been working both together and separately in these projects. No doubt our objective resembles your own: to find, in a divided world, in a divided society, a coherence between faith and life. What a simple project, and yet, how ambitious! As a church of prestige, a church of belligerence, recedes, we see a yeast, a leaven, at work, not outside the human family, but at its very heart! We know too that the message of the gospel is not bounded by the limits of our programs or the walls of our church buildings. And we rejoice in that, too!

Through our delegates, we shall be following the progress of your conference with great interest. We hope that this meeting will be, for our churches too, a bearer of challenges, yes, but also of signs of hope.

2

Emílio J. M. de Carvalho

Opening Statement

"Doing theology in a divided world" is the theme of this conference. As put forward in the invitation letter of May 15, 1982, the conference "is the result of a long process of search for and reflection on a relevant theology for the different contexts wherein Christians live."

The idea of dialogue among theologians from outside Europe and North America goes back to the mid-1970s, when three young theologians—Oscar Bimwenyi, L. Marmora, and Enrique Dussel—met in Louvain in October 1975. Since then there have been quite a few international ecumenical dialogues for promoting the "doing of theology" in the context of our differing social, political, economic, religious, and cultural backgrounds, bringing together independent theologians and representatives of Christian communities committed to justice, social change, and liberation. The aim has been the "contextualization of theology" and the definition of liberation in its sociopolitical and cultural perspectives.

In fact, EATWOT (Ecumenical Association of Third World Theologians) started in Dar es Salaam, Tanzania, in August 1976, as an international, systematic, ecumenical dialogue. From that historical beginning EATWOT "has provided an independent ecumenical forum for dialogue, challenge, and mutual enrichment among Third World theologians."[1] It was not until the end of that meeting in Tanzania that EATWOT came into existence, its original purpose being that of "doing theology in a new way relevant to the Third World context."[2] Later on, as groups of theologians in some countries of Europe and North America came to participate in a number of such dialogues,[3] that original purpose was enlarged, "to see Christians of the Third and First worlds working together to overcome forces of oppression and aiming at . . . a new theological reflection."[4]

5

Thus, EATWOT has played a remarkable role as "facilitator of dialogues." The "working together" of theologians from around the world has brought mutual sharing of concerns and experiences.

As theologies from outside Europe and North America made their impact on the Christian conscience and on traditional Western thinking, many professional theologians and lay persons, as well as grassroots groups in Europe and North America, began listening and became sensitive to the voices of Third World theologians. Not only did they take seriously the contextualization of theology, they entered into solidarity with struggles for justice, social change, and liberation. They involved themselves in rank-and-file movements for the change of mentalities and institutions. This led them to reevaluate their own theologies and feel the urgent need for new theological reflection. That theological renewal is at work in some sectors of the Western world is very evident today.

On the other hand, theologians from Africa, Asia, Latin America, the Caribbean, and from minorities in North America want to get an honest and sincere response to their critique and rejection of the long dominant theologies from Europe and North America. They also want to gain from the reflections of other committed Christians living in situations of poverty and oppression, so that they too can rethink their new role in a divided world.

Both the irruption of the Third World and the future of Europe and North America are a challenge to theology. Hence the need felt for an honest and open dialogue on how the concrete struggles and dreams of the oppressed and of the poor against all forms of injustice can lead to a better understanding of God and of God's salvific action in history and in different global contexts. And as far as EATWOT is concerned, this was set as a priority in its five-year plan of work for the future.[5]

We can see and discern "the signs of the times." There are signs of hope; they constitute the real context of our theologies. The poor and the oppressed of the world, both in the Third and in the First worlds, are emerging invincibly from their silence and passivity, struggling in different ways against unjust structures, institutions, and values in their societies, which for centuries or decades have dehumanized and dominated them. Theologians from those situations of oppression are now protesting strongly against (even rejecting) "prefabricated" theologies from the outside to articulate their own reflections, spirituality, formulations, methodologies, and understanding of the Bible, without any official authorization. They are "doing theology" from and in their own situations of struggle. It is a new theology that speaks to them, to their way of living the message of the gospel more meaningfully. As James H. Cone put it in one of his reflections, "the cries of oppressed peoples are becoming essential sources for Christian theology."

This very interesting new development can be epitomized as "the decentralization of authoritative statements about meanings" or "a change of the locus for theologizing."[6] Today we can verify what Sergio Torres saw as "a change in the geographical location of theology."[7]

The Third World reevaluation (even rejection) of what was for centuries considered to be "the only valid theology for the church universal" and Third World resistance to dependence on foreign theological initiative are realities that are bringing with them church renewal—from within the oppressive structures of neocolonialism. In the First World, the irrelevance of traditional theology, as far as social movements constituted by Christian activists and liberationists are concerned, is also calling for a reinterpretation of the gospel of Jesus Christ within a situation of generalized crisis.

The signs of the times are calling for a "theology from the oppressed," not secluded from the struggles of the people. It is the irruption of the oppressed and of the poor that constitutes an exciting challenge to committed Christians, to theology, and to everything else.

Let me end by affirming that we are here to begin a new era in theological reflection, "to share our experiences for mutual critique and to look together for new ways of doing theology and being disciples of Jesus Christ." We are here to begin "a new theological existence."

Dialogue can take place only on the basis of our identities and experiences. It is only when each one of us acknowledges the others, with their differences of theological and practical orientations, that dialogue can take place. To quote Jacques van Nieuwenhove, dialogue can be conceived as "a search for real reciprocities." There are mutual riches to share, in the spirit of faith, honesty, and solidarity. Even confrontation and tension can help to make dialogue more honest, exciting, serious, and profound. We need an openness to reality and reflection on the reality of the situation of others if we are to become truly partners in dialogue.

The process has just begun, and we should not envisage immediate success. But we must now move to new types of relationship, with the Spirit of the Lord guiding us. We live in a divided world; as committed Christians we cannot ignore complex areas of struggle for justice and theological issues that arise in such struggle. We would simply discredit theology should we ignore these challenges.

As followers of Jesus Christ, let us struggle together for a new society in a divided world.

NOTES

1. New Delhi, August 1981, "Proposal for the Future of EATWOT."
2. Preamble, EATWOT Constitution.
3. "Theology in the Americas" is one such group. It is one of the few groups in North America that has shown a sustained interest in linking critical social analysis and theology. See Sergio Torres and John Eagleson, eds., *Theology in the Americas* (Maryknoll, N.Y.: Orbis, 1976).
4. Sergio Torres, Accra, 1977.

8   *Emílio J. M. de Carvalho*

5. New Delhi, 1981.

6. O.K. Bimwenyi, "Displacements. A l'origine de l'Association Oecuménique des Théologiens du Tiers Monde," *Bulletin de Théologie Africaine,* vol. 2, no. 3, Jan.–Feb. 1980, p. 51.

7. Dar es Salaam, 1976.

3

Philip Potter

Doing Theology in a Divided World

An attempt was made by the World Council of Churches (WCC), in a meeting organized by its Program Unit on Education and Renewal in 1973, to promote dialogue between First World and Third World theologians. It was a brave effort, but also a painful experience of mutual incomprehension. After these ten momentous years of very intensive theological reflection in the midst of costly witness in our divided world, I hope that this present encounter will be more fruitful, and will open up fresh dimensions of doing theology in a truly ecumenical way. Certainly we in the WCC have been greatly enriched by the work of EATWOT as we have endeavored to carry out our ecumenical mandate and as we prepare for the sixth WCC assembly in July 1983 on the theme "Jesus Christ—the Life of the World."

I must confess that, although I readily agreed to address this meeting, I have gone through agonies about what I could say that has not already been said by the many Third World theologians in their now formidable array of books, articles, and manifestos—not to speak of the position papers, analyses, final statements, and evaluations in the five published volumes resulting from the five previous EATWOT conferences. I can hardly claim to have read, let alone mastered, the vast output of theological writing by Third World scholars during these last twenty years. However, I do feel a deep sense of solidarity with them, being myself a Third World person from the Caribbean, trained especially in biblical and historical theology, against a background of the practice of law and the study of history. My real apprenticeship in doing theology was my service as a pastor in Haiti in the 1950s.

As is well known, Haiti was the first Latin American country to free itself from slavery and colonial rule by a popular uprising. The French were routed in the field of battle in 1803 precisely in the area where I worked, in Cap-

Häitien. This was quickly followed by the independence of several other Latin American countries. Alas, though Haiti led the way, it ended up as the poorest and most exploited country in the Americas.

In 1950, when I went there, 90 percent of the population was illiterate and living in desperate circumstances under an oligarchy dominated by the U.S.A. There was no freedom to speak directly about the political and economic situation. But I could tell the stories of the Bible, and do so in such a way that my hearers immediately understood their own situation in the light of the biblical message of God's dealing with Israel and the nations, and of the life and ministry of Jesus. Then I would listen to them tell their own story in relation to the message of the kingdom of God and of their own history. Their consciousness was awakened and so was mine. They began to form new communities of prayer and action with and for one another. I immersed myself in their history both oral and written, studied their economic and political plight, listened, received, and shared. My faith was tested almost to the breaking point.

Of course, I did not go to Haiti without some preparation. In the Student Christian Movement I had learned that we must have the Bible in one hand and the newspaper in the other. There was not much news available in print in Haiti, but there was the news of the people—what I heard, saw, and felt. I had also learned that theology is the encounter of *theos*, God, through the word revealed in scripture and especially in the Word made flesh in Christ, and *logos*, the words of a people, the harsh realities in which a people lives, and its anguished cries. My calling was to enter into this encounter and to invite the people to participate in it. And as I tried to do so, I began to understand the cry of agony of Jesus on the cross: "My God, my God, why have you forsaken me?" Theology was not an intellectual exercise; rather it meant entering into the fellowship of the sufferings of Christ in the power of his resurrection, and entering in anguish and hope into the sufferings of the people.

But my most significant preparation was my participation in the first WCC assembly in 1948 and the message that was sent to the churches and that we pledged to make our own as we covenanted to stay together and go forward together as the whole church with the whole gospel to the whole person in the whole world. The words of that message that kept ringing in my ears all the time I was in Haiti and ever since are the following:

> We have to remind ourselves and all men that God has put down the mighty from their seats and exalted the humble and meek. We have to learn afresh together to speak boldly in Christ's name both to those in power and to the people, to oppose terror, cruelty, and race discrimination, to stand by the outcast, the prisoner, and the refugee. We have to make of the church in every place a voice for those who have no voice, and a home where every man will be at home. We have to learn afresh together what is the duty of the Christian man or woman in industry, in

agriculture, in politics, in the professions, and in the home. We have to ask God to teach us together to say no and to say yes in truth. No, to all that flouts the love of Christ, to every system, every program and every person that treats any man as though he were an irresponsible thing or a means of profit, to the defenders of injustice in the name of order, to those who sow the seeds of war or urge war as inevitable. Yes, to all that conforms to the love of Christ, to all who seek for justice, to the peace-makers, to all who hope, fight, and suffer for the cause of man, to all who—even without knowing it—look for new heavens and a new earth wherein dwelleth righteousness.[1]

It is out of this experience and all that has happened to me in the course of these tumultuous years that I have tried to understand what Third World theologians have been saying and writing, out of the anguish of their own involvement in the struggles of the poor, the deprived, the marginalized—who form the great majority of the world population and in whose name they speak and write. In particular, I have tried to digest the statements coming out of the five EATWOT encounters at Dar es Salaam (1976), Accra (1977), Colombo (1979), São Paulo (1980), and New Delhi (1981). It might therefore be appropriate to indicate and comment on what I have learned from these statements.

INSIGHTS OF THIRD WORLD THEOLOGIANS

In the Third World, theology has to be done in a context of the most tragic and devastating history of domination, exploitation, and destruction that humanity has ever known and perpetrated. For the last nearly five hundred years, and particularly since the industrial revolution of the eighteenth century, Europe and later North America, and the outposts of Europe in South Africa, Australia, and New Zealand, joined in this century by Japan, have been engaged in a massive onslaught on the peoples, lands, and resources of the Third World. Although slavery had been practiced in many parts of the world, the slave trade of the seventeenth to the nineteenth century conducted by Europe from Africa to the Americas and the institution of slavery represented a new demonic phenomenon in history, the effects of which still remain, not least in the form of white racism. These events took place around the time of the Renaissance, the Reformation, and Counter-Reformation in Europe, and were accelerated in the era of the Enlightenment of the eighteenth century and the French revolution in the name of liberty, equality, and fraternity.

These are the historical facts, and those of us who come from the Third World know those facts from within. They are the fabric of our existence, even if we, who are represented here, thanks to our bourgeois privileges, cannot speak about it with the same agony and pertinence as the vast millions of sufferers. But on the other hand, our very status as bourgeois intellectuals has enabled us to make use of the now available tools of historical and socio-economic analysis. We are aware of the whole tangled web of crushing oppression to which our peoples have been and are being subjected. We also know that our own societies were predisposed to be the victims of this onslaught, because of our own inherited history of oppression backed by sexism, caste, tribalism, and religio-cultural structures. For example, Africans sold their fellow Africans into slavery for next to nothing. Asians were transported to other countries as indentured laborers without much protest. The exploitation and domination of women has been a crying shame on us all. As Christians and church officials, we know the role that was played by the churches in justifying, furthering, or acquiescing in these events. Theology was consciously or unconsciously the handmaid of the whole process.

There is therefore an awesome responsibility laid upon us as Third World persons to receive, proclaim, and interpret the biblical faith in this context with all the rigor and passion that it demands. Otherwise, we are being totally unfaithful to the gospel, and we turn God into a lie. The text of the gospel of the kingdom of God and God's justice must be read and conveyed in the context of our catastrophic situation—context, indeed, because it accompanies (the sense of the prefix "con") the text. Necessity is laid upon us, and we have at last taken on this task in the last twenty to thirty years.

It is significant that we were forced to it by the largely secular tools of analysis that have become available, especially Marxist analysis. We have finally perceived the global character of the dehumanizing injustice in our world, and the extraordinary interlinkages of oppression that have become more evident and strident since World War II.

This has been a period of political decolonization and of the awakened consciousness of our peoples, but also of the incredible acceleration of the effects of science and technology developed in the West. Through transnational corporations, the sale of sophisticated armaments, and the rapid means of communication, it has brought about new and more powerful forms of exploitation and domination. At the world conference on "Faith, Science, and the Future" at the Massachusetts Institute of Technology in July 1979, I drew attention to a report of the Club of Rome entitled "Reshaping the International Order," which states:

Nowhere is the disparity between the industrialized and Third World countries more marked than in the field of scientific research and technological development. Although 90 percent of all technologists and scientists that have ever lived are alive today, over 90 percent are at work in the industrialized countries. Over 90 percent of their activities are concentrated on research for the rich world and on converting their findings into protected technical processes. The rich minority thus commands an overwhelming proportion of techno-scientific development.[2]

I went on to remark that it is estimated that over half of all scientists and technologists are engaged in arms research and development. The arms produced form one of the major exports to the Third World. Since World War II nearly all the more than 130 wars that have taken place and are going on have been in the Third World and have cost over 25 million lives, and have further destabilized all our societies.

I do not need to go on with this litany of woe. But our fellow Christians and theologians in the First World and Second World too (because especially Russia took part in the imperialist grab of Asia and the Middle East, and the socialist states are themselves involved in various ways in the economic and political conflicts in the Third World), yes, our fellow Christians in these two worlds must understand that we have no other option than to be engaged and to do theology in this context of the idolatrous denial of God's purpose for humanity and creation. They must also appreciate that we shall have to do so even more intensively now and in the dangerous years that lie ahead of us.

That is the first and most persistent point that Third World theologians have been making. And they are not going to be silenced by accusations of being political, Marxist, or communist, or by any other hysterical epithets coming precisely from the First World and echoed by power elites in the Third World.

This leads me to the second insight we have learned about doing theology in the Third World. Doing theology means becoming the messengers of the gospel of good news to the poor and liberation for the oppressed. Doing theology means being missionary, evangelistic, in the spirit and style of the Hebrew prophets and especially of Jesus. Our stance has to be one of confrontation with and resistance to the forces of evil. But this confrontation and resistance start with ourselves. We have to be constantly challenged and purged from all our complicity in attitude, thinking, and involvement with sexual, racial, and class oppression and from our ignorance or denigration of our own religious and cultural history. But this confrontation and resistance means putting ourselves on the line, committing our whole person in word and deed to the battle of God against the forces of evil in our midst and in the world. This demands great discipline (the way of life of the disciple) and a spirituality that enables us to place ourselves at the disposal of the Holy Spirit. The Holy Spirit corrects, illumines, and empowers us in the secret places of our being, as also through the people of God, and, indeed, through those who belong to other faiths.

This is not new. The prophets long ago took this stance and in doing so experienced the agony of rejection and persecution. Jeremiah was even forced to argue with God about his calling; but there was no way out:

> O Lord, thou hast deceived me, and I was deceived;
> thou are stronger than I, and thou hast prevailed.
> I have become a laughingstock all the day;
> every one mocks me.

> For whenever I speak, I cry out,
> I shout, "Violence and destruction!"
> For the word of the Lord has become for me
> a reproach and derision all day long.
> If I say, "I will not mention him,
> or speak any more in his name,"
> there is in my heart as it were a burning fire
> shut up in my bones,
> and I am weary with holding it in, and I cannot
> [Jer. 20:7–9, RSV].

Jesus made this very clear to us in his life and teaching. It is nowhere clearer than in John's Gospel, especially chapter 15, about his being the vine and we the branches that must bear fruit. Our calling is one of abiding in Christ in love and therefore carrying out his commandment of love, which means laying down our lives for each other: "You did not choose me," says Jesus, "but I chose you and appointed you that you should go and bear fruit and that your fruit should abide; so that whatever you ask the Father in my name, he may give it to you. This I command you, to love one another" (vv. 16–17). We usually end our reading of this chapter here. But what is significant is that Jesus goes on to say:

> If the world hates you, know that it has hated me before it hated you. If you were of the world, the world would love its own; but because you are not of the world, but I chose you out of the world, therefore the world hates you. Remember the word that I said to you, "A servant is not greater than his master." If they persecuted me, they will persecute you; if they kept my word, they will keep yours also. But all this they will do to you on my account, because they do not know him who sent me [John 15:18–21].

I have referred to John 15 partly because of an interesting and tragic fact of history. One of the three earliest writings of Karl Marx is an essay he wrote for his matriculation (*Abitur*) when he was seventeen years old on "a demonstration, according to St. John's Gospel, chapter 15, verses 1–14, of the reason, necessity, and effects of the union of believers with Christ." Marx came, from both sides of his family, from generations of Jewish rabbis, but he was brought up as a Christian. He starts his essay by saying that "history is the great teacher of humanity" in raising human nature to a higher ethical state:

> Thus the history of mankind teaches us the necessity of union with Christ. Also when we consider the history of individuals, and the nature of man, we immediately see a spark of the divine in his breast, and enthusiasm for the good, a striving after knowledge, a desire for truth.[3]

The essay is filled with an enthusiasm for the development of one's personality to the full by giving up ideas of power and glory, and working with self-sacrifice for the good of humanity as a whole. Marx received a pat on the shoulder for that essay, but neither his pastor nor the church in Germany at the time, 1835, was anywhere near understanding or acting on the words of Jesus in this sense. The gospel was preached and understood in personal, pietistic terms and with reference to very restricted circles. No wonder Marx later described religion as opium for the people. What Third World theologians are discovering in the storms of their engagement in the struggles of the people is that the biblical faith is yeast, leaven, for the people.

The early fathers of the church also saw theology as an activity that took place in the immersion of the person in adoration and prayer to the triune God revealed in the Word, and which was for the sake of mission. In the seventh century Maximus the Confessor wrote that "a theology without action is the theology of demons." In the same spirit Martin Luther wrote: "Not reading and speculation, but living, dying, and being condemned make a real theologian." This is what Third World theologians are learning by hard experience. C. S. Song sums it all up when he writes that the beginning of theology is the aching of the heart as God's heart aches for sinful, suffering humanity and that "theology is the love of God-and-man in action."

If theology is the love of God-and-humankind in action, then all who are branches of the vine, all who accept God in Christ in love, are engaged in doing theology. This is the third insight that has emerged from the writings of Third World theologians. They do not do theology *for* the people but *with* the people. The poor themselves in the grassroots Christian communities are doing theology in their stories as they relate the biblical story to their own cultural stories, legends, myths, songs, and theater that have arisen from their lived history of struggling for justice. These communities are creating new songs, new liturgies, new prayers, and are forming new groups of solidarity for their rights as human beings with and for others. This is particularly so in Asia and Latin America.

They know what "living, dying, and being condemned" means. They are witnesses, martyrs in love, and are bringing out the inner, revolutionary message of the gospel of the kingdom of God. They are the *laos*, the whole people of God, who discern God's will as they seek to do it. They respond to Paul's exhortation to the Corinthians, following what he says about the gifts of grace (*charismata*), and about the body and its members that have their own identity but are bound together and indispensable for one another in love. Paul says: "Make love your aim, and earnestly desire the spiritual gifts, especially that you may prophesy. . . . Whoever prophesies speaks to others for their upbuilding and encouragement and consolation . . . and edifies the church" (1 Cor. 14:1, 3–4). That is doing theology and doing it so that the church may become a prophetic, caring, servant community in the world.

The fourth insight that Third World theologians are bringing to our attention is therefore the need for a new ecclesiology of the whole people of God.

In the Third World this means, in great majority, "the wretched of the earth," as my fellow Caribbean, Frantz Fanon, called them in his book with that title. This was particularly brought out in the São Paulo EATWOT conference on "Ecclesiology of Popular Christian Communities." The question is how do we understand the marks of the church in a new and liberating way in relation to the reality and goal of the kingdom of God? How is the church one, holy, catholic, and apostolic in both belief and action?

We are learning that the unity of the church is being built on the basis of the common calling to a mission of liberation through life and action in communion with God in Christ and with each other. Unity is both given and is a task. But the task is carried out in the design of God to unite all persons and all things in Christ (Eph. 1:10). The unity of the church as the body of Christ, the fullness of him who fills all things, is inextricably bound up with the struggle for unity in the diversity of humankind, in justice and peace.

The holiness of the church has to be seen in the biblical meaning of holy. The Hebrew word *godesh* literally means "separation." It signifies separation *from*, taking our distance from everything—both within and around us—that denies God's sovereign purpose, and separation *to* God, total commitment and availability to God in making God's kingly rule known and acknowledged. The church is holy insofar as it takes its distance from demonic and idolatrous powers, and commits itself to God's creative will for good. And, as has been rightly said, the good is that which increases communication and multiplies responsibilities. The spirituality that such holiness requires is one that overcomes the dualism of faith and life, prayer and action, contemplation and struggle.

The catholicity of the church is its concern for the whole world and the whole of life in space and time, in full recognition of the rich diversities of culture and of the expressions of faith and life, and yet held together in mutual sharing and communion. This is what the peoples of the Third World are yearning for and seeking to express in the manifoldness of the grace of God.

The apostolicity of the church is its very raison d'être. The *ecclesia* is the assembly of the people of God called out by God and belonging to the Lord (*Kyriake*, hence church, *Kirche*, kirk) in order to be sent out (apostolic). Such a church is not fixed and attached in time and place, but is a pilgrim, diaspora church living in the midst of the people as the people of the Lord, Yahweh, he who is present. The diaspora nature of the church is also a sign of its provisional character—always being renewed, recalled, and sent. We are learning afresh the insight of the Reformers that the church should be the *ecclesia reformanda*, the church always in process of being reformed. As the third WCC assembly in New Delhi said in 1961:

> The assembly wishes only to urge that those who know themselves to be
> called to the responsibility of Christian witness in their own locality
> should examine afresh the structures of their church life with a view to
> meeting the challenge and opportunity of a new day. In a spirit of peni-

tence and of willingness to be led by the Spirit of God into new ways of witness, the whole church must recognize that its divine mission calls for the most dynamic and costly flexibility. . . . [Thus] the church may become the pilgrim church, which goes forth boldly as Abraham did into the unknown future, not afraid to leave behind the securities of its conventional structures, glad to dwell in the tent of perpetual adaptation, looking to the city whose builder and maker is God.[4]

This expresses the eschatological nature of the apostolicity of the church as the agent and sign of the kingly rule of God that is active now, but for which we work, wait, and pray the whole of our lives as the people of God. God will inaugurate the final reign when and how God wills.

ELEMENTS FOR FIRST WORLD/THIRD WORLD DIALOGUE

This brings me to the purpose of this meeting, a dialogue between First World and Third World theologians. In the light of what has emerged in doing theology in the Third World, what are the elements for such a dialogue? They are implicit in what I have already said. I can point them out only in summary fashion.

First, we share a common humanity and live in one world, which at the same time is deeply divided between North and South, East and West, rich and poor. It is also divided sexually and racially, divided into castes, tribes, and nations. We face a common threat of the annihilation of the whole human race. The realities I have earlier described are global realities—that is, what happens in one part of the world affects all the other parts.

What is called in question is the centralizing history and tendency of the rich industrial North and especially the First World, a centralizing that means domination. But, as Booker T. Washington said early in this century: "You can't keep a person down in the gutter without remaining there yourself." Domination reduces dominators to being captive to their dominating. They dare not let go, and in the process they are diminished. Moreover, domination by the First World is conditioned by its dependence on the Third World for raw materials and for markets. There is a common agenda here.

The question posed to First World theologians is: Are they seeking to do their theology in context—that is, with a radical analysis of the socio-economic and religio-cultural realities in the First World? From my long experience in Europe, I have the impression that most theologians, at least in this second half of the twentieth century, have not come to terms with the nature and consequences of the two major revolutions that have transformed the world—the industrial revolution and the French revolution, as well as with the two world wars that were waged by Europe. Genuine dialogue can take place only when both partners face their contexts and recognize that these contexts are interrelated.

Secondly, we have the common ground of biblical tradition, and the tradition of the whole church throughout the ages. But we have to discuss together the ways in which we interpret scripture and our understanding of ecclesiology. What Third World theologians have been saying is that the theological tradition in which they were trained and which comes from the First World is alienated from reality and is based on an interpretation of scripture that is alienating. In this respect it is interesting to notice that those Western theologians who have tried to liberate themselves from this alienating theological tradition have themselves often been marginalized by their colleagues and especially by the churches.

As regards ecclesiology, we have to deal with the captivity of the church in both North and South, East and West, to static structures. The posture of *ecclesia reformanda* is yet to be, or is manifest only here and there. Efforts as ecclesiological renewal are regarded with great suspicion in both North and South.

Moreover, we are witnessing today the emergence of a militant, reactionary but sophisticated politico-religious movement that is challenging theological tradition in the North in a way that is alarming for the Third World, because it is providing theological justification for a type of nineteenth-century capitalistic thrust of social Darwinism: the survival of the fittest. This dangerous tendency calls for urgent dialogue between First World and Third World theologians.

To this must be added an observed tendency, with notable exceptions, toward a regressive confessionalism in the churches in the First World that is being exported to the Third World. One of the effects of this confessionalism is to put pressure on theologians to do theology in certain clearly defined traditional ways.

Lastly, both First World and Third World theologians have to reckon with the fact of the ecumenical movement and especially with the World Council of Churches and with the consequences of Vatican II. All that Third World theologians have been saying and writing has been the substance of the statements, programs, and activities of the World Council and have been its task and calling since its inception. What is the significance of the existence and work of the World Council for doing theology? How can the World Council provide a genuine and permanent forum for dialogue between First World, Second World, and Third World theologians? I am not sure that these questions have been explicitly faced by many theologians and by institutions that are engaged in theological education and discussion. This is not a criticism. It is a plea and a cry for mutual help and support.

I am sure that Third World theologians would be the first to admit that they are only at the beginning of a long process. Their work still touches but a small segment of the life of the church. There are burning issues that have not yet been squarely faced, such as the fact and use of power for social change toward a more just, more participatory and sustainable society, and for the renewal of our churches; and especially the issue of the interpretation of scripture and tradition as regards the identity of women, and the full community of women and men in church and society.

The spirit in which we meet here can best be expressed in the words of Paul to the Corinthians:

> For it is the God who said, "Let light shine out of darkness," who has shone in our hearts to give the light of the knowledge of the glory of God in the face of Christ. But we have this treasure in earthen vessels, to show that the transcendent power belongs to God and not to us. We are afflicted in every way, but not crushed; perplexed, but not driven to despair; persecuted, but not forsaken; struck down, but not destroyed; always carrying in the body the death of Jesus, so that the life of Jesus may also be manifested in our bodies. . . . So we do not lose heart [2 Cor. 4:6–10, 16a].

NOTES

1. "Amsterdam Report," p. 10.
2. "Faith and Science in an Unjust World," p. 26.
3. Cited in David McLellan, *Karl Marx, His Life and Thought,* Modern Masters Series (New York: Penguin, 1976), p. 11.
4. "New Delhi Report," p. 28.

PART II

CASE HISTORIES OF STRUGGLE

4

Wil Blezer van de Walle

The Netherlands: Women Seeking Equality

Although the case history I want to present is the story of a group of persons, I think it better to introduce myself first.

I am a woman, forty-six years of age. I still belong to the Catholic Church (with many ups and downs). I was a religious missionary for eighteen years, until 1972. I got married in 1974 and am now the mother of two children. I am a pastor in the deanery of Valkenswaard and a feminist theologian. My husband is a pastor in the same deanery.

As a missionary sister I lived one year in North Africa, from 1958 to 1959, in Algeria, almost two years in England, and from 1962 to 1971 in Tanzania, East Africa.

In Tanzania I worked very closely with African women, both lay and religious, and I dare say that they modeled me more than I could ever have foreseen.

Living next to the major seminary of Tanzania, in Kipalapala, I had frequent contacts with the African theology students and the staff. As such I came into contact with their search for a new African theology. It has been a blessing for me to be able to live for such a long time in a rich African culture. In Tanzania I learned to understand the Bible and everyday life in its light. This was also thanks to the inspiration of Dr. Julius Nyerere, the president of Tanzania and one of the greater prophets of our time.

After so many years I dare say now that the roots of my being a feminist were laid in Tanzania. This was mainly due to the experience of living so closely to African women who were able to bring about real revolution in their own surroundings, on whatever small scale, due to their cooperation, their care for one another, the encouragement they gave one another, the sharing and mutual encouragement.

In Tanzania, too, I became more "religious minded" than I had ever been

before. The more natural life we lived was imbued with a religious undertone.
All the happenings and encounters of everyday life were seen in the light of or
related to God, *Mungu*, the creator and source of all life. It was not rules and
regulations that mattered, but *life*. Here in western Europe, I am afraid, it is
the other way around.

Upon my return to Holland, I was deeply shocked by how materialistic
almost everybody had become. It took me a long time to become reaccli-
mated. First I took up social work, but felt very unhappy in it because I felt I
could not really help others. After a year I took up studies in theology and
pastoral ministry. As one of the first women in Tilburg, I met with many
problems. The same was true of fieldwork in a parish. Again, it was not life
that really mattered, but rules and regulations, and abstract ways of thinking,
in disregard of the real needs and beliefs of the people.

Gradually I came into contact with feminist theology. Here I felt at last
again "at home." Why? Because the starting point was not abstract theories,
but the praxis of women, individuals and groups, who felt the need for new
forms and from that need started working for them.

I am very much aware of the fact that I, as so many other women in Europe
and North America, have many more material possibilities and chances than
do women in other parts of the world. Nevertheless it is also true that European and North American women are deprived of many opportunities that
men are accorded without question.

Because of all the foregoing I decided to try to get an official appointment
from a bishop of a diocese as a pastor for a pastorate for and with women,
something that would be totally unique in Holland, as much in the Catholic
Church as in the other churches. Why? Because women have been disre-
garded as "full" persons for two thousand years of Christianity; they are
oppressed, humiliated, exploited, and marginalized. It is time that they climb
out of their graves, stand straight, and become aware of who they are and the
power that lies within them.

In August 1979 I received, not a pastoral appointment at once, but a commission to undertake study and research in order to prove that such a pastorate was necessary. I found this humiliating, but I accepted it. The first year
proved the need beyond any doubt. It took another six months of hard struggle to get the appointment through. I was treated by church officials in such a
deplorable and inhuman way that I almost lost courage to carry on with the
struggle. Thanks to the encouragement of other women I could go forward.

The third year of my pastoral appointment has just begun and I wonder
how long I will be able to go on. Men in the church and in the almost exclusively masculine structures of ecclesiastical institutions are becoming afraid.
They fear they will loose power as women stand up and are no longer afraid to
speak out, demanding their rightful places.

The case history I want to present to you consists of a group of women
struggling in the situation of oppression sketched above. They are women of

the deanery I am working in. I think that they are quite representative of Holland as a whole. They range in age from thirty to sixty-five. They belong to different churches, or no church at all, because many left the institutional churches long ago, but their faith is strong. They come from all levels of society and I meet them in various settings—women's centers, church groups, and the like.

They all have in common that they feel and experience that the real values of life are manipulated. As a result, they look upon themselves as "used" and "misused," regarded as "inferior" because of being female, an inferior branch of the human race that society and the churches do not have to take into account seriously. These women, and I with them, feel daily exploited, marginalized, humiliated. And now as Western economy tarnishes, women become its first victims.

As such we are irrupting from the underside of history into the Western world of male-dominated culture and local elites who want women to remain servile. The same can be said of the churches in western Europe. Although the Bible says that God created woman and man alike and in God's image, the churches disregard this in practice and treat men as *the* human beings, and women as less than secondary. In this regard the churches and society still go hand in hand; "Christian politics" confirms this status quo and consolidates it in legislation.

But women are becoming more and more aware of who they are. They now demand official recognition of themselves, and equality and equal treatment—in society and in the churches.

What Are Our Contentions?

• That women are human beings completely equal to men.
• That we have our own personalities and that we should no longer be looked upon as sex objects, confronted and restricted to the role of "playmate," wife, and mother. In other words, that women are not only "derivative" persons—that is to say, the mistress of . . . , the wife of . . . , the mother of. . . .
• That we have our own rights, besides all our duties.
• That we should not be asked to take up responsibilities only when shortage of men becomes apparent.
• That we should be accorded equal treatment in all sectors of social and public life, and also in the churches.

With *local government* we have been struggling to get official recognition as an organization. It has been a hard and long struggle. Our numbers are great and when organized we become a power men are afraid of. Very subtle means have been used to keep apart women's groups and organizations that wanted to unite.

In the *churches* the struggle is even more difficult. Women are simply not regarded as full and capable human beings. Ecclesiastical institutions are almost exclusively controlled by men and they want it to remain that way. Women may do volunteer assignments and work that men disdain. We are consequently struggling for more, and equal, places for women in strategy-planning and decision-making groups, parish councils, committees, and so forth. The struggle is hard. Sometimes men walk out when women walk in.

Very subtle ways are over and over again used by church leaders to find fault with women who work efficiently. Even blasphemies are not unknown. In the name of God everything seems to be permitted to keep women out of church government. According to church leaders, women have to be shown again their place in the kitchen, with children, serving their husbands in submissiveness.

What Discoveries Have We Made?

- That we do not need the established ecclesiastical institutions as much as was thought.
- That faith is not the exclusive possession of instititions, but that they have appropriated it.
- That the sacraments too are not the possession of institutions, and that the claim of exclusively male administration of the sacraments is fallacious and pretentious. Whether there be two or seven sacraments has become irrelevant.
- That women united together are "church" and we experience that the Spirit works in and through us. Spontaneous pastorate arises quite naturally from a group. A nonsexist exegesis of the Bible becomes very much the inspiration of various groups. Hidden parts of the Bible suddenly take on a new, a different, meaning. From this another, a new, theology becomes possible.
- That ordinary women are capable of theologizing and are not afraid to elaborate a new ecclesiology.
- That women are well qualified to bring symbols back to life, discover new ones, and so create a new spirituality.
- That women dare to assert that the double-standard morality within the churches should be abolished, and that a new ethic should emerge and be formulated.

One conclusion I may draw is that feminist theology springs mostly from women's groups and as such it is a theology of the people, with its own language and vocabulary. Of women theologians it is asked—as it should be of all theologians—that they remain with their peers and think with them, and not, as many male theologians do, *for* the poor and oppressed. Women theologians can do so because they themselves are part of an oppressed group and they experience the same problems and inequities everywhere they turn.

A very concrete experience of this struggle has been the way the Dutch delegation was formed for the Woudschoten Symposium and the Dutch paper on feminist theology. Feminist theologians talk from within; our male colleagues, or most of them, do not really share from within the struggle of the people they work with, however much they try.

We are struggling against two groups—namely, the dominant male group, and those women who have so interiorized and are content with the stereotyped female image that they help to continue its reign. Our tactics differ. Resistance comes from both groups. Resistance from other women is more painful. It frustrates other women and withholds them sometimes from going forward.

We are struggling with all women in the most varied places, women's organizations, women in political parties—and with the few men who also work for a new, more human society.

5

Pablo Richard

Nicaragua: Basic Church Communities in a Revolutionary Situation

I have been involved in the Nicaraguan revolutionary process since 1978. My work has been basically theological: with Christians having a militant commitment to the revolution, in revolutionary organizations, and with basic church communities. Since the triumph of the revolution, on July 19, 1979, a systematic theological project has been launched under the auspices of the Centro Antonio Valdivieso. I have also worked with youth, and, most recently, with *campesino* communities.

My prevailing theological concern has always been educational: that of faith seeking a revolutionary conceptualization. My point of departure has been the concrete experience of Christians in the revolution. The vast majority of Nicaraguans are Christians—the same who participated in the uprising. It would have been impossible without at least some consistency between religion and revolution.

In the basic church communities, we are initiating a process of education in the faith, to strengthen and develop this basic compatibility between religion and the revolution. My work has consisted in setting up workshops and training courses for lay ministers and Christian leaders. Our general task has been to form men and women who will testify, by their lives, all over the country, that there is no incompatibility between Christianity and the revolution. A massive participation by the people in the revolution would, we saw, necessarily require this labor of education in the faith on the popular level.

A more delicate and demanding task has been our work with Christian youth who are totally involved in revolutionary praxis—with all the organic, theoretical, and political impact of that praxis. I have devoted myself most energetically to the creation of a new synthesis of faith and politics in the concrete Nicaraguan situation. Here the most important thing for me has been to live this synthesis myself. Invariably, the young express their Christian identity by identifying with someone they know and admire. But it is also necessary to establish a very rigorous theological basis for this synthesis of faith and revolution. To this purpose, then, I began a study of the original roots of Christianity. But we must also study the rationale of revolution, and this involves a study of Marxist tradition. Pitched battles have had to be waged against a "conservative," dogmatic Marxism that seems to have lost all revolutionary creativity.

I have devoted a great deal of time to this theoretical work of theology, both with the masses and with militant youth. Experience has taught that, without a mature synthesis of faith and revolution, those whose revolutionary commitment deepens will sooner or later leave the church—and those who remain faithful to their Christian identity will sooner or later abandon the revolution, or at least refrain from taking on tasks calling for deeper revolutionary commitment. Theology can be born and develop in Nicaragua only if it is capable of educating the faith of revolutionary Christians— educating those who are becoming more and more integrated into the revolution and in ever greater numbers. I have invested all my theoretical energies in this project, seeking at the same time to form Nicaraguan theologians who will spread this work throughout the country and give it native roots.

NICARAGUA: POLITICAL AND ECCLESIAL ANALYSIS

On July 19, 1979, the revolution led by the Sandinista Front for National Liberation (the FSLN) triumphed. Now began the difficult task of national reconstruction. The program launched was one of a mixed economy (with some 60 percent of the means of production in private hands), using a model of diversified external dependence (divided among the United States, other capitalist countries, the Third World, and socialist countries), and based on a broad coalition of social classes (including the middle class and sectors of the bourgeoisie that had not been partisans of the ousted dictator, Somoza) in which the popular classes hold the hegemony—all led by the FSLN and the revolutionary government.

In August 1980, the "second uprising"—the National Literacy Crusade— came to a successful end. In 1981 all organs of popular power were bolstered with a view to ensuring a direct democracy, one in which the poor would be the protagonists of their own history. In 1982 the national defenses had to be consolidated, for a counterrevolution was now underway. It was especially the popular militias that were developed at this time, so that the armed defenders of the revolution could be the citizens themselves. In 1983 the direct intervention of counterrevolutionary armies began, attacking from Honduras with the support of the United States government—which also unleashed a full-scale economic, political, and ideological attack on the revolutionary process.

During the first year, the Catholic Church supported the revolution. On November 17, 1979, the bishops' conference published its pastoral letter "Christian Commitment for a New Nicaragua," the most advanced magisterial document in the history of the Latin American church. The church had also supported the literacy crusade, taking its official position in August 1980. For its part, the FSLN, on October 7, 1980, published a communiqué on religion, a document unique for its open position toward Christians and the churches. Never in the history of revolution had the church enjoyed such opportunities as it now possessed in the Nicaraguan revolutionary process. And yet the hierarchy was unable to seize this historic moment, this moment of grace and conversion. Very soon the Catholic hierarchy took an aggressive position vis-à-vis the revolution and the people, the majority of whom are Catholic.

The first serious confrontation occurred on June 1, 1980, when the bishops' conference issued an ultimatum to priests holding official posts in the revolution, and withdrew ecclesiastical approbation from centers of Christian reflection having ties with the revolution. On February 19, 1982, matters came to a near breach: the bishops took advantage of the racial problem for a virulent, unprecedented attack on the government, while continuing to upbraid all pastoral ministers carrying on apostolic work within the revolution. There have been revolutions that persecuted the church; in Nicaragua, the church persecutes the revolution—a revolution being carried forward, perhaps for the first time in history, mostly by Christians.

Among the reasons for this situation we can mention the traditional ones: the diffidence of the Catholic hierarchy with regard to any revolutionary process, and the practically connatural alliance of the hierarchy with the dominant classes down through four centuries of Latin American history. But in Nicaragua there are two specific causes as well. First, CELAM, the Conference of Latin American Bishops, inspired by a Polish model of the church, sketched for Nicaragua a "strategy of confrontation" between the church and the revolution, in hopes of preventing this revolution from having any influence in the rest of Latin America, where a mighty "church of the poor" flourishes. Secondly, the classes that had been dominant during the old dictatorship, now, with the support of neoconservative groups in the United States (such as the Institute for Religion and Democracy, which invited Archbishop Obando y Bravo on a tour of the United States in January 1982), sought to implement a "strategy of manipulation" of the church. These groups, ousted from control of the economy and the political machinery, now sought to control civil society. In order to do this, they saw they had to manipulate the church, the media, education, the family, the human-rights question, the ethnic problem, and so on, for their political ends. Manipulation of the church in Nicaragua is a counterrevolutionary strategy for controlling civil society, with a view to dividing the people and bring it into confrontation with its vanguard, the FSLN.

In this situation, all our theological efforts have been devoted to a strengthening of the basic church communities. In this endeavor we have enjoyed the support of some of the Nicaraguan bishops, and the solidarity of a great number of other Latin American bishops, other Christian groups, and theologians of the First World. Our work has sought to vindicate the full ecclesiality of the church of the poor in Nicaragua. We have sought to defend the right to live the gospel and faith in Jesus at the heart of the revolution. We have not sought to divide the church, still less to create a state church. On the contrary, we have sought only to carry on a defense of the gospel and of the future of the church, which is the future lived today in Nicaragua by the church sprung from the people by the power of God.

AN EMERGING THEOLOGY
OF THE BASIC CHURCH COMMUNITIES

What is the special nature of this theology of the basic church communities? There are two special things about it, and I should like to conclude with a remark on each.

First, we seek to foster a new theological rationality. All theology uses reasoning. Faith seeks to understand. We are called upon to be ever ready to give "the reason for this hope" of ours (1 Peter 3:15, NAB). The rationality of the emerging theology of the basic church communities in Nicaragua is becoming progressively more identified with the rationality of the praxis of liberation itself, and its content is always the life of the people. The rational element, the logical element, the truth element, is always that the people may live. The death of the people is the maximal expression of the irrational.

Theology develops its epistemology—its criterion of truth and its mode of knowledge—from a point of departure in the contradiction between death and life, as experienced in revolutionary praxis. This life, the life of the people, is defined by us in very concrete terms: bread, housing, health, education, and security for all. These basic needs are economic and political imperatives, of course—but they become spiritual, theological, and ethical imperatives as well. In the revolution, theology takes on an economic rationality, and this transforms it into a theology of life. This theology also defines the status or position of the theologian in society and in the church.

The second special characteristic of our theology in the basic church community has to do with its divine object. All theology has God as its object and center. And the theology that is emerging today in the revolution is *theo*logy as never before. For it is a theology that seeks to discover the presence of God in the struggle of the poor—in their pursuit of liberation for all society. This theology does not seek to demonstrate the existence of God so much as to demonstrate that God is present in our revolutionary processes.

One of the things that plays an important role in this discovery of the meaning of God in the revolution is a rereading of the Bible. The Bible does not reveal the word of God to us mechanically. It reveals to us how and where God engages in self-revelation in our history. The faith of the poor finds, in the Bible, a basic criterion of discernment of the presence of God in their fight for full humanity.

The church lives this *theo*logy as a new, liberating spirituality. It has a new experience of the transcendent in the revolution: God, completely gratuitous, transcends every human impossibility, and becomes the root of a hope, a limitless hope, for a promised land, a new country, a new city. The church is a space of spiritual encounter in the revolution. And this is its finest contribution to integral liberation.

—Translated by Robert R. Barr

6

Lakshman Wickremesinghe

Sri Lanka: The Devasarana Movement, 1970–1983

The experience of and struggle for liberation by the Devasarana movement and its articulated religio-ideology is not something in which I am myself directly involved. My personal connection with it from its inception stems from the fact that it is based on land owned by the church, functions mainly within the area covered by the diocese of which I am the bishop, and also because its animator and leading figure has been a long-standing friend and a senior clergyman in the diocese.

Devasarana was originally an indigenous monastic foundation of which I was a close associate. With regard to the development of this ashram into a base for a liberation movement, I have been present when required, and have given support and advice when requested. It is from this standpoint that I venture to present a case history of it.

The primary or core group has consisted of educated, unemployed, and alienated rural youth. A smaller number of young persons from the urban intelligentsia, with more middle-class backgrounds, joined them. They have been inspired by a priest-monk who is from an elite sector in society. In addition, older rural workers and rural Buddhist monks have slowly been drawn into the Devasarana movement.

Originally their struggle was primarily against local and regional elites, in successive stages. The young personally experienced not only alienation and frustration but also disillusionment. They were daily aware of exploitation by local landowners, traders, and wealthy farmers, of corruption in political leaders and government officials, of rough treatment by the police when crime occurred or disputes arose, of marginalization by elitist groups, of indifference on the part of local religious leaders, and of a passivity based on long experience and fear on the part of their parents and others of their parents' generation.

The young were gripped by a maturing political consciousness that ruled out passivity. They had experience of the electoral process (franchise had been in effect in Sri Lanka since 1931); they heard radical speakers at political rallies and read radical literature (literacy was high even in rural areas); there was an emerging secularism that made belief in fate or the consolation of religious devotion unacceptable to them; and there was an incipient awareness that the social system was operating against them.

They wanted their rightful share and place in society and they also believed that those in positions of power and privilege could be persuaded to make the necessary changes to realize these goals. But their increasing experience was that those in authority would not do so. They became more and more convinced that entrenched leaders had to be displaced and replaced by others who would do what was needed.

Members of local and regional elites spoke English as a second language and many were placed in the higher rungs of the caste system, whereas many of the rural youth knew only their mother tongue and were placed lower down in the caste hierarchy. The gap they wanted to overcome was not only that of class, but also of caste and culture.

Some young persons felt that leadership at the local level could come from their ranks. But the insurrection or rebellion in 1971 led by radical and educated rural youth made them aware that there were others among them who could be leaders at the regional and national levels also. The desire to radically alter the existing social system became more dominant among those associated with the Devasarana movement, as a result of both the rebellion and of incarceration after its suppression. Marxist ideas became pervasive, and have remained so.

At the local and regional level there has been a growing alliance of Devasarana adherents with professional writers, both monastic and lay, with radicals employed as civil servants, and with members of rural-based radical political groups. More recently there has been wider linkage with trade unionists of urban and estate background, and with leaders of small radical political parties seeking a peasant or rural base. Linkage at the local and regional level was forged by young rural radicals and rural intelligentsia; national and international linkage was facilitated by the priest-monk with his contacts and social position.

Other radical Christian groups in Sri Lanka and other Asian radical groups with a rural base have been linked with the struggle and experience of the Devasarana movement. The original procedure of meeting for discussions and for planning strategy and tactics at the local level remains, but alliances for joint action, especially at the regional level, though not excluding the national level, have become more important. Joint action on common issues, processions and presentation of petitions, campaigning at election time, and joining in May Day rallies in the capital are some concrete examples of the mass mobilization of liberative aspirations through a network of alliances.

The abortive strike of 1980 in Sri Lanka, which left in a vulnerable situation those middle-class trade unionists who had lost their jobs, deepened linkage at the national level through support and solidarity. Communication is effective, transportation readily available, and translation into three languages not a major problem. The point to note is that by these linkages, both national and international, rural youth and some older Sri Lankans with a mainly local base became more aware of the national and international dimensions of socio-cultural oppression.

What the Devasarana movement is struggling for, and how, is best explained in terms of the two discernible stages in its historical devolution.

1. A COLLECTIVE FARM

The original idea was that of a collective farm as a socialist model within a capitalist system—an oasis surrounded by the dehumanizing desert. It was the era of resplendent Maoism with its immense attraction for radicals in Asia and elsewhere. It was also the period when the influence of the suppressed armed insurrection of 1971, led by radical rural youth, had its impact on the policies of the government then in power. As a result of land-reform measures, collective farms were begun on nationalized plantations allocated for rice cultivation, animal husbandry, subsidiary crops, and agro-based industries. The era of appropriate technology had also dawned.

In the Devasarana center there was a genuine attempt to run a collective farm on a socialist pattern. There was sharing of manual labor and of the income obtained from the produce of the land; use of scientific methods and appropriate technology to increase productivity and satisfy the reasonable expectations of the collective farmers; an appeal to the dedicated service that overcomes selfishness; regular, almost daily, meetings for criticism, including self-criticism, and corporate meditation; and practice of a para-liturgy at regular intervals in connection with a ceremonial partaking of ordinary food and drink—namely, rice and tea.

Some foreign donations were accepted, along with those of local well-wishers. The money was used to give the poor and the landless whatever kind of help was relevant. This included the extension of credit, a fair-price shop, and the loan of tractors at low rates in order to avoid exploitation by money-lenders and traders. Arrangements were made to get advice from personnel in government agricultural research stations and training schools in the vicinity; joint-labor activities were begun in order to improve roads, set up a medical clinic for women, and establish a community health service. Local youth also had a recreational center with a library and the opportunity to learn English.

Regular meetings of the core group and larger meetings with others in the local community and supporters were also held. The intention was to conscientize the people and draw lessons for strategy and tactics while fostering a sense of comradeship. Keeping a balance between the articulate intelligentsia and the practical but generally inarticulate wisdom of the seasoned peasantry was not easy. Consensus was sought as in the rural tradition, but it was not easy to interpret accurately the silence of those who listened and said nothing.

A major component in this collective farm stage was the place given to meditation and devotion. Devasarana (meaning "refuge of God") had originally been an ashram engaged in ecumenism with Buddhists in the locality. The para-liturgy named "the new world liturgy" was the fruit of the shared experience of both religious traditions, of secularized insights, and of the creative articulation of them all by the priest-monk with an instinctive liturgical sense. In it were readings from the scriptures of the major religions on the island and from radical contemporary writings, expression of gratitude, confession of faults, remembrance of others in situations of oppression, aspirations toward the "new person in the new society," and commitment to the struggle for liberation. Periods of silence, time for personal sharing of experience or dialogue, the ritual sharing of rice and tea—the common food and drink of the countryside—were other aspects of this liturgy.

However, this stage was brought to an end. The government that had begun the collective farms was replaced. Even before this, the experiment had failed, for a number of reasons. There was the corruption of project managers and politicians, the inexperience of the young, problems between the articulate who took over positions of leadership and the inarticulate youth who did most of the manual work, the question of higher income for better work, the inadequate place given to women, and an emerging sexual license. The government farms did not increase material wealth enough to satisfy the increased expectations of the young for better living standards. The new government disbanded these farms, lured some of the young members to other jobs in exchange for reversing their political loyalties, and harassed the radical youth who had worked against them in the elections.

The Devasarana collective farm fared better than others, owing to greater dedication and honesty, along with the guidance of the resident priest-monk. But even for it, increased production did not bring self-reliance or enough profit to improve living standards. Increasing inflation due to the policies of the new government made recourse to foreign aid more and more inevitable, both to maintain the farm and those associates who were relocated with the disbanding of the government farms.

The model was seen as incapable of realization in the de facto context. The need for greater political struggle within society and in the local community also became evident, when the welfare basis of Sri Lankan social policy was increasingly undermined by the capitalist policies of the new government and its repressive policies against trade unions. The new thrust was seen to be toward issue-based mass mobilization. The project model was replaced by the program model; development was replaced by political action as the main strategy. Society had first to be socialized in order for collective farms to be viable.

2. A PROGRAM CENTER

Devasarana farm became a center for issue-based programs and support for struggling groups of former collective farmers in other centers. The main focus was on resistance to unjust policies and struggle for a changed social order, in addition to keeping the socialist vision alive in the face of the alternative vision offered by the new government. The dormant All-Island Peasants' Organization was resuscitated for this purpose. Cadres were recruited from harassed radicals, and later from urban radicals after the abortive strike. A newspaper was published as a vehicle for exposition, to share news and views, raise immediate issues, build up awareness of oppression all over the island, and publicize the power of mass-mobilization to meet specific issues or crises. Practical efforts were also made at regional levels across the island to demonstrate the value and effectiveness of mass power to obtain redress.

In addition, plays, songs, folk tales, historical incidents, and stories from religious scriptures that formed an integral part of the peasant folk memory and mentality were radicalized and used to awaken and strengthen liberative aspirations. The indigenous and religious dimension was so used as to draw into the struggle a series of alliances with groups of Buddhist monks with liberal and nationalist ideas.

New programs were added. Articulate and educated women were now given a due place in the struggle for a socialist society. Scholars were encouraged to draw out radical aspects of struggles in past history. Links with radical Tamil youth in the northern part of the island were fostered, especially among those low in the caste hierarchy. There began an attempt to link radical groups in the rural, estate, urban, and northern sectors for mutual support.

Setbacks had to be faced. Youth left for employment that would give them better living standards. Politicians faced with mass demonstrations on issues at the local or regional level exploited caste, family, or political differences to split alliances. Government repression and police harassment became more systematic. Older rural and urban citizens, although more aware of the real nature of oppression in the social system, remained uncommitted unless they foresaw that their participation in the region where they lived would in fact bring benefit rather than retaliation. Their attitude was ambivalent.

All these programs, promotional literature, and organization of mass-mobilization campaigns involve a large increase of foreign aid. This creates problems. The lifestyle of the cadres begins to become somewhat divorced from those on whose behalf they claim to work, unless strict self-regulation and group control are exercised. Authoritarianism can emerge in the decision-making process if those who have power to disburse funds can abuse their power. How much progress has been made in animating liberative aspirations and engendering mass power, and how much of what is seen as mass-mobilization results from a judicious use of money for transportation, promotional literature, and ancillary methods, now becomes a real question.

THEMES, ASSUMPTIONS, AND QUESTIONS FOR THEOLOGY

Analysis elaborated by articulate members makes use of neo-Marxist notions. The Maoist tradition, adapted to the local situation, predominates. The practice and literature of the Devasarana movement highlight the following themes: class analysis of rural society; the peasantry as the vanguard of the liberation movement and its relation to other oppressed groups sharing in the struggle; the value of joining in national struggles against imperialism in all its forms; the need to single out the chief enemy in a given situation and to forge a network of alliances with others to form a common front; the need to be aware of what are the real contradictions in planning strategy and tactics; the way practice and theory should blend; the demand for cadres to be dedicated and to listen to the people in a continual dialogue; the use of folktales and indigenous traditions so as to serve radical ideas as they are communicated to the masses. The experience of the rebellion in 1971 is also evaluated to draw lessons for ongoing struggle.

Certain meta-empirical perspectives are also evident. They are empirical experiences interpreted by presuppositions and presented as indubitable facts of history. One is the view that there is an underlying trend in the historical process leading ultimately to liberation and socialism, in spite of all setbacks. Another is that the cadres form an elite that can be trusted to serve the people and help it seize the opportune moments to bring this trend to fulfillment. Finally, there is the view that in the masses there is an experience and wisdom that will enable them to become subjects of their own historical destiny. The people will pursue its own destiny.

In the Devasarana experience and its articulation, the Chinese tradition, with its puritan moralism and emphasis on reforming motivation from self-interest to selfless service for the people, is given a transcendental dimension. The Indian notion of a transcendental *Dhamma* (suprapersonal *logos*) immanent in the cosmo-historical process, and its spirituality of interiorized contemplation to enable liberation from self-consciousness, give a religious basis to Maoist ideology without lessening its radical thrust. This *Dhamma* is immanent in history, struggling to enable human beings to overcome evil at both personal and structural levels, and to create a new person in a new society within a new natural environment. The purely secular and radical is accepted and given a wider and deeper dimension consonant with the Sri Lankan mentality.

The Christian theologian will note that the Devasarana liberation struggle is articulated not in theologico-ideological but in religio-ideological terms.

Salvation and national histories other than biblical and ecclesiastical are given equal status within the all-encompassing *Dhamma,* which can be viewed in either nonpersonal or personal imagery. Paradigms serving as inspiration for liberative socialism are taken from all religious scriptures, secular writings, and historical traditions. Liberative heroes or models are taken from the same sources. There is a comprehensiveness that includes and relativizes each, with the main focus on liberation and socialism.

Two theological questions must be posed. First, it is an open question whether Jesus Christ is given centrality and universality in relation to other liberative heroes. It is an equally open question whether biblical history and the community of the church are given normative status in relation to other liberative histories and communities, though the latter can no doubt enrich a Christ-based normativity that is central rather than absolute. They can enrich but not replace what is christocentric.

Secondly, it is an open question also whether the liberative hero is a prophet-martyr-victim who judges the oppressor and liberates the oppressed, or a prophet-martyr-savior-victim (*satyagrahi,* as viewed in the Indian tradition), who judges and liberates both but at their different levels, giving liberation of the oppressed a primacy of status. I do not see in the writings of the priest-monk the notion of an "agonized violence of love" that concedes nothing to the oppressor but that also does not break the bonds of love, as affirmed by Kim Chi Ha of Korea.

Our theological task is to appreciate and assess this liberative experience, struggle, and articulation, with Jesus Christ as the central paradigm or historical root-model.

7

Per Frostin

Sweden: The Union of Christian Labor Members

The first strike in Sweden was led by Pietist revivalists. In 1879 the sawmill owners of Sundsvall decided to lower workers' wages. The six thousand workers responded in a quite unexpected way: they refused to work for the reduced wages. For the first time in the history of Swedish industry, workers vacated their place of work. They settled down in a camp outside the town. Liquor was prohibited because alcoholism was considered a great threat to the morale of solidarity. Every evening the striking workers met for prayer and worship in a revivalist-type meeting.

The strike was vehemently condemned by Christian leaders in Sweden and bishops of the established church; revivalist preachers were unanimous in their outright condemnations. The striking workers were forced to choose between the institutional Christian community and proletarian solidarity.

This event is important for understanding the dilemma of being a Christian socialist in Sweden. Even if Christians choose socialism as an act of obedience to Jesus Christ, they will face a painful conflict of loyalties: either a Christianity embedded in middle-class morality or a rather economistic and antispiritual labor movement.

In spite of this dilemma there have always been *some* Christian workers. One of them was my grandfather, the son of a peasant. He worked in a huge limestone quarry in the city of Malmo until he had to quit because of silicosis. This disease developed into tuberculosis, which killed him. When he left the limestone quarry he had to earn his living as a crofter. He was not a card-carrying member of the Labor Party but he voted for it. Yet he felt some uneasiness about its technocratic and economistic narrowness, as can be illus-

40

trated by an episode: when he was cared for at a sanatorium some years before his death, he wanted the socialist leaders to experience the same love that he had experienced from the nurses, "so that they can believe in the existence of angels."

THE CHRISTIAN LABOR MOVEMENT

In 1926 Christian workers, some socialist pastors, and radical members of the middle classes formed the Union of Swedish Christian Labor Members, popularly called "the fraternity movement." The union differs from organizations of religious-minded socialists in other parts of Europe. Its political aim is not to establish a specific religious brand of socialism but to participate in the struggle for socialism together with persons of other faiths and world-views. It incorporates a socialist interpretation of Luther's doctrine of the two kingdoms. Its members all belong to the Labor Party. Their main political work is done outside movement structures, in party organizations and in local, regional, and national government. Some fifteen members of the movement are members of parliament.

Today the movement is one of the officially recognized branch organizations of the Labor Party, on an equal footing with the youth branch, the women's branch, and so forth. The branch organizations are important as forces of renewal in overcoming the inertia of an established structure. The Swedish Labor Party is an established structure and rather bureaucratic, though it is the only genuine workers' party in Sweden (communist groups are mostly recruited from the middle classes).

The union movement represents 5 percent of the 200,000 active church members who vote Labor. Half of its membership comes from the working class and the other half from the middle classes, where the churches have their social base.

A major problem in the movement is the imbalance between the generations. The older members are mainly industrial workers but the younger ones are to a great extent from the middle classes. During the last fifteen years quite a few radical intellectuals have joined the movement. I myself belong to this group and I know how much we have learned from the older workers, from their struggles in the factories and in political institutions. But unless the recruitment of younger workers is increased, the movement will lose its character of being a popular movement.

Between the Working Class and the Middle Classes

I was raised in a middle-class setting. My father was a rural pastor, and he remembered how as a child, he had been mobbed, scratched with nettles, and so on, by middle-class children who had already picked up the arrogance of a classed society. The fact that my grandfather had worked in a limestone quarry was a social taboo, as was the relationship between the working conditions there and the tuberculosis that finally killed him. The social contradictions between the working class and the middle classes were thus present in the home of my childhood.

This dilemma was deepened when I faced the possibility of higher academic studies. On the one hand I appreciated the resources of academic research: all the books in the libraries, discussions in seminars, the discipline of source criticism, and so forth. These resources were valuable as tools in the struggle for justice. And there was the thrill of intellectual excitement in the process of research. On the other hand I felt from the beginning a vague fear of the university: "This is not my place. If I want to stay there, then I must learn *their* language." And my sister warned me sternly: "Your words will be quite incomprehensible to ordinary persons if you become a researcher." It was a difficult decision!

In retrospect I would formulate the problem differently. I felt a deep anger but I could find no "scientific" channels to express it. The detachment and frostiness of academic language, as also the superficiality of cheap reconciliation in middle-class piety, barred the way. When the universities—or the churches—teach persons to suppress their anger, they paralyze and depersonalize them.

As a boy I learned from my father to distinguish carefully between language that really gives the people something, and glamorous, glittering phrases without substance. When we went home from a church meeting he could tear a speech apart, showing that it lacked content, though it had been applauded and praised. At the university I made the same observation: you could be respected and promoted just by conforming to the rules of the established authorities, without creating anything of value to the people. I wanted to criticize this wrong. But when I tried to translate my anger into the detached and aseptic language of the liberal ideology at the universities, I defeated my own purpose.

In the labor movement I found the way to a language that could voice the anger we have in common. This help was not given by party officials, who often resort to a rather technocratic and aloof mode of expression, but by the rank and file of the labor movement. When I used their language of commitment and anger, I found that the problem of suppressed anger was not mine only. I shared it with many others. For example, when speaking at a demonstration in a township, I could clearly sense in the air the different reaction to reading the dull guidelines supplied by party headquarters, with their endless statistics, and speaking straightforwardly about injustices in the Swedish welfare society.

A worship service could be the occasion for Christians to muster up the courage to acknowledge their suppressed anger caused by injustice. But it generally serves to draw attention away from any such anger. There is a striking difference between the psalms and contemporary liturgies and prayers: the psalmist voices his anger over injustice *coram Deo* ("to God, face to face"), whereas contemporary religious language glosses over social and economic contradictions.

We have tried to re-create prophetical language in worship in different ways: in house liturgies, political Bible studies, services on the first of May. It is a very difficult undertaking, especially because it easily generates heated feelings in bourgeois Christians who are firmly convinced that the liberal stand on the separation of faith and politics is correct; religion is, and should be, politically neutral.

Pilot Studies

The Union of Christian Labor Members functions at the juncture between two large and rather disparate movements, the churches and the Labor Party. Its main work inside movement structures aims at mediation between the visionary language of the biblical, prophetic tradition and political praxis. In this context pilot studies are of special importance. They are used by branch organizations to renew and radicalize party politics.

A pilot study is a document of some fifty pages, analyzing a certain field of politics. The analysis of each chapter is concluded by specific political demands that can be implemented by—for example—the parliament. The union movement produces, on the average, one pilot study a year, on international economic justice, social welfare, family policies, culture, mass media, environment questions, drugs, energy questions, and the like.

The pilot studies are the fruits of a comprehensive work. The pilot study committee, elected by the congress of the movement, appoints an ad hoc committee to write a draft after one or two years of study. The draft is discussed by the pilot study committee and sometimes by the national board before it is sent to local groups and regional conferences for their reactions. The draft can be revised on the basis of these reactions before it is submitted to the congress.

My first contacts with this work entailed some cultural shock. Coming from the individualism of the universities, I had to learn the discipline imposed by research based on collective cooperation. By way of example, I served as the secretary of the ad hoc committee on social welfare. I had a lot of radical ideas before starting that work. It was a revelation to discover how laborious it was to translate those ideas into concrete, political demands. In the process I had to take into account the richness of the experience of other members.

Something similar is true of theological work: academic theology can neglect the complexity of social reality. But in the pilot study approach, theology does not make sense unless it can be incarnated into political demands, which are rooted in material reality.

TOWARD A SPIRITUALITY OF AWARENESS

During one of my first years in the labor movement I had some heated discussions in a workshop with an older worker. I disliked his conservatism and he could not stand my talking about "socialism," "class struggle," and so forth. Just by chance I happened to hear his personal history. He had sacrificed his health by starting a trade union branch in his factory against the will of the factory owner. It was a hard struggle for many years and even took him to the Labor Court! But my talk about "class struggle" had not tied in with his experience.

With this example I do not mean to deprecate Marxist concepts; I think they are essential in a scientific analysis of the contradictions in existing societies. But I suspect that all concepts can be used in an oppressive way, even when they are created with the best of intentions.

Before joining the movement and the Labor Party in 1968, I belonged to the radical left. It was no easy decision to join Labor. I was already a Marxist by that time and thus rather skeptical about many decisions taken by the party leadership. Yet I was more and more wary of the elitist and authoritarian methods of the radical left when it tried to "conscientize" the people from above.

Idealism—be it bourgeois, be it revolutionary—is oppressive when it ignores or denies the concrete experiences of the people. Awareness is of basic importance from both the spiritual and political point of view. Awareness is at the same time both a gift of the Holy Spirit and the basis of a materialistic understanding of history.

8

Frances Arbour

Canada: The Inter-Church Committee on Human Rights in Latin America

Between 1968 and 1971 I was introduced to the reality of Latin America while working as a Canadian missionary in a working-class urban area in Mexico. For me it was an awakening to a vibrant culture and a dynamic political environment. It was also a profound faith experience—an experience of the search by Christian communities to integrate faith and work for social transformation.

It was an experience of great hope that there were real possibilities to change exploitive economic and political structures and to challenge the dominant international relationships between rich and poor nations. My own commitment to my faith, to the Latin American peoples, and to my own country was nurtured and advanced by a sense of historical progression throughout the continent that paralleled my own maturing as a person. The experience was also one of darkness, of sharing through the exile, torture, imprisonment, and sometimes death of dear friends and colleagues in the repression and dictatorship to which Latin America is subjected.

Both of these experiences—of hope and of darkness—challenged me to return to Canada to try to change North American policies and economic structures as one of the most important acts of solidarity requested by the persons with whom I had worked. In my opinion, the Canadian churches in the early 1970s were realizing their potential for common action on social issues. They were a valid point of insertion to continue my commitment to Latin America and in so doing to contribute to the development of a social faith in Canada. The Inter-Church Committee on Human Rights in Latin America, ICCHRLA, has been for me an expression of that commitment.[1]

45

PAST AND PRESENT

The ICCHRLA was a natural outgrowth of an earlier ad hoc ecumenical project, the Inter-Church Committee on Chile, ICCC, born following the coup d'etat in Chile in September 1973. The experience of that committee established a framework of Canadian church analysis and action that would later mature in the ICCHRLA.

The ICCC was an early response by Canadian churches to urgent pleas from church partners and friends in Chile. Through the testimonies of Chilean exiles, through fact-finding missions by Canadian church representatives to Chile, and later through the visit to Canada by Chileans we became aware of the urgent need to assist in the defense of human rights and in the denunciation of repression and dictatorial rule. From the outset, our response to those needs led us into a dialogue, and sometimes a conflictive encounter, with those responsible for the formulation of Canadian foreign policy.

In early conversations with the Canadian government, the ICCC urged Ottawa to accept large numbers of refugees from Chile. We also urged the Canadian government not to grant early recognition to the military junta. Our representations were not at first successful. The government failed to respond rapidly to the plight of the refugees and quickly accorded diplomatic recognition to the new government. Later, the Canadian churches, along with other Canadian organizations, succeeded in encouraging the government to open its doors to Chilean refugees. Over seven thousand refugees arrived in Canada during the 1970s. Later still, the Canadian churches urged the authorities in Ottawa to create what would become a precedent-setting political prisoner program. The potential for Canadian churches to influence governmental policy toward Latin America was established.

As the ICC continued its work over the course of almost three years, we were challenged by reports of increasingly grave and widespread violations of human rights in other Latin American countries. By 1976 the Chilean economic "model" and the ideology of the "national security state" appeared to be extending their influence throughout the continent. In that year, the Canadian churches decided to transform and expand the mandate of the ICCC.

The ICCHRLA was formed in January 1977 to assist Canadian Christians to respond more fully to the reality of all Latin America. Since then our mandate has drawn us to address as a major focus of work the human rights concerns of Central America—Guatemala, El Salvador, Nicaragua, and Honduras. But the committee also sustained a commitment to the southern cone region of Latin America while developing new efforts related to situations in Bolivia and Peru.

As ICCHRLA work expanded dramatically from a concentration on Chile in 1973 to a continental concern by 1983, it became necessary to create a new organization to deal adequately with continuing refugee issues. In 1980 the

Canadian churches created the Inter-Church Committee on Refugees, with which ICCHRLA continues to collaborate actively.

What Have We Learned from Latin America?

Our work on human rights issues in Latin America has been a dynamic process. It has evolved from immediate and concrete reactions to emergency situations, from engagement with North American foreign policy makers, from an ongoing dialogue within Canadian church institutions and with their constituencies, from reflection on our mistakes and successes, on our powerlessness and on our real ability to have an impact.

Our experience did not begin from abstract perceptions about development, social justice, and human rights. It has most often grown out of responses to persecuted trade unionists, *campesinos,* community workers, indigenous peoples, dedicated professionals, political prisoners, the disappeared and their relatives, human rights advocates and their organizations. These responses have led us to share in the painful experience of torture, disappearance, and death of Latin American sisters and brothers.

Our solidarity with those struggling to break the bonds of oppression has led us to a clearer identification of the enemies of human liberation—financial, industrial, and landed elites and their military and police structures that shore up an unjust status quo. These powerful groups have international allies in the large transnational companies and banks whose investment decisions are made without concern for basic justice for the people. Powerful elites in Latin America also survive and flourish in association with governments of the First World whose policies support them in the name of "protecting strategic interests."

This identification of those we serve and of those we oppose has helped us shape and reflect on the link between work for justice and the defense of human rights. We have begun to see more clearly that human rights are not solely and primarily the civil and political rights so cherished by Canadian and other Western societies. Human rights include the fundamental economic and social rights necessary to ensure life, dignity, and participation for the human person and the human community.

This relationship between social justice, fundamental human rights, and struggles for liberation is the substance of how we understand the Christian "preferential option for the poor." That option commits us to developing, with our Latin American partners, a social and political analysis that uncovers the basic causes of economic injustice and political repression. And it commits us to coordinated action to change oppressive structures in Latin America, in Canada, and throughout the hemisphere.

The Impact of the ICCHRLA

The ICCHRLA assesses its own work not only on the basis of the quality of its educational programs and the integrity of its prophetic vocation, but most importantly on the effectiveness of its response to the violation of human rights in Latin America. Although we have not succeeded in changing many aspects of Canadian foreign policy, the committee has become one of the most reputable and critical contributors to public debate in Canada on foreign policy vis-à-vis Latin America. Our efforts have greatly increased the degree of parliamentary scrutiny of Latin America policy, as manifested in the recent work of the Parliamentary Sub-Committee on Canada's Relations with Latin America and the Caribbean.

The ICCHRLA has also developed human rights documentation and policy recommendations of a sufficiently high quality that they are employed by United Nations bodies and other international human rights organizations. In these and other ways, the ICCHRLA has been an important agent in the deepening of Canadian public awareness of its relationship with the social justice struggles of Latin America.

Our work has also had an important impact within the Canadian churches in advancing the mission of evangelization, in stimulating theological reflection, in supporting new modes of social analysis in Canada, and in fomenting change within our church institutions and participation among our constituencies.

Many Canadian Christians have been inspired by the way many Latin American Christians, committed to their people's authentic struggle for liberation, integrate dedication to justice for the poor with an evangelical mission to preach the good news of the gospel of Jesus Christ. This combination, this social faith, obliges us to become part of historical processes in order to transform the world and make more visible the kingdom of God. We have been moved by the tremendous faith of Latin American Christians who, despite great pain and suffering, live with a profound hope in life and resurrection.

Vincent Menchu, a Guatemalan rural leader killed in the massacre at the Spanish Embassy in January 1980, told us shortly before his death that he was no longer afraid to die, because such a sacrifice sows the seeds of life for his children and his people. This kind of witness, a witness we have seen repeatedly throughout Latin America, has been for many of us a conversion experience.

Our faith has been challenged, strengthened, and deepened by the living historical witness of the paschal mystery. We have come to recognize that theology is being done by these martyrs, prophets, and witnesses through their integrity and dedication to the gospel of Jesus as expressed by their lives, their work, their accomplishments, their deaths. In communicating these learnings to Canadians and in engaging them in follow-up activity, the ICCHRLA has contributed to the mission of evangelization entrusted to the churches.

In a similar way, ICCHRLA expressions of solidarity with Latin American struggles for justice has contributed to theological reflection in Canada. The ICCHRLA has been a channel for the transmission of theological insights from Latin America to Canadian Christians and theological institutions. Perhaps more importantly, our educational material, human rights documentation, and field experience have become the subject of study in theological colleges and a contributing element in the ongoing process of developing a theology rooted in Canadian experience.

The analysis we have been developing of the linkage between human rights and integral development, of the national security state, of the impact of militarism, and of international structures of domination has also reinforced new modes of social analysis of Canadian society. Our ongoing analysis of Latin American realities, of the nature of dependency, of the consequences of elitist economic and political models, and of the strategies of great economic and political concentrations of corporate and state power has helped Canadians evaluate more precisely the role of Canada in international relations. We have come to understand that Canada as a developed country shares many similarities with dependent ones, that oppressed peoples in Canada—the unemployed, native peoples, citizens of depressed regions, workers, and women—share common struggles with their sisters and brothers in Latin America, and that exchanges of experiences and analyses between Canadians and Latin Americans can be a dynamic contribution to the effort for more just societies.

Our study and adaptation of Latin American modes of analysis have assisted the formulation of Canadian church positions on issues of unemployment, militarism, and development as evidenced in recent public statements by church leaders. Unlike similar work carried out by other organizations, ICCHRLA efforts are representative of church institutions. This characteristic of our work means that at times it can have a great impact. It also means that our work requires that Canadian churches continuously develop precise policies and action strategies on many crucial issues. The ICCHRLA is a coordinating body for such denominational policies and action strategies.

We are also part of an important network within the Canadian churches dealing with various social justice concerns. The ICCHRLA works with the Task Force on the Churches and Corporate Responsibility on issues of economic relationships and human rights. It works with the Ten Days for World Development program and the Canadian Catholic Organization for Development and Peace in educational programs aimed at an everwidening Canadian public.

The ICCHRLA is one of several social action bodies that both manifest and stimulate ecumenical cooperation. The committee has provided a wealth of information and experience from many Christian churches in Latin America. Both the ICCHRLA and its denominational members have been more effective for drawing on the strength of an ecumenical approach in the arena of social justice. Although marked by inadequacies and some frustrations, this ecumenical experience has been a gift to the Christian community in Canada.

FOR THE FUTURE

Despite the success and contributions of ICCHRLA work, the future holds many challenges. Issues of human rights and social justice in both Latin America and Canada confront Canadian Christians with new challenges, ones that touch on the confluence of church-state relationships and the very purpose of church institutions. The current economic crisis and political tensions within Canada may test the commitment of the churches to issues of justice and ecumenical cooperation. This could lead to the exaggeration of the differences that exist between the churches, especially as they confront those interest groups both within the church and in society that attempt to deny historical, prophetic expressions of Christian mission.

These challenges, as well as those coming from our Latin American sisters and brothers, call us to deepen our conversion to the gospel of Jesus Christ who came to bring life to all members of the human community.

NOTE

1. The ICCHRLA is one of several national ecumenical coalitions in Canada created by Christian churches to address urgent social issues. It is comprised of representatives of the mainline Christian churches in Canada—Anglican, Lutheran, Presbyterian, Roman Catholic, United, and the Quakers. Several Roman Catholic religious orders are also members of the committee and, since 1982, the Christian Reformed Church has participated with observer status. The Canadian Conference of Catholic Bishops and the Canadian Council of Churches both participate actively in the ICCHRLA. The committee has enjoyed a long-standing working relationship with the Montreal-based Comité Chrétien pour les Droits Humains and with the Latin American Working Group of Toronto.

PART III

ANALYSIS:
THE INTERRELATEDNESS
OF OPPRESSION
AND EFFORTS FOR LIBERATION

9

Bonganjalo Goba

A Black South African Perspective

My task is not an easy one. To engage in any analysis of the South African situation is always dangerous and in many instances incomplete, because we are dealing with a dynamic situation—one continuously under different kinds of pressure. Before I move on to consider the topic before us, I must emphasize that apartheid has not disappeared. Nor has the overall situation changed in South Africa. Many persons in the West have the impression that the situation is changing in South Africa. This view is associated with the constitutional proposals currently being studied in South Africa.

While the world believes that things are changing, South Africans are dying in detention. A classic example is that of Newil Eggert, a trade unionist. Many continue to be banned—or rebanned—such as the leading white Reformed theologian, Dr. Beyers Naudé, and Father Smangaliso Mkhatshwa, secretary of the Catholic bishops' conference.

Apartheid continues—a very sophisticated ideology that destroys human lives. As I am speaking to you, a number of my fellow blacks are dying of cholera and other diseases related to malnutrition—a result of apartheid. More and more blacks are removed to the so-called resettlement camps, such as Crossroads and Dimbaza. Many of them continue to be harassed by police, especially those who live in shacks near Crossroads. There is a move among government officials to introduce a bill that would strictly control the movement of blacks under the influx control system. Security laws are much harsher than before. Those who oppose the system face daily harassment by security police. But in spite of all this there is greater support of the South African regime by Western countries—a subject that I shall return to later.

The fundamental crisis facing South Africa is that of the ongoing political conspiracy of Western countries in supporting the system of apartheid. Con-

53

spiracy is not something new; it has been experienced by many Third World countries. What is rather shocking is that some Third World countries are also participating in this conspiracy, countries in Latin America, as well as the Republic of China. As we continue to struggle against oppression, we are becoming very much aware of who our enemies are and what kinds of methods they use to perpetuate our domination.

This conference is very important in that we are brought together with some of our friends from those countries who are on our side in the search for lasting and concrete liberation. It is my hope that together we shall discover practical strategies in which to express our solidarity in working for a just world social order.

As oppressed peoples of South Africa we know that our enemy is apartheid and that Western societies are not committed to dismantling this system, for reasons that I shall explore later. We are also aware that apartheid as a racial capitalistic ideology is adopting very sophisticated methods to sell itself to the Western world. This we see in the flourishing economic presence of Western corporations.

Within the South African situation itself there is the sophisticated process of political and economic domestication. Part of this domestication we see in the creation of the so-called independent states, such as Transkei, Bophu-tatswana, Venda, and Ciskei—used by the present government to make sure that there is an abundant availability of cheap labor for the South African economy. Many black South Africans are being systematically deprived of their birth rights and land rights. Many of us have become virtually for-eigners in the land of our birth.

Another aspect of this political domestication is that more and more blacks are being drawn into the capitalistic system via the creation of a black middle class. This is promoted by Western business interests with the support of the South African government. Although this is not something to have far-reaching consequences for a while, it is a dangerous situation. Some blacks are becoming apologists for the current political system. This we see espe-cially in urban areas.

Apart from domestication, there are disturbing signs among various groups that are committed to working for change: serious ideological rifts are resurfacing.

There are those within the black community who are critical of the black consciousness movement because of its lack of critical analysis and its refusal to collaborate with white progressive movements, especially among students. On the other hand there are others who refuse to emphasize the racial charac-ter of the struggle but who engage more and more in economic analysis of the situation. Within this camp there is more collaboration among so-called pro-gressive elements. Because of these ideological differences there is an unfor-tunate polarization among students as well as persons in the trade union movement. One would hope that these differences will be transcended when a genuine grassroots movement emerges in the South African context.

Apart from these movements there are those that have opted to try to change the system from within. Here I am thinking of the Black Alliance consisting of groups that have accepted government-created political platforms—for example, the Colored Labor Party, the Inkatha movement, whose leader is Chief Gatsha Buthelezi. Although some of these movements enjoy popular support from the masses, they offer no real opposition to the system.

Against this rather sketchy background, how do the churches come into the picture? The church is in a situation of crisis. The South African Council of Churches, under the leadership of Bishop Tutu, continues to be vocal in opposing the policy of apartheid. As a result it is being investigated by a commission appointed by the government. But the real problem with churches that are members of the South African Council are conflicting political visions among its members. Many of the white (liberal) members support the existing status quo, even the co-called constitutional proposals of the president's council.

On the other hand the majority of the black constituency is committed to change, although some among them have already been forced to opt for the so-called independent states. On the other hand we have the Afrikaans-speaking churches of the Reformed tradition who openly support the policy of apartheid. The church on the whole is becoming irrelevant to the struggle for liberation owing to internal problems and the lack of a prophetic vision and commitment of its leaders and members.

Despite these problems, nothing will stop the struggle for liberation from racism in South Africa. There is hope in the student movements, and in the new young leaders who are emerging with a clear commitment to radical change. There is also hope in the trade union movement despite the obstacles in its way. I believe the political future of South Africa will be shaped to a large extent by the struggle maintained by workers.

On the other hand the system of apartheid is also consolidating itself in what is known as a total strategy: marshaling all available power resources to challenge all programs of radical, meaningful change. This is why there is close cooperation between the business sector, the military, and the government. All this suggests to me that there will continue to be struggle on both sides. On the side of the regime, First World countries are involved for economic and political reasons. On the side of the oppressed our hope is the support of progressive forces in Third World countries as well as in First World countries.

THE INTERRELATEDNESS OF OPPRESSION IN SOUTH AFRICA

The concept of the interrelatedness of oppression may be examined from a number of perspectives. One perspective would focus on the different expressions of oppression within the same socio-political context—for example, racism and sexism in the same given context. The other perspective would focus on the expressions of oppression within a global context identifying all agents involved in a program of domination, be it political or economic. This means that a study of the agents of oppression would also call for an examination of action strategies among the oppressed.

Both those perspectives are very important for the South African context. One of the fundamental problems associated with South Africa is the ideology of apartheid, which represents a system of institutionalized racism to be found nowhere else in the world. This may sound like an exaggeration but it is not. Apartheid is enshrined in the legal order of South African society from top to bottom. Despite many challenges to it, it continues to thrive as an ideology because of the economic benefits it bestows on the western countries that support the South African government. It must be understood that Apartheid as a form of institutionalized racism is a continuing legacy of white imperialism in the southern part of Africa. There is no clear commitment by Western countries to eradicate the system. Too many of those countries do not regard apartheid as a crime against humanity, but simply as an unfortunate inconvenience.

There is ample evidence to support this view. One good example was the resolution passed by the General Assembly of the United Nations in 1973 to establish an international convention on the suppression and punishment of the crime of apartheid. The resolution was ratified by thirty-eight countries— none of them in the West. Another good example is the strong European opposition to the WCC Program to Combat Racism under the pretext of not wanting to support violent revolutionary movements. This I believe is just a farce; what it really reflects is the stubborn unwillingness of Western societies to deal with the problem of racism. For those of us who are victims of racial domination, apartheid is an open wound in the body of humankind, a cancer that continues to destroy many lives. So many black lives have been sacrificed because of this demonic system of institutionalized racism.

It must be remembered that apartheid in South Africa is a viable political policy with interesting economic consequences. Apartheid as a racio-capitalist system provides cheap labor not only for the present South African economy but also for those Western countries that have vested economic interests in South Africa. These countries will not commit themselves to the dismantling of apartheid, but will continue to support it. When apartheid is examined from this perspective, we begin to appreciate that it is a world problem, promoted by Western powers, in which there is a clear commitment to the maintenance of white economic interests.

Institutionalized racism is part of the Western political and cultural ethos. The problem of racism is deeply engrained in the psyche of Western society. Patterns of white racial domination are apparent in Latin America, Australia, and the United States of America. Any approach that underestimates this pattern of racial domination is misleading and misled.

Apartheid as a racist, capitalist ideology has serious implications for the whole southern part of the African continent. Because of the prevalence of important mineral resources in this area, there is a commitment by South Africa to ensure that it maintain economic dominance, thus forcing all neighboring countries to be its economic hostages. This program is supported not only by the whole business community in South Africa, but by many Western countries. Their governments believe that as long as South Africa perpetuates the policy of apartheid, the West will be assured of cheap economic resources and benefits. The will to perpetuate the policy of apartheid is supported by an aggressive program of militarization to ensure that no other power has access to the economic wealth of this region.

Hence the struggle against apartheid is not just a struggle of black South Africans. It is one in which all the peoples of southern Africa and of other Third World countries should be involved.

THEOLOGY AND THE CHALLENGE OF RACISM

Apartheid as a form of institutionalized racism has been criticized by Christian churches in South Africa, but their statements and resolutions have not posed any serious challenges to apartheid. A good example is the "Message to the People of South Africa" and the open letter of the 129 theologians of the Dutch Reformed churches. Such resolutions and statements suggest that it has become routine to condemn apartheid as a form of idolatry or sin, but without encouraging Christians to engage in any program of change. As a result no one takes these statements to mean anything. Many of us in the black community are becoming deeply suspicious of the condemnation of apartheid that leads nowhere. We see no commitment on the part of white Christians and theologians to challenge the system.

The challenge of apartheid as a form of institutionalized racism has created or provided a very interesting context for doing theology, for apartheid is also a theological ideology that has been promoted by the Christian community, especially the churches of the Reformed tradition. There is a sense in which we can say that apartheid was born within the Reformed tradition. In our theologizing one of the challenges we confront in our struggle against racism is that of reinterpreting the meaning of the Christian faith from a black perspective.

The first duty of black theology has been to debunk or discredit the theology of oppression that has promoted our systematic dehumanization. This has been done by emphasizing black cultural values within the struggle against apartheid. The struggle against apartheid has given birth to a new way of theologizing in South Africa.

The Christian message has acquired a new meaning that emphasizes the determination of black Christians to work for the creation of a new social order. Black theological reflection has broadened its approach by collaborating with other secular movements working for change. This is an interesting development: racism as a form of oppression is not examined in isolation from other oppressive situations but is seen in the broader context of the struggle for liberation in which workers, women, and other marginalized sectors of the population are involved.

Traditional Christian attitudes in South Africa have been enslaved to the theology of white supremacy. This is further complicated by the negative attitude Christianity has had against African cultural and religious values. Theology as pursued in the West has become a joke to many of our young black persons involved in the struggle for liberation. In that struggle a neocolonial theology is just as irrelevant as is the institutional church. What we are discovering is that true theological reflection takes place as we respond concretely to the needs and the struggles of the people. This kind of theology is more issue-oriented and takes place outside official church structures.

The theological challenge to racism involves for us a fundamental quest to affirm our black humanity and dignity. It is a challenge to name the world for ourselves, for even our present names are not really our own. All of life is tarnished and disfigured by apartheid.

For us theology is not an academic exercise, but a struggle against the demon of white racism. We are convinced that only the exorcising of this demon in all its manifestations in South Africa and in other parts of the world will make it possible for both blacks and whites to celebrate in a concrete way their common humanity. Racism is a demonic force in the world used by the powerful to divide the powerless, and to destroy human life. In South Africa racism is also part of the strategy of separate development—promoting forms of tribalism—further destroying the political solidarity of the people.

Because of the tremendous challenge posed by racism in the form of apartheid, programs of conscientization are not enough. Our theological dynamism must develop new strategies for change and project visions of a new society. This means that as we develop our theology we have much to learn from others who are struggling against white racism. But our contribution will be unique because our historical situation is unique.

Our struggle as blacks in South Africa is a struggle in concert with all other black peoples in the world and those who identify with us. In racism we see a fixed determination to relegate us to a state of perpetual servitude. It is for this reason that blacks everywhere are committed to declare war on racism in its many forms and invite all progressive movements to join them in eradicating this evil from the world.

10

Julio de Santa Ana

The Perspective of Economic Analysis

In his introductory address to this conference, the secretary general of the World Council of Churches, Dr. Philip Potter, indicated the need for theologians to take into consideration two major revolutions that influence our world: the industrial-technical revolution begun in the eighteenth century and the French bourgeois revolution. I think that we should also take into consideration the process of socialist revolution that has been going on in the twentieth century. The all-important point, however, is that theology should be done with awareness of what is happening in the world and why it is happening.

THE IMPORTANCE OF PERSPECTIVE

It is with this awareness that we need to analyze situations of oppression/ liberation. The perspective from which this analysis can be made is always important. That is, we do not analyze historical reality from a point disengaged from history: we are historical beings and we take part in historical processes in one way or another. In my case, my perspective is given from the fact that I come from Uruguay, a small country between Argentina and Brazil that declared its independence in 1925 and had it accepted by British imperialism in 1928. But imperialism continued to exert a decisive influence on the history of Uruguay ever since then. For the rest of the nineteenth century British imperialism prevailed; in the twentieth century (after 1920) American imperialism has taken its place.

For my generation the question was: "Would a liberated Uruguay be a viable entity as a nation?" For most of us the answer was yes, but in the context of a liberated Latin America. Thus, since the time of our youth, it has been very important to be aware of liberation struggles in Latin America first, and then elsewhere. We followed with sympathy the struggles for independence in Indonesia, India, Ghana. We celebrated the Bolivian revolution in 1952, and we suffered with the suppression of the Guatemalan revolution by the U.S.A. and the United Fruit Co. in 1954. This is the perspective for our analysis.

However, it can be questioned whether this perspective is valid for the analysis of socio-economic and political situations. That is, it could be that from the perspective of revolution we could look at things not as they are, but as we should like them to be. In this case, we would be dealing with illusions instead of realities.

In order to avoid the trap of wishful thinking, a perspective can be valid if it is confirmed by historical fact. That is, a point of view taken from a people struggling for liberation is valid if the fact of struggle for liberation is verified. In the case of Latin American peoples, this perspective has been confirmed by the irruption and permanence of the Cuban revolution. It proved that liberation from imperialism is possible. More importantly, it proved that a society oriented to freedom, the satisfaction of basic human needs, full employment, and human dignity could be created in Latin America.

When this conviction was shaken because of the repression carried on in the name of the "national security state," during the period from 1972 to 1978, the struggle of the Nicaraguan people represented a reaffirmation of this perspective. History, to be sure, can be understood as a field of conflicts, but the initiative for betterment is—has been—taken by peoples who long for and are ready to pay for justice and liberation.

MEANINGFUL STRUGGLES

Analysis, then, should have as a starting point situations of conflict and confrontation. It is possible to discern in them the forces that aim at liberation and the forces that try to retain power and control. Of course, confrontations are happening everywhere: at the level of family life, the neighborhood, the village, the factory, society at large. For the given forces and interests that try to overcome the oppression that they suffer, the conflict in which they are involved is the most important one. However, for those who want to analyze situations where many struggles are occurring at the same time, more or less interrelated, it is necessary to focus on what are the most meaningful struggles, disregarding those that are not so significant. Meaningful struggles are those that manifest in themselves the possibility of overcoming oppression and bringing about liberation.

Liberative forces become significant when they challenge, disturb, and affect the powers that be. Because of this it seems necessary, for this type of analysis, to pose, and to try to respond to, questions such as the following:
•Who are those struggling for liberation?
•Where are they in action today?

•What are they achieving? How can their effectiveness be assessed?

•Are they breaking the framework of control that entrenched powers try to perserve? How?

I want to single out here what for me are three meaningful processes of confrontation going on in the world today. There are, of course, more cases of this kind, some of them known to many, limited to the framework of very concrete situations. The three examples that I shall highlight are illustrative of the fact that liberation struggles at present participate in the ambiguous character implicit in all historical events. But these three examples are meaningful for me because each of them is disturbing, challenging, and possibly affecting the powers that control the situations where they are active.

1. Southern Africa

The geopolitical importance of this part of our world is very clear: a very significant part of the globe can be controlled from there, and traffic between the Atlantic and the Indian Oceans can also be kept under surveillance. This region is also very rich in minerals necessary for modern technology and trade.

The struggle of the peoples in South Africa and Namibia must be seen in the context of the process of liberation that is going on in Zimbabwe, Angola, and elsewhere in southern Africa. It is rejection of the terrible injustices of racism, but also an affirmation of self-identity and self-reliance.

In spite of the support given to the white government in Johannesburg by Western powers and others (including many Third World governments), these peoples continue to struggle. Sooner or later they will succeed in their effort for liberation. This will bring about many changes in southern Africa and elsewhere (the worldwide gold market will certainly be affected by it).

2. Central America

There is also the confrontation that the rural poor in Central America, together with other progressive forces, are carrying on against their national oligarchies—oligarchies supported mainly by Western interests, especially the U.S.A. In Guatemala those who strive for liberation are mainly Amerindians, heavily oppressed for many centuries. But the Central American struggle is not only classist; it is also a struggle against sexism: established patterns of sexual domination by men over women are being challenged.

This struggle must be seen in a comprehensive way: what is going on in El Salvador, Guatemala, and Honduras cannot be dissociated from what is happening in Nicaragua. It incarnates the age-old demand of the peoples in the region, mainly those of Amerindian origin, to be free and to live in community. As in the case of the struggle of the peoples in southern Africa, the changes that they are making will certainly affect and influence the overall situation.

3. Islamic Peoples

We have also observed in recent years the phenomenon of a resurgence of Islamic peoples, to be understood as part of the general uprising of the poor of the world. However, it would be a mistake to regard the Islamic resurgence as a monolithic phenomenon with a single center. There is a great deal of variety and plurality in the numerous manifestations of Islam in various countries and continents. Islam is the majority religious faith in many countries of Asia and Africa, and a large but minority faith in many other nations.

The implications of Islamic claims must be understood at the national, as well as at the international, level. For example, some Islamic forces are calling for a total restructuring of economic and political power to shape a world where Islamic nations could find a more meaningful place and play a more significant role. If collective self-reliance of the Islamic world is achieved, it may lead to an important redistribution of worldwide power, and to the creation of new tensions and possibilities in international relationships.

THE TENACITY OF DOMINATION

It must be noted that among forces struggling for liberation there is a lack of clear inter-relationship and coordination. But perhaps more important is the fact that, in spite of the efforts, inventiveness, and generosity of those struggling for liberation, it seems very unlikely, at the beginning of the 1980s, that radical changes will be made in prevailing situations, or that systems of domination will be deeply affected.

This demands a careful study of systems of domination. The fact that this conference is between First and Third World theologians suggests that I not give an analysis of how domination exists and is implemented in the Second World.

In the capitalist world the system of domination has a very solid framework, after the manner of an iron jacket. It has been built up on colonialism and imperialism, since the end of World War I. There are two major compo nents of this system of domination.

The Bretton Woods Conference (1944), in which forty-four nations took part, designed the prevailing world economic order. The aim of those who met in Bretton Woods was to avoid a repetition of the world economic recession like the one that occurred between 1928 and 1932, and which created conditions that led to World War II. Bretton Woods agreed on a world order aiming at free trade, free exchange, where a world (transnational) market could be created. Need was expressed for the end of protectionism.

Two institutions were created for the implementation of these agreements: the World Bank and the International Monetary Fund. Little by little the system became consolidated but, at the same time, the domination of capital and the poverty and dependence of those nations that lacked the strength and means to share power were accentuated. The internationalization of capital—and labor—(results of the system) has not led to development of Third World countries, but rather to the loss of their possibilities for self-reliance. The magnitude of the foreign debt of Mexico, Brazil, Argentina, India, Zaire, Tanzania, and other Third World countries, is sufficient proof. It seems very difficult, though not impossible, to break with this system.

The second major element that has built up conditions of domination came from the Yalta Declaration agreed upon by the U.S.A., Britain, and the U.S.S.R. in April 1945, when zones of influence were assigned. Since then, and in spite of the existence of the United Nations Organization and the Association of Non-Aligned Countries ("the 77"), the fate of the world seems to be largely in the hands of the great powers, the U.S.A. and the U.S.S.R. especially.

The development of militarism, of armament production and sales, of military technology and of new doctrines of national security that gave to the military a more prominent role in government are results of the agreements made at Yalta. They provide elements for a situation that now seems more and more difficult to change.

It is within this framework that there has been emerging little by little a new type of power—or amalgamation of powers—that surprises and confounds those who struggle for justice and liberation. Here, as Karl Barth pointed out in the first version of his *Römerbrief*, the important thing is not to analyze power per se, in abstract terms, but to penetrate reality in order to discern who are the subjugated and who are the subjugators.

The reality in which we live is not transparent, is not clear, and when we do an analysis of it we should try to bring into the open what is hidden and dark. I stated above that, in spite of so much effort and generosity, meaningful changes are so difficult to achieve. The search for an explanation of this predicament has to take into account that at the beginning of the 1980s we are witnessing the manifestation of a kind of power that results from the combination of—at least—four different kinds of interest (and, behind each interest, forces): international capital, military might, technological knowledge, and international alliances.

The constellation and coordination of these forces shows their interrelationship. A clear attempt made during the 1970s for their coordination was the creation of the Trilateral Commission, gathering very influential persons of political, academic, military, and business circles from North America, western Europe, and Japan. If it is true that since the end of the 1970s the Trilateral Commission has not been as visible as it was during the period from 1974 to 1979, it should also be noted that some of the reports produced for it continue to be very influential—for example, "The Crisis of Democracy" by Crozier, Huntington, and Watanuki. It proposes the idea of "limited" or "restrained" democracy (hence, marginalization of persons from the exercise of their rights).

Another example of the coordination of interest and forces wielding power is, in the realm of religious studies and religious activities, the organization of conservative politicized centers—for example, the Institute for Religion and Democracy, in Washington, D.C.

The emergence of this kind of power surprises and confuses organized popular movements. This does not mean that they are giving up. But it seems that the instrumentalities used to date in popular struggles to counteract domination are not enough. For example, in Latin American countries where self-expression is possible, there has been a manifest rejection of the doctrine of "national security" and the crimes perpetrated in its name. But this is not enough to change the situation. Something similar happened in South Korea. In southern European countries where a majority has demanded change (Portugal, Spain, Greece, etc.), barricades to substantial transformation have immediately been put in place.

I conclude by saying that what I have presented cannot be taken as anything other than an introduction to an analysis. Even as an introduction it has been very short and, in the case of national and local situations, it should be complemented by a "conjunctional analysis," aiming to clarify how forces that operate in a given situation are in dynamic interrelationship. It is precisely this aspect of reality that presents the best opportunities for those aiming at justice and liberation to be creative and inventive in their struggles.

I want to reiterate that for me, and in spite of the prevailing trend toward rigidity in many places, peoples still have the initiative. They are not giving up; they continue to struggle for their rights and for the fulfillment of their hopes. Their struggles introduce the variables of change even in a world where the constant and the fixed discerned by analysis do not leave much room for the possibility of social transformations.

11

Rosemary Radford Ruether

A Feminist Perspective

The question of sexism in the struggle against oppression and for liberation constitutes what Mercy Amba Oduyoye has called "an irruption within an irruption" (within the irruption of the poor). It is the cry of protest of another yet more invisible and marginalized group—women—within the communities of the oppressed.

Over the last decade and still today there has been resistance to dealing with this question seriously in liberation theology and social analysis. This resistance takes several forms. It is said that the issue of sexism is trivial. It is an issue of middle-class and First World women. Or it is said that the issue, although real, is a luxury for Third World movements. Often this implies that the issue of sexism will be automatically resolved through the movement for national liberation, through the movement of socialist reconstruction of the social order.

So, the first, and main, point that I wish to make in this introductory statement on the relationship of sexism to the other structures of oppression—racism and classism—is that sexism is not a trivial issue. It is not an issue only for middle-class or First World women, even though, until now, it has been dealt with primarily by middle-class and First World women, and it has been trivialized by the Western media. Moreover, sexism will not automatically be taken care of by a nationalist or socialist revolution, if such revolutions remain male-centered in theory and practice, and do not take into account gender-specific types of oppression within a socio-economic and cultural system.

Sexism exists as a universal system of marginalization of women within various cultures and at every class level, although it has taken and takes different forms in different cultures and socio-economic systems, and at different class levels. To explicate this thesis I should like to analyze two systems of patriarchy: (1) classic, preindustrial patriarchy, and (2) liberal capitalist patriarchy. For the purposes of this discussion, I shall refrain from analyzing patriarchy in present systems of industrialization under state socialism. Suffice it to say that such systems have ameliorated some of the contradictions between patriarchy and industrialism, but they have not succeeded in overcoming the basic patriarchical structures that subordinate women both in the domestic and in the public work economy.

CLASSIC PREINDUSTRIAL PATRIARCHY

I shall be speaking here primarily of patriarchy within west European society as that society has been mandated in biblical law, as well as Greco-Roman law, and carried forth in medieval and early modern Europe. Some other cultures, particularly in Asia and Africa and among Amerindians, have preserved elements of motherright that balanced patriarchal dominance. It would be important, as a part of the ongoing EATWOT agenda, to study the way in which non-Western cultures preserved some areas of motherright (not to be confused with matriarchy, which probably never existed). Motherright means that women, as a group, have spheres of control over property, production, and culture independent of men. But this does not mean that women are dominant. In most of these cultures patriarchal elements still predominate. However, in west European culture and social structure by the early modern period, few traces of motherright customs remained. In this sense it can be seen as an example of classic patriarchal culture prior to industrialization.

The general characteristics of such a preindustrial patriarchal society are the following. Women in such societies are denied civil or legal rights in their own name. They cannot vote, represent themselves in law, make contracts, or in other ways be recognized as an autonomous adult with legal standing. They have the permanent legal standing of children or dependents, and are defined as quasiproperty of their fathers and later their husbands or other male relatives who are the "head of the household" where they reside. They can be physically punished, sometimes even killed, and sometimes sold or bought by males. They also have restricted rights to own or inherit property. They may be able to hold a dowry as a security against divorce or widowhood, but most of the property and titles in a family pass from father to son. The property of a woman is held or managed by her husband or other male relatives. Her children belong to her husband. Men can divorce women, but women cannot divorce men. At marriage she loses membership in her own family and becomes a member of her husband's family. Her identity is seen as legally merged into that of her husband who represents her and exercises headship over her.

Such patriarchal societies also deny women higher education. The public offices of war, politics, and culture are seen as belonging exclusively to men.

Women are denied access to the universities and other institutions that prepare men for professions and leadership in the public order. Religion reinforces this subordination of women in its symbolic systems and ecclesiastical codes, and excludes women from theological education and official religious leadership.

The woman, then, is restricted to the home. There she plays a double role as wife and mother who bears and nurtures children, and as a worker in the domestic economy. In preindustrial society this domestic economy was very extensive: most of the goods of society were produced in the home or in workshops and farms attached to the home. Thus woman played an extensive role as an economic worker (or as manager of domestic work), but lacked legal ownership to the fruits of her own labor. Her work belonged to her husband.

There were and are, of course, exceptions to this system in the cases of individual women, and women find means of secondary power and influence within it through other roles and relationships. But in this short treatment, this will have to suffice as description of the main outlines of women's status in classic patriarchy.

WOMEN IN CAPITALIST PATRIARCHY

The fundamental change that takes place in industrialism is the loss of the economic role of the family or the domestic economy to a collectivized and industrialized form of production outside the home and no longer owned by workers as family units. Women thus lose more and more of their productive economic role in the home. Instead, woman's role in the family is converted into being the manager of consumption, the nurturer in an intensified and prolonged system of child care (i.e., children remain economically dependent longer), and the housekeeper. Housekeeping now includes much more rigorous standards of cleanliness. With the loss of domestic servants, this role is taken over by the wife. The family shrinks from the extended to the nuclear family, so the adult woman is left as the only adult in the household in the absence of the husband who works outside the home.

A new ideology of the feminine arises to idealize this extended and intensified role of the wife and mother as nurturer who is mandated to provide a compensatory sphere of rest and recuperation for the working males, as well as take care of their physical needs and raise the children. Industrialization creates a new, rigid separation of spheres—separation of male from female, work from home, secular or public work (war and politics) from the domestic realm of compensatory nurture. Religion is disestablished, privatized, and identified with the woman's sphere—the home. Religion comes to be seen as "feminine" rather than "masculine," as it was in classic patriarchy.

Poor women or working-class women are incorporated into the new industrial economy at doubly exploitive wages. This was also true of children, although reform movements endeavored to eliminate child labor. Working women seldom do the same work as men, but are drawn into special women's sectors of the industrial economy where they work equally long hours, but typically at 50 percent or less of comparable male wages. They are used as a marginal and superexploited sector of the labor force. Such working women are still expected to play the roles of wife, mother, and housekeeper in relation to husband and children, as the nonworking middle-class housewife.

The nonworking (i.e., doing only unpaid domestic work) housewife sets the official standards of "femininity" of the culture. The working-class woman is called to aspire to these same standards, although society makes it impossible for her to actually do so. She is therefore regarded as not really a "lady"—that is, her womanhood is denied respect, which is given to the women of the ruling class who conform to the standards of normative "femininity."

As the industrial economy develops, more and more middle-class and married women are drawn into the labor force. Liberal reform movements ameliorate some of the bad conditions and poor wages of workers, although their primary answer to the problem of the exploitation of women is to remove them from the labor force by providing men a wage high enough for only them to have to work.

Liberal reformers also dissolve many of the structures of traditional patriarchal law that denied women civil rights, property rights, and access to higher education and the professions. This reform of traditional patriarchal legal systems is brought about particularly by the women's movement within liberalism and generally is seen as culminating in granting women the vote (i.e., officially recognizing them as legal persons in their own right).

But this reform of women's position, legally and educationally, masks the new system of economic oppression of women that is being forged by industrialism. This system of patriarchy in liberal capitalism has several characteristics. First, all working women at whatever class level are expected to work a double shift. That is to say, paid labor is defined in terms of a male workday based on a wife who provides the domestic support structure for paid work. Working women must work the same workday as the male (part-time work being so marginal and poorly paid as not to be a viable option for most women). But they also are expected to do the same domestic work in childcare, housekeeping, and providing the domestic support structure for the workers in the family as the normative "wife." Even in advanced industrial countries this work sector amounts to about twenty-five to forty hours a week.

This double work load fragments and defeats a woman's competence in both areas. On the one hand, she is blamed for being an inadequate wife and mother. All sorts of social evils are attributed to the fact that she works outside the home, although this work is essential for women who are single heads of household and increasingly necessary for married women as well. Secondly, her domestic work role structures her out of the more demanding professions that require extensive education, high mobility, extended hours away from the family, and so forth. Thus women are kept at the bottom of their various professions.

Women who work are structured primarily into gender-segregated sectors of the economy that have low status, poor working conditions, low pay, and few fringe benefits. Women's work is seldom unionized. In the U.S.A. about 90 percent of women workers work in economic sectors that are entirely or predominantly female. This work at whatever level is thought of as auxiliary and inferior to the male labor to which it is related—secretary to boss, nurse to doctor, waitress to owner or even headwaiter. The cultural stereotype of women's auxiliary and inferior relationship to men is thus preserved in the paid labor structure, as well as the relationship of women to men in the home.

Only a tiny percentage of women (about 3 to 5 percent in Western countries) work in professions regarded as of high status and pay—lawyers, university professors, doctors—and even these women are found in the lower-paid sectors of these professions. Thus it is somewhat misleading to speak of middle-class or ruling-class women as if they were comparable to middle-class or ruling-class men.

Women, in fact, do not possess class status in the same way as men. Most women belong to particular classes because of their dependence on males as parents or husbands. Very few women could maintain upper-class status by their own means, on the basis of independent income, apart from this dependency. This means that many women become impoverished when they are widowed or divorced. It has been shown that the fastest growing poverty sector in American society is that of female heads of households, whether white or of racial minorities. Such female-headed households account for the majority of families living in poverty.

One of the defects of the feminist movements in the Western middle-class context is that they have concentrated on promoting the equal pay and equal opportunities of women within the small sector of women working or aspiring to work in high-status male professions. This orientation of middle-class white feminism obscures the total economic and cultural structure of sexist oppression. Black and Third World women thus justifiably conclude that the feminist movement has nothing to do with them.

The sort of feminist movement that is compatible with a liberation theology perspective must explicate the total system of women's oppression, looking at this question from the perspective of working-class and Third World women.

DOUBLE OPPRESSION:
SEXISM WITHIN OPPRESSED CLASSES AND RACES

It has often been said that women of the working class and Third World suffer from "double oppression"—oppression both as women and as members of oppressed classist and racial groups. But the meaning of this phrase has not been fully explicated.

"Double oppression" does not mean simply one kind of oppression as women and another kind as members of oppressed groups, but, in addition, doubled kinds of *sexist* oppression that come from the multilayered oppression experienced by women of oppressed groups. One can analyze this compounding of sexist oppression on various levels.

On the level of their sexuality and sexual roles, oppressed women suffer double sexist oppression. On the one hand, they suffer the traditional kinds of oppression through their sexual roles in relation to the men of their own class or race (family). Their impoverished condition intensifies these problems—for example, means of birth control may not be available to them, the frustration experienced by men of their community may cause these men to take out their anger on women through sexual violence and wife battering, and so forth. Secondly, they experience a denigration of their womanhood at the hands of men (and women) of the dominant classes and skin color. They may be expected to be sexually available to dominant males in the places where they work, and are punished if they do not comply. As poor and minority women they are not granted the respect reserved for "ladies" of the dominant class and are humiliated by their inability to achieve the standards of the dominant "feminine" image and role.

On the economic level, poor women carry the double work role of both homemaker-mother and the paid job. But they carry this double work role under the most unfavorable conditions. They work in the most exploited sectors of the labor force—those reserved for minority and poor women. They receive the lowest pay and endure the worst working conditions. Their low pay, in turn, makes it even more difficult for them to fulfill their domestic role. They cannot pay for adequate food and shelter, much less for childcare. Their children are often left alone at home or in the streets, without adequate supervision. They cannot be sure whether their children will still be alive or well, or the house intact, when they return. Their place of work may be far from where they live, and they must take long bus rides or walk long distances to their work. Thus the double work load is exacerbated in myriad ways for the woman of the poor.

At the level of culture, minority and Third World women also suffer a double oppression. This is a particularly complicated area. It would be important for EATWOT to consider the effects of christianization and westernization on women of the Third World. For example, a particular African culture might have had practices of polygamy, but also of women's associations through which women marketed their own produce and had economic independence. Christianization and westernization seek to abolish polygamy, regarding such practices as immoral. Western Christians may do so believing that they are actually elevating the status of women. Liberal reforms dissolve some of the traditional disabilities experienced by native women and bring the vote and university education for women. But such reforms are available primarily to a small elite of upper-class native women.

Meanwhile, the poorer women experience the disruption of a traditional system of marriage without any adequate substitute, so that many former wives are left destitute. Also Western agricultural and industrial aid give the tools of modernization to men, in the Western capitalist assumption that it is men who are the productive class. Thus women are deprived of the economic power that they once had enjoyed.

Third World women of the poor are caught between two patriarchal systems and often suffer the worst of both worlds, losing the traditional areas of power they once enjoyed, and not being able to aspire to the new "rights for women" brought in for the upper classes.

Moreover, men of their own country, who lead and define the agenda of the anticolonial liberation movement, may see themselves as throwing off the effects of westernization and liberalization in such a way as to rescind some of the new rights won for women through this influence. They call for women to return to their traditional subordination in the name of affirming the traditional culture. Women are enjoined to step back and put on the veil or go back to other such customs of subordination in the name of patriotism and commitment to the liberation struggle. This is why it is essential that the women's agenda be included in the liberation agenda, and also that Third World women be the primary advocates for the women's agenda.

It is very important to contextualize this issue of double oppression in various specific cultural and historical contexts. What this means in certain cultures in Africa might be quite different from what it means in certain contexts in Asia or Latin America. This would be an important area for development of dialogue between Third and First World women within EATWOT. One has only begun to glimpse the complex patterns set up for women by the double structures of oppression created by the superimposition of Christianity and Western industrialization on top of traditional cultures within the context of colonial dependency. What is needed within EATWOT is real dialogue across classist, racial, and cultural lines to explicate more fully the actual meaning of the double oppression of women within the systems of classist, racial, and international economic oppression.

12

Engelbert Mveng

A Cultural Perspective

This is the first meeting of EATWOT with colleagues from the First World. What we are witnessing is surely an ecumenical event—a meeting of Christians divided by cultural traditions that are all-inclusive, closed, and intransigent.

At the origin of Christian division is a confrontation of cultures, with their claims that they have reduced the faith to ideological discourse—victorious, imperialistic, invasive. Dialogue is precluded, for the systems deny one another. Faith in one and the same Lord Jesus Christ, membership in one and the same church, have finally surrendered to the arrogance of theological discourse.

CULTURE AND ARROGANCE

Theology is the product of culture. The church, become an institution, is also the product of culture. Thus a dialogue of theologians is a confrontation of cultures. Here in Geneva we see it very well. The oppressed, the abandoned, the voiceless of the Third World have come to meet the masters of Western theology, those who have monopolized Christ, the church, the faith, and the world, and who claim that their discourse is universal theology. At long last, the Third World has found itself face to face with the oppressed, the abandoned, and the voiceless of the First World—in other words, with its own image in a Western version.

And the masters of the West? Oh, we have seen a fleeting silhouette or two, condescending, magisterial, almost disdainful, too busy for a greeting, and much too busy to stop and listen.

Are we to think that dialogue had been rejected? Or only that it was too early to speak of dialogue? Frankly, have we not had only monologue—the monologue of the poor and those left out of account? But now those of the Third World and those of the First World have met at last in this improbable encounter.

Perhaps it is precisely there that we have the major event of this Geneva meeting. Something has appeared on the horizon, something like a mysterious hand inscribing in the firmament the "Mene, Tekel, Peres" (Dan. 5:25) that yesterday's masters of thought dared not decipher.

The problem is that the dialogue of divided Christians, for centuries now, has never been able to pierce the walls of arrogance of their cultural bastions. The Second Vatican Council made dialogue possible, because for the first time a wall of arrogance was denounced. But those who have divided Christendom are the very ones who today divide the world into blocs. A dialogue among Christians, in a like universe, remains problematic.

What, then, can we say of the Third World and the First World? There has never been dialogue between them. There has been only, on the part of the First World, a monologue of arrogance, derision, and domination addressed to the Third World.

Culture is essentially a way of conceiving the human being, the world, and God. It is culture that bestows on faith its categories and its language. The culture of the West has never accepted the exsitence of other cultures. Its conception of the human being and the world reduced the rest of humanity to simple instruments for the realization of its own projected undertakings: its intentions for the human being, its intentions for society, and its intentions for the political, economic, and cultural organization of the world.

The fact that evangelization—Western-style—embraced the same undertaking is borne abundant witness by history. And in that embrace evangelization was poisoned in its roots. In the face of the anguish of the Third World the language of mission has been one of derision, arrogance, and domination. Faced with the thousands of years of art, culture, wisdom, spiritual life, and holiness amassed by the peoples of the Third World, the language of mission ignored all of it in the proclamation of the good news of salvation in Jesus Christ.

Yet the Christ of the gospel was the Christ of the marginalized, the poor, the oppressed, the Christ of a people of calamity and dereliction! The Christ of the gospel was the one come to fulfill Moses, not to destroy him. And the Third World had many a Moses. The Christ of the gospel was the suffering servant, filled with the Spirit of Yahweh, and sent to proclaim the good news of liberation to captives, to the oppressed. And liberation is what the Third World has need of most.

To tell the truth, between the culture of the West and the message of the gospel, the contradiction has been flagrant. The gospel preaches compassion where the West preaches derision and arrogance. The gospel announces deliverance where the West preaches domination and subjugation.

It thus becomes clear that if dialogue is possible, it can be only between the gospel and the Third World. Not between the culture of the West and the Third World, for the former is the denial of the latter. Theology being a product of culture, the mediation of the theology of the West becomes an obstacle to dialogue.

Thus the problem of the inculturation of the gospel is posed for us, first and foremost, in terms of "deculturation." The gospel must be de-westernized and restored to the peoples of the Third World.

The problem is perhaps not an altogether simple one. The attempt at dialogue between the First World and the Third World is revelatory. It is not by accident that those who are the commissioned representatives of Western theology have evaded dialogue. But, you will retort, how do you know that they were the ones with whom we wanted to speak? What is sure, you will be constrained to admit, is that they, ever since the birth of the Ecumenical Association of Third World Theologians, have spoken to us in terms of annoyance, demand, and arrogance—not of dialogue.

It is no accident that those of the First World whom we have met in Geneva have reflected to us our own image. They are the presence of the Third World at the heart of the First World. That is why our attempt at dialogue has revealed to us that, at bottom, there is a radical crisis between the gospel and the culture of the West. The good news of Jesus Christ, for the establishment, has ceased to be the message of salvation and liberation for the oppressed, and has become an instrument of domination in the service of the mighty of this world. God's word, the sacred scriptures, the church of Jesus Christ have been perverted. Here is where Pablo Richard's recent article, "La Bible, mémoire historique des pauvres" ["the Bible, the historical memoir of the poor"] is so pertinent.[1]

The poor must be given back the word of God. It is addressed to them, it is written for them, and it is they who have the preparation to receive and understand it.

CONVERSION AND DIALOGUE

And so the Geneva dialogue turns the page to a new chapter in postconciliar history. Instead of being a podium for academic dissertations and sterile polemics, it is a conscientization and call to conversion.

To speak of dialogue between the First and Third Worlds is before all else a denunciation of the arrogance of the former and the demagogy of the latter. It is recognition of the fact that all human culture is liable to the judgment of the gospel challenge. Next, it is the proclamation that everyone has the right to be different: it is the recognition that the other is in partnership with God. As God's partners, we are called, first and foremost, to conversion, as a prerequisite to any dialogue. And in this face-to-face encounter with God, there is no one but we of the Third World, and no one but they of the First World, to answer the very precise questions that God poses to us today. For them as well as for us, there are our respective cultures to be evangelized, so that through them we may encounter Jesus Christ. In the encounter with Jesus Christ we shall encounter one another, and this will be dialogue indeed.

The level on which the Geneva meeting is taking place is not difficult to discern. Whatever may have been its antecedents, its preparation, and the echoes awakened on either side, for us African delegates this meeting is a direct challenge on the part of the gospel, as we confront a world where all other dialogue is falsified in advance. The context, really, is that of the "dialogue" between North and South, a dialogue of the deaf, actually a cynical stage show in which the weak of this world are immolated to the God Moloch by the all too powerful worshipers of Mammon.

The first challenge tells us that dialogue between churches should be something different from the self-styled "dialogue" between North and South. Let this be a warning to those who, within our churches, still dream of theological triumphalism, which is but cultural triumphalism in an idolatrous form.

The second challenge tells us that authentic theological research is always the search for Jesus Christ. But the mystery of Jesus Christ is in our midst, in this universe of the Beatitudes called the Third World. The road walked by Jesus Christ today does not run north and south. That way is the way of exploitation, oppression, denial of God, and rejection of humankind.

In order for a North-South encounter to be possible, the North, as North, must encounter Jesus Christ, and the South, as South, must encounter him in its own turn. We continue to hold that Jesus Christ is the one possible hyphen that will tie our meeting together. The call, then, is a call to conversion and thus the theologian's mission becomes evangelization. It is not by accident that in the West there is more and more interest in theologies of liberation.

The presence of the Third World in the heart of the First World is a sign of hope. For the First World, this is the finger of God pointing to an opening through which Jesus Christ can make his way in. For us, it is assurance that it will be possible to meet Jesus Christ, one day, in the First World.

Dialogue between theologians of the Third World and those of the First World is just beginning.

NOTE

1. *Coeli*, no. 32 (Sept. 1982), pp. 3–8.

PART IV

HISTORY OF THEOLOGY

13

Dorothee Sölle

Dialectics of Enlightenment: Reflections of a European Theologian

What was the response of European Christianity to the challenges of the modern world? How did European churches respond to the scientific, the industrial, and the political revolutions during the last two centuries? What is relevant from this European heritage for us today?

I should like to ask these same questions in a less neutral language—on a deeper level. I have to ask myself about my European heritage as I face persons from the Third World, non-Europeans. The first thing that comes to my mind is guilt. My country participated in colonialism until 1918, and in neocolonialism since the 1950s and the German economic miracle. Today West Germany has excellent economic relationships with the leading powers in South Africa, Chile, Argentina, Turkey, and with many other countries whose governments perpetrate atrocities.

My country has participated in the exploitation of colonized peoples and in the raping of the earth. My country developed a unique form of racism by gassing six million Jews; it has hidden massive unconscious forms of sexism behind a liberal facade; it was the decisive force in the European militarism that led to two world wars. And the churches kept silence during the long dark night of European imperialism. My tradition is almost hopeless, and I ask myself: Is there anything to be proud of? Is there anything to remember happily or to offer others as a means of humanization?

THE LIBERATING EFFECTS OF THE ENLIGHTENMENT

The Enlightenment was rooted in the best intentions of the Judeo-Christian tradition. Galatians 3:28 says: "There are no more distinctions

79

between Jew and Greek [national or religious identity], slave and free [class identity], male and female [sexual identity], but all of you are one in Christ Jesus'' (JB).

Enlightenment refers to "light." When we pray "Light of light enlighten me," we mean: Make our thoughts clear, make our feelings conscious, make our actions consistent. The tradition of the Enlightenment is a liberating one. Its message was liberation from oppressive structures, and it enabled persons to engage in a thorough-going critique of the powers that be.

Kant defined the Enlightenment as "the outgoing of humankind from self-inflicted dependencies." In the context of the church, it meant new forms of criticism directed against impenetrable traditions such as those encasing the Bible, authoritarian institutions such as the church had become, and undemocratic domination by the state.

Christian tradition was rendered transparent by the double-pronged critical approach developed by Enlightenment theologians. One thrust of their criticism was the historico-critical approach to scripture, which freed Christians from the hitherto enforced limitation of their own thought and experience. The other was a substantial form of criticism that, for example, would eventually allow us to reject Paul's understanding of homosexuality and his teaching about obedience to the state. The spell of the immutability of tradition was broken and persons were set free to use their own consciences as well as the best parts of tradition as opposed to its oppressive tendencies.

The Enlightenment prompted the educated to do a sociological critique of given institutions such as the church, the school, the court of law, the hospital. They saw that none of these institutions were sacrosanct or holy, and none of them were the exclusive province of experts. The Enlightenment plunged the class that profited most from it—namely, the liberal bourgeois class—into political criticism of an oppressive state and a nonemancipatory society.

How did the church respond to these offerings of liberation from oppressive structures? After long struggle, Protestant churches embraced the historical and substantial criticisms of the Bible. However, Protestantism only partially embraced the sociological criticism of the church—some denominations more, some less. In general, Protestantism withdrew from the question of state domination by recourse to two ideological mechanisms: the doctrine of the two kingdoms and the liberal concept of the separation of church and state.

FAILURES OF PARTIALLY ENLIGHTENED LIBERAL CHURCHES

Of the different weaknesses and blindnesses of the liberal, enlightened churches, there are just a few fundamental ones that I should like to mention briefly.

Sexism

Protestantism failed to integrate women into the emancipatory process. In the romantic period, Schleiermacher was an exception and provided some hope for women. But in mainstream Protestantism, patriarchy in the form of a neo-Lutheran "orders of creation" metaphysics triumphed over emancipation.

Capitalism

The challenge of industrialization was not answered by the churches. They ignored the social consequences of rapid industrialization, including the massive migration of rural poor to the cities. The working class remained invisible to them.

The result of this numbness was a reduction of spirituality to a personal, individualistic, "Jesus and me" type of piety. Individualism was considered the deepest strength of the capitalist mentality. The sense of having, however, kills our very being, destroys human relationships, and produces the "Ice Age" (one of the favorite images of pop culture) in which mainstream European culture exists today.

Militarism

The enlightened interracial, nonsexist, international tradition failed to denounce and to confront militarism, which in Germany raised its head after 1871 with the Bismarck Reich—an early manifestation of the military-industrial complex. Liberal Protestantism enthusiastically applauded the beginning of World War I, and the Protestant church in Germany today is still not ready to adopt a clear antimilitaristic stance.

The shortcomings and failures of liberal bourgeois religion, which reduced the Enlightenment tradition to mere individualism, are obvious. Today there is a search for a different type of religion among our youth. They are looking for a God who is not at peace with sexism, capitalism, and militarism. As liberation theologians, what do we have to offer?

CONSEQUENCES FOR THE CHRISTIAN CHURCH TODAY

I should like to make you aware of the pain evoked by the phrase "a divided world." Our life achieves its deepest meaning in the overcoming of divisions and separations. All human beings seek unification and they suffer, consciously or unconsciously, from divisions, even more so if they have encountered Jesus Christ.

The most fundamental divisions in the church are based on worldly—in other words, socio-economic—conditions. How can we talk about the undivided love of God if we are rich and becoming richer at the cost of the poor?

How can we give our lives totally to God's life in the world if we do not allow our vision to interfere with the powers that be? How can we talk about unity while our governments do anything to increase the annihilation potential that divides the human community into "first-strikers" and "second-strikers" who harbor a deep death-wish and a desire to exterminate the so-called enemy?

Christians in South Africa have developed a specific form of dividing and separating the human family called apartheid. I construe the concept of apartheid in terms of both political and spiritual disunity, which permeates the institutions and the lives of South Africans.

Our own First World theology is tainted by our living in apartheid: we do not allow our brothers and sisters from the Third World to enter our thoughts and feelings, our singing and praying, our reading of scripture, and our theologizing. We manipulate our ideas about family life and privacy, about clinical pastoral education and family counseling, to hide ourselves from those whom we exploit. Living in the rich countries of the First World means participating in apartheid through lifestyle and ideology.

Rich nations wage a permanent and relentless war against poor nations. During the last twenty years, a profit-centered economy has demonstrated its incompetence in the face of the problem of hunger. Instead of feeding the hungry, we in the First World arm ourselves against them. Under the pretext of East/West conflict, we escalate the arms race as the major dynamic in North/South conflict. "The bombs are falling now," states the U.S. peace group, Mobilization for Survival.

Militarism aims to protect capitalism, and capitalism uses racism and sexism as helpmates. It is not an international balance of deterrence, but the new political doctrine of national security, that underlies the global master plan of the Trilateral Commission: unity by silencing the oppressed, peace without justice, and suppression and regulation of those who thirst for justice.

A cheap unity divorced from and defended against historical struggles is a danger for the church. It is not up to us to decide as a matter of preference whether to establish or to neglect the relationship of Christ to the present situation. To neglect this relationship is to deny Jesus. We must tug, draw him into the flesh; or, as Luther put it, we must draw him into historical flesh, into what is happening to persons today.

Currently the most important religion in Western industrialized countries is individualism and the attempt to make more out of one's life. Education and career are subsumed under this prevailing rubric. The praxis of this new religion is consumerism: the compulsive drive to shop, to get, to own, to possess, to use—all in a frantic pursuit of that which is advertised to guarantee the full meaning of life.

The Judeo-Christian tradition affirms that the deepest human need is to be needed and to be loved. Post-Christian corporate capitalism has completely destroyed a culture once built around these personal and humanistic needs. It has transformed the need to be into the wish to have, thereby completely alienating persons from their own spirituality. It does not foster a vision that goes beyond individual well-being. It does not prompt interference in behalf of others' and one's own dignity. Health has become a religious value. Future and past, which once were the framework of reasonable beings, have lost their human and divine meaning; post-Christian corporate capitalism has driven out both memory and hope in favor of the "right now" of consumerism.

An African friend told me, "I don't want to grow old in West Germany," because of the way we segregate the old from others. We have something to learn from other cultures about this issue. "Reverse mission" becomes a necessity in a culture that has sold out to individualism.

More and more persons in Western metropolises rebel against what has been done to them. *Wir haben schon Grund genug zum Weinen, auch ohne euer Tränengas* ("we have reason enough to cry, even without your tear gas") was one of the slogans of young rioters in Zurich in 1980. This cry—this weeping—is the best thing that west Europeans can give to the human community right now. These are the tears that Christ wept over Jerusalem. The renewal of the human community takes place where the cry is heard and the last—namely, the unemployed, uneducated, futureless youth—become the first.

Ignazio Silone writes: "We are saved today by freeing our spirit from resignation to the existing disorder. Spiritual life has always meant a capacity for sacrifice. In a society like ours a spiritual life can only be a revolutionary life." The existing disorder corresponds to the prevailing disbelief. The existing disorder comes from the fact that we rape the earth, lead a war of annihilation against the poor, betray the Spirit through the godless dream of individualism, and maintain sexist oppression, thereby disconnecting persons from one another.

The most natural and unconscious response to these facts is resignation to the existing disorder. The "flesh" seduces us into believing that human life has never been different. For many, faith is not considered to be an alternative, because of the ambivalence of the established churches on the issues of ecology, militarism, individualism, and sexism.

A spiritual response to these facts is possible, however. It is a response that emerges from a different vision of life, one handed down to us from biblical tradition and constituting a more daring interference with the powers that be. It seems that from the side of the citizen of the First World the concept of resistance is becoming more and more relevant in the latter part of the twentieth century. "Trust in God and resist" is becoming the new imperative.

To create resistance groups inside the belly of the beast is the new missionary task. To follow Christ at least up to Gethsemane if not, as some have done, to Golgotha is the way. The historical situation in Europe changed when NATO decided in December 1979 to "go nuclear." There is no way in which the theological situation could have remained unchanged. The first mission commandment of Jesus was given when he sent the disciples out with the message "the kingdom of heaven is at hand."

"Heal the sick, raise the dead, cleanse lepers, cast out demons" (Matt. 10:8) are imperatives for resisters today. Those who do so are the true followers of Jesus; they raise the dead apartheid folk, they conscienticize them, they cast out the demons of militarism.

Churches that are on the side of resistance groups could give them support and encouragement as they move from one place to another. Churches then would understand themselves as civil rights movements for peace and justice.

If we do not teach and live resistance as Jesus did, we shall die either as victims of preemptive first-strikes or as psychic casualties in the midst of our apartheid fortresses. We are in search of a nondivided world. There is no way to go around the cross, to avoid it. The crosses we busily avoid descend on our neighbors. If we look for the spiritual reality grounded in Jesus Christ who loved all things and with his whole being, there is one place to find unification—namely, in the struggle. In the cross. In resistance.

14

Johann Baptist Metz

Standing at the End
of the Eurocentric Era of Christianity:
A Catholic View

My starting point is a hypothesis that embraces all the six theses to follow, and qualifies them theologically: *We are standing at the end of the European-centered era of Christianity*. This standpoint enables me to look back at European/Western Christianity and to look forward to the future of Christianity and to the future of the churches in our divided world. The Catholic Church and its theologies are the main concerns here—in terms of both their European history and their present trends.

Thesis 1: The course of Western Christianity in the modern age has been stamped above all else by the Reformation, Enlightenment, the French and American revolutions, technological civilization, secularization (the so-called occidental rationality), and by the spirit of capitalism.

There is a dark side, a *colonialist underside,* to these processes: the anthropological pattern stamping them, the anthropology of domination, starting with an anthropology of subjugation vis-à-vis nature.

Thesis 2: There has been a more offensive *assimilation of this course of the modern age by Protestant Christianity (combining the opportunity for productive contemporaneity with the danger of overadaptation); and there has been a more* defensive *assimilation of it by Catholic Christianity (combining the opportunity to remain sensitive to the "dialectics" of the Enlightenment with the danger of a sterile, unproductive noncontemporaneity or backwardness).*

In any case this European development resulted in a profound crisis for Christianity and its theologies:

1) by the reduction of Christianity to the private realm, the *privatistic reduction* of Christianity in the modern age (the "modern consensus" between the bourgeoisie and Marxism);

2) by the *rationalistic reduction* of Christianity—that is, by an ever increasing desensitization, a radical suspicion of symbol, memory, and myth under the anonymous pressure of the modern world of technological reason (secondhand symbols).

Thesis 3: There was a special dilemma for Catholic Christianity and Catholic theology in the development of the modern age in Europe.

Catholicism not only did not take part in the fight for bourgeois freedoms (civil liberties); indeed, on the whole it resisted the bourgeois history of freedom. The so-called Catholic ages within modern European history were always periods of "countering," of "being against": against the Reformation (Counter-Reformation), against revolution, against the Enlightenment; they were also periods of political restoration and political romanticism.

How is this historical process to be evaluated? Are Catholics simply recalcitrants in the school of the modern age (with its lessons in bourgeois freedom and enlightenment)? Is Catholic resistance anything other than backwardness? Is there any other alternative for Catholics besides simply retrieving the testimonies of the Reformation and the bourgeois history of freedom, as liberal Catholic theologians recommend? Is it even possible to retrieve a missed moment of history? Or could there perhaps now be something like a new reformation situation in which Catholicism learns to invoke grace as liberation and thus learns to live?

I am assuming that this last question can be answered positively. The positive answer, however, points beyond the monocultural sphere of European Christianity. The hour of reformation is the hour of the poor churches in our world. The fundamental reformational situation is being defined by the emergent churches of the poor countries. The second Reformation will come from neither Wittenberg nor Geneva nor Rome, but from the poor churches of the Third World.

Thesis 4: Within Western Catholic theology there are three types of reaction to the "European dilemma" of Catholicism.

I mean this in terms of ideal types; in reality there are quite often mixed forms.

1) Resolution of the dilemma by means of a utopia turned backward to the

past—that is, by retreating from the Reformation and modern developments (the mentality of the Counter-Reformation, of a recatholicizing traditionalism).

a) *Its theological expression:* social criticism oriented to the past; the triumph of classic political theology.

b) *Its ecclesial expression:* the traditional "people's church" as a church *for* the people (not *of* the people) with predominantly feudal structures.

c) *Its ecumenical expression:* controversial theology, apologetics vis-à-vis Protestantism; primacy of concepts, of systems, not of experience, praxis.

2) Resolution of the dilemma by identifying with the plausibilities of "liberal"/bourgeois society and by trying to "catch up with" the Reformation and the Enlightenment within Catholic Christianity and the Catholic Church.

a) *Its theological expression:* liberal theology (including its great services to theology, for example in the debate with historicism); criticism of the church without criticism of society (criticism of the church according to the standards of the bourgeois history of freedom).

b) *Its ecclesial expression:* a supply church servicing the needs of the people, filling personal and group demands; Christianity as a bourgeois religion (overidentification of the bourgeois subject with the Christian subject, of bourgeois freedom with Christian freedom; God as a "value" that arches over the preconceived bourgeois identity; Christianity as the political religion of the bourgeois middle class).

c) *Its ecumenical expression:* dialogue between Catholicism and Protestantism—on the basis of Christianity as a bourgeois religion.

3) Resolution of the dilemma by productive or creative participation in forming a new social identity and by instigating a "second reformation" in Christianity in order to "interrupt" the development of Christianity as a bourgeois religion.

a) *Its theological expression: new* political theologies, basically ecumenical (i.e., from their very beginning).

If I am right it started with a shocking experience in our European, in particular in our German, context: the experience that, for me, being a Christian meant being a Christian *in the face of Auschwitz, in the face of the Holocaust;* doing theology meant doing theology in the face of Auschwitz, in the face of the Holocaust.

It meant the end point of any kind of theological idealism (by which we tried to dominate world theology), with its burden of apathy and its lack of sensitivity to historical catastrophes and "interruptions." The system is no longer the locus of theological truth—at least not since the catastrophe of the Holocaust, which no one, under pain of cynicism, may ignore or allow to disappear in an objective system of meaning. For me, there is no truth that could be defended with one's back turned to Auschwitz, no "meaning" that could be salvaged with one's back turned to Auschwitz, no God to whom one could pray with one's back turned to Auschwitz, no Jesus whom one could follow with one's back turned to Auschwitz.

It meant the end point of bourgeois religion. After becoming theologically aware of my post-Holocaust situation, I also asked myself what sort of faith it must have been that allowed us to go on believing and praying undisturbed during the Nazi period with our backs turned to Auschwitz. Was it not a purely "believed" faith, faith as a "superstructure" of our bourgeois identity, and thus faith as bourgeois religion? Was it not a faith that does not really follow but believes in following, and under the mantle of believing that it was following went its own way? Was it not a faith without compassion but with a belief in compassion, and under the mantle of believing that it was compassion cultivated the apathy that allowed us Christians to go on believing and praying with our backs turned to Auschwitz? Here is the decisive reason for my criticism of Christianity as bourgeois religion.

We European Catholics saw the catastrophe of Auschwitz—our lack of resistance—as a result of the reductional privatization of Christianity in the modern European experience. In the light of this shocking experience we began to reread the Bible. We rediscovered that the messianic God is never a "superstructure" that could be superimposed on any given situation without contradiction. God is represented rather by the idea of *intervention, resistance. God's grace is the ability to resist in time—and constantly.*

That is what we have tried to learn from our catastrophe: if Christianity is to regain its messianic power, it must overcome the situation of privatization. As a private matter it cannot be a messianic matter. So we must try to overcome our privatization—not from above, but from below, from the base of our society, by developing a new politico-religious culture at the ground level.

This new type of messianic church and Christianity is already at work: in the poor churches of the Third World where the struggling basic communities sprang up. It became an inspiration for our own European situation.

b) *Its ecclesial expression:* the basic community church moving into the center of the process of forming Christian identity, with its new productive unity of social and religious identity-formation, with its new creative unity of religion and politics, of redemption and liberation— a unity that can be represented neither by the old theocratic monism nor by the modern bourgeois-liberal dualism.

c) *Its ecumenical expression:* not primarily oriented toward unity among the Christian denominations (as in Europe), but rather toward unity among the churches of the First World and the Third World. The breakdown of church unity in the sixteenth century thus appears primarily as an inner-European event that can be overcome only indirectly, by overcoming the Eurocentrism of the church.

An orientation toward the universal or world church is envisioned here in two ways. First, by perception and theological acknowledgment of the fact that the Third World has historically and socially already entered the First World—not as a partner, but above all else as a victim.

Secondly, by perception and theological acknowledgment of the fact that since Vatican II the Catholic Church is moving away from a culturally mono-centric European church to a culturally polycentric world church.

Thesis 5: The Catholic Church is changing from a culturally monocentric church (Europe and North America) to a culturally polycentric world church.

This is perhaps the most profound break or hiatus in the history of the church since the earliest period of Christianity. It is important to pay attention to the very first marks or traces and beginnings of this transition and to the significance it has for the relationship between the churches of the First World and the Third World.

Empirically, the Eurocentric age of the church is coming to an end. The Catholic Church of the present does not *have* a Third World church, it *is* a Third World church with a European/Western origin.

In order to highlight the theological significance of this new situation, I would divide church history into three epochs as does Karl Rahner: the brief period of Judeo-Christianity; the very long period within one culture (the period of Hellenism and of European culture and civilization); and the period of a culturally polycentric, truly universal or world church that had its beginnings at Vatican II.

Signs in Vatican II of this new period are to be found in: (1) the composition of the council: multicultural for the first time; (2) liturgical reform for the whole church (liturgy in the vernacular); (3) doctrinal statements:

a) For the first time a cautious, positive assessment of the great world religions is begun in the Declaration on the Relationship of the Church to Non-Christian Religions.

b) In the Declaration on Religious Freedom the principle of tolerance for the spread of other faiths is proclaimed (important for witness against such countermovements as Khomeini's fundamentalism).

c) In the Pastoral Constitution on the Church in the Modern World there is an understanding of the world that modifies the prevailing identification of the universal church with the Eurocentric church.

This transition entails many far-reaching consequences:

1) With regard to the churches of the Third World, especially in Latin America, ecclesial processes and conflicts (some observers are already talking about "two churches") must be judged in the light of this epoch-making transition. The question is not principally one of a conflict between an ortho-dox church bound to tradition and a heterodox church of liberation de-nounced as communist or communist-inclined. It is rather a question of the painful process of changing from a Eurocentric church to a culturally poly-centric world church. During this transition those who consider themselves

particularly orthodox and faithful to the Vatican are in danger of betraying just that mandate or message that lies well-founded in the universal memory of the church—namely, the epoch-making transition to a culturally polycentric world church: "You will be my witnesses . . . to the ends of the earth" (Acts 1:8).

2) With regard to the new situation of the European churches and European theologies, the transition to a culturally polycentric world church does not mean that the church and theology break down into a historically and politically innocent pluralism. There are two reasons why this is not so.

First, the European church is an essential and lasting element of the original history of the new world church. The almost two thousand years of European church history has its own undeniable truth; without it there would be no truth for the whole church.

Secondly, the European church is connected to the polycentric world church not only by this original history, but also by a history of guilt: ecclesial colonialism (Christianity as an export), economic colonialism, cultural colonialism, and political colonialism.

Thesis 6: This cultural polycentrism within Christianity must be grounded in a culture of resistance/liberation. *Otherwise we shall never contribute to a culture of peace.*

Is cultural polycentrism a viable assumption? Are there any great and living cultures that have not been touched and deeply changed by European/Western colonialism and its technological civilization?

"European/Western" includes capitalism, multinational corporations, exported consumerism, but also classic marxist anthropology. It bespeaks a technological civilization that entails a condensed history of Europe and a condensed European anthropology. Technology embodies not only political but also historical and anthropological colorings.

At any rate, the essential fact remains that if there is to be cultural polycentrism it must be based on cultures of resistance to and liberation from all overt or covert forms of European colonialism. In this regard, the projection of European East-West conflict into the Third World is probably the last and most deadly form of European colonialism.

Resistance/liberation must have an authentic cultural basis; otherwise its "liberation" would be nothing but "conversion to Western civilization."

Resistance/liberation will succeed only if "conversion" succeeds within European societies. This conversion is also a kind of resistance/liberation—liberating us Westerners not from a state of oppression, but from our apathy; not from powerlessness, but from our particular forms of power and militarism.

This can be considered our common basis for contributing to a culture of peace—inspired by faith and discipleship as a productive, unifying force in our divided world.

PART V

REFORMULATION OF THE METHODOLOGY AND CONTENT OF THEOLOGY

15

James H. Cone

Black Theology: Its Origin, Methodology, and Relationship to Third World Theologies

The concept "black theology" refers to a theological movement that emerged among North American blacks during the second half of the 1960s. During the early part of the 1970s, North American black theology began to make an impact in South Africa.[1] I shall here limit my analysis to the origin and meaning of North American black theology, with special reference to its methodology, as defined by its dialogue with the Third World theologies of Africa, Asia, and Latin America.

ORIGIN OF BLACK THEOLOGY

The origin of black theology had three major contexts: (1) the civil rights movement of the 1950s and 60s, largely associated with Martin Luther King, Jr.; (2) the publication of Joseph Washington's book, *Black Religion* (1964); and (3) the rise of the black power movement, strongly influenced by Malcolm X's philosophy of black nationalism.

Civil Rights Movement

All persons involved in the creation of black theology were also deeply involved in the civil rights movement, and they participated in the protest demonstrations led by Martin Luther King, Jr. Unlike most other contemporary theological movements in Europe and North America, black theology did not originate in a seminary or university setting. In fact, most of its early interpreters did not even hold advanced academic degrees. Black theology came into being in the context of the struggle of black persons for racial justice, which was initiated in the black churches, but chiefly identified with such civil rights organizations as the Southern Christian Leadership Conference (SCLC), the National Conference of Black Churchmen (NCBC), the Interreligious Foundation for Community Organization (IFCO), and many black caucuses in white churches.

From the beginning black theology was understood by its creators as Christian theological reflection upon the black struggle for justice and liberation, strongly influenced by the life and thought of Martin Luther King, Jr. When King and other black church persons began to relate the Christian gospel to the struggle for justice in American society, the great majority of white churches and their theologians denied that such a relationship existed. Conservative white Christians claimed that religion and politics did not mix. Liberal white Christians, with few exceptions during the 1950s and early 60s, remained silent on the theme or they advocated a form of gradualism that denounced boycotts, sit-ins, and freedom rides.

Contrary to popular opinion, King was not well received by the white American church establishment when he inaugurated the civil rights movement with the Montgomery bus boycott in 1955.[2] Because blacks received no theological support from white churches and their theologians (who) were preoccupied with Barth, Bultmann, and the death-of-God controversy!), blacks themselves had to search deeply into their own history in order to find a theological basis for their prior political commitment to liberate the black poor. They found support in Richard Allen (founder of the African Methodist Episcopal [AME] Church in 1816), Henry Highland Garnet (a nineteenth-century Presbyterian preacher who urged slaves to resist slavery), Nat Turner (a slave Baptist preacher who led an insurrection that killed sixty whites), Henry McNeal Turner (an AME bishop who claimed in 1898 that "God is a Negro"), and many others.[3]

When blacks investigated their religious history, they were reminded that their struggle for political freedom did not begin in the 1950s and 60s but had roots stretching back to the days of slavery. They were also reminded that their struggle for political justice in the United States had always been associated with their churches. Whether in the independent northern churches (AME, African Methodist Episcopal Zion [AMEZ], Baptists, etc.), or the so-called invisible institution among slaves in the south (which emerged with the independent black churches after the Civil War), or blacks in white denominations, black Christians have always known that the God of Moses and of Jesus did not create them to be slaves or second-class citizens in North America. In order to forge a theological witness to this religious knowledge, black preachers and civil rights activists of the 1960s initiated the development of a black theology that rejected racism and affirmed the black struggle for liberation as consistent with the gospel of Jesus.

Joseph Washington

When black preachers and lay activist Christians began to search for the radical side of their black church history, they also began to ask about the distinctive religious and theological contributions of black persons. It was generally assumed, by most whites and many blacks as well, that black culture had no unique contribution to make to Christianity in particular and humanity in general. Indeed white liberal Christians understood integration to mean assimilation: that blacks would reject their cultural past by becoming like whites, adopting European cultural values. The assumption behind the white definition of integration was the belief that African cultural values among North American blacks were completely destroyed during slavery. Therefore, if blacks were to develop a cultural knowledge of themselves, they had to find it in their identification with white American values.

Joseph Washington, a black scholar, wrote his *Black Religion* in the context of the hegemony of integration in black-white relationships in America. Contrary to the dominant view, Washington contended that there was a unique black culture, a distinctive black religion, that can be placed alongside Protestantism, Catholicism, Judaism, and secularism. Black religion is not identical with white Protestantism or any other expression of Euro-American Christianity.

Washington, however, was not pleased with the continued existence of black religion, and he placed the blame squarely upon white Christians. He contended that black religion exists only because blacks had been excluded from the genuine Christianity of white churches. Because blacks were excluded from the faith of white churches, black churches are not genuine Christian churches. And if there are no genuine Christian churches, there can be no Christian theology. Blacks have only folk religion and folk theology. In Washington's own words: "Negro congregations are not churches but religious societies—religion can choose to worship whatever gods are pleasing. But a church without a theology, the interpretation of a response of the will of God for the faithful, is a contradiction in terms."[4]

Although *Black Religion* was received with enthusiasm in the white community, it was strongly denounced in the black church community. Indeed, black theology, in part, was created in order to refute Washington's thesis. Black preachers wanted to correct two misconceptions: (1) that black religion is not Christian and thus has no Christian theology; and (2) that the Christian gospel has nothing to do with the struggle for justice in society.

Black Power Movement

After the march on Washington in August 1963, the integration theme in the black community began to lose ground to the black nationalist philosophy of Malcolm X.[5] The riots in the ghettoes of U.S. cities were shocking evidence that many blacks agreed with Malcolm X's contention that America was not a dream but a nightmare.

However, it was not until the summer of 1966, after Malcolm X's assassination (1965), that the term "black power" began to replace the term "integration" among many civil rights activists. The occasion was the continuation of the James Meredith "march against fear" (in Mississippi) by Martin Luther King, Jr., Stokely Carmichael, and other civil rights activists. Carmichael seized this occasion to sound the black power slogan, and it was heard loud and clear throughout the U.S.A.[6]

The rise of black power had a profound effect upon the appearance of black theology. When Carmichael and other radical black activists separated themselves from King's absolute commitment to nonviolence by proclaiming black power, white church persons, especially members of the clergy, called upon their black brothers and sisters in the gospel to denounce black power as un-Christian. To the surprise of white Christians, some black ministers refused to follow their advice and instead wrote a "Black Power Statement" that was published in the *New York Times,* July 31, 1966.[7]

The publication of the "Black Power Statement" may be regarded as the beginning of the conscious development of a black theology in which black ministers consciously separated their understanding of the gospel of Jesus from white Christianity and identified it with the struggles of the black poor for justice. The radical black clergy created an ecumenical organization called the National Conference of Black Churchmen (NCBC) as well as black caucuses in the National Council of Churches and almost all white churches. Black church leaders denounced white racism as the Antichrist, and were unrelenting in their attack on its demonic presence in white denominations. It was in this context that the term "black theology" emerged.

BLACK THEOLOGY AS LIBERATION THEOLOGY

It is one thing to proclaim black theology and quite another to give it theological substance. Many white Christians and almost all white theologians dismissed black theology as nothing but rhetoric. Inasmuch as white theologians controlled the seminaries and university departments of religion, it gave the impression that only whites, Europeans, and persons who think like them could define what theology is. In order to challenge the white monopoly on the definition of theology, many young black scholars realized that they had to carry the fight to the seminaries and universities where theology was being done.

I wrote the first book on black theology: *Black Theology and Black Power* (1969). The central thesis of that book was its identification of the liberating elements in black power with the Christian gospel. One year later I wrote the second book, *A Black Theology of Liberation* (1970) and made liberation the organizing center of my theological perspective. I wrote: "Christian theology is a theology of liberation. It is a rational study of the being of God in the world in the light of the existential situation of an oppressed community, relating the forces of liberation to the essence of the gospel, which is Jesus Christ."[8]

After my works appeared, other black theologians joined me, supporting my theological project and also challenging what they regarded as my excesses. In his *Liberation and Reconciliation: A Black Theology* (1971), J. Deotis Roberts, although supporting my emphasis on liberation, claimed that I overlooked reconciliation as central to the gospel and black-white relationships. A similar position was advocated by Major Jones' *Black Awareness: A Theology of Hope* (1971). Other black theologians claimed that I was too dependent upon white theology and was not sufficiently aware of the African origins of black religion. This position is taken up by my brother, Cecil, in his *Identity Crisis in Black Theology* (1975), and it is also found in Gayraud Wilmore's *Black Religion and Black Radicalism* (1972).

Although my perspective on black theology was challenged by other black scholars, they supported my claim that liberation was the central core of the gospel as found in the scriptures and the religious history of black Americans. For black theologians the *political* meaning of liberation was best illustrated in the exodus; its *eschatological* meaning was found in the life, death, and resurrection of Jesus. The exodus was interpreted to be analogous to Nat Turner's slave insurrection and Harriet Tubman's emancipation of an estimated three hundred slaves. Slave songs (often called "Negro spirituals"), sermons, and prayers expressed the futuristic character of liberation found in the resurrection of Jesus.

Because many black male theologians were reluctant to take up the subject of sexism and others were openly hostile when black women raised the issue as a critical theological problem, a black feminist theology is emerging as an open challenge to the patriarchal nature of the current perspectives of black theology. Jacquelyn Grant and Pauli Murray are prominent examples.[9] Black feminist theologians accept the liberation theme of black theology, but they reject the narrow limitations of that theme to racism, as if sexism were not an important problem in the black community.

Because of the urgency of the problem of sexism, black women have begun to insist on doing theology out of their experience. Black feminist theology is both a challenge to the sexist orientation of black theology and a deepening of the black struggle against racism.

THE METHODOLOGY OF BLACK THEOLOGY
AND ITS RELATIONSHIP TO THIRD WORLD THEOLOGIES

In the early 1970s, black theologians in North America began to have some contact with other forms of liberation theology in Africa, Latin America, and Asia.[10] Black theology in South Africa became a natural ally. Black and Latin theologies became copartners in their identification of the gospel with the liberation of the poor, although one emphasized racism and the other classism. A similar partnership occurred with black, African, and Asian theologians regarding the importance of culture in defining theology.

When we black theologians dialogued with Third World theologians, the striking difference between the theologies of the poor and the theologies of the rich became very clear to us. As long as our dialogue was confined to North American whites who oppressed blacks, and to European theologians whom our oppressors venerated, our understanding of our theological task was determined too much by our reactions to white racism in the United States. African, Asian, and Latin American theologians enlarged our vision by challenging us to do theology from a global perspective of oppression. Third World theologians urged us to analyze racism in relation to international capitalism, imperialism, colonialism, world poverty, classism, and sexism. For the first time, black theologians began to seriously consider socialism as an alternative to capitalism.

We began to see the connections between the black ghettoes in the U.S.A. and poverty in Asia, Africa, and Latin America, between the rising unemployment among blacks and other poor minorities in the U.S.A. and the exploitation of the labor of Third World peoples, and between the racist practices of white churches of North America and Europe, and the activities of their missionaries in the Third World. These discoveries deeply affected our political and theological vision, and we began to see clearly that we could not do theology in isolation from our struggling brothers and sisters in the Third World. As oppressors band themselves together in order to keep the poor of the world in poverty, the poor of the world must enter into political and theological solidarity if they expect to create a movement of liberation capable of breaking the chains of oppression.

Early in our dialogue, black and Third World theologians realized the importance of building a common theological movement of liberation. Although we encountered differences with each other (especially with Latins during the early stages of our dialogue regarding race and class analyses), our mutual commitment to do theology in solidarity with the poor held us together. We had too much in common to allow our differences to separate us. Furthermore, it became increasingly clear that our differences were largely due to a difference in context and to our mutual internalization of the lies that our oppressors had told us about each other.

After seven years of dialogue under the auspices of the Ecumenical Association of Third World Theologians, including five major conferences, the differences between black and Third World theologians have diminished considerably, and our similarities have increased to the extent that we are now engaged in the exciting task of creating a Third World theology of liberation that we all can support.[11]

When the question "How do we do theology?" is asked, black and Third World theologians agree that theology is not the first act but rather the second. Although our Latin American brothers and sisters, with the use of

Marxist class analysis, were the first to explicate this methodological point,[12] it was already present and now reaffirmed in all our theologies.[13] The first act is both a religio-cultural affirmation and a political commitment on behalf of the liberation of the poor and voiceless of our continents. Our cultural identity and political commitment are worth more than a thousand textbooks of theology. That is why we do not talk about theology as the first order of business in EATWOT. Rather our first concern is with the quality of the commitment that each of us has made and will make for those about whom and with whom we claim to do theology. We contend that we know what others believe by what they do, and not by what they say in their creeds, conference statements, or theological textbooks.

Praxis—a reflective political action that includes cultural identity—comes before theology in any formal sense. Therefore, the initial motivation that compels us to do theology is not our desire to place books in university and seminary libraries for professors and their graduate students. On the contrary, our reason for doing theology arises from our experience in the ghettoes, villages, and churches of the poor in our various countries. We do not believe that it is necessary for our peoples to remain poor. Something must be done about the misery of our peoples. Doing and saying are therefore bound together so that the meaning of what one says can be validated only by what one does. Theology for us is critical reflection upon a prior religio-cultural affirmation and political commitment to solidarity with the oppressed of our continents.

Because the starting point of black and Third World theologies is defined by a prior cultural affirmation and political commitment to solidarity with the poor, our theologies bear the names that reflect our affirmations and commitments. We call our theologies black, African, Hispanic-American, Asian, red, Latin American, minjung, black feminist, and a host of other names that still sound strange to persons whose theological knowledge has been confined to European and white North American theologies. The identities of our theologies are determined by the human and divine dimensions of reality to which we are attempting to bear witness.

We do not begin our theology with a reflection on divine revelation as if the God of our faith is separate from the suffering of our peoples. We do not believe that revelation is a deposit of fixed doctrines or an objective word of God that is then applied to the human situation. On the contrary, we contend that there is no truth outside or beyond the concrete historical events in which persons are engaged as agents. Truth is found in the histories, cultures, and religions of our peoples. Our focus on social and religio-cultural analyses differentiates our theological enterprise from the progressive and abstract theologies of Europe and North America. It also illuminates the reasons why orthopraxis, in contrast to orthodoxy, has become for many of us the criterion of theology.[14]

Many European and North American critics have accused black and Third World theologians of reducing theology to ideology, but their criticism is misplaced. It glosses over the human character of all theologies and particularly the ideological option for the rich that our critics have made. Unlike our critics, we do not claim to be neutral in our theology, because the enormity of the suffering of our peoples demands that we choose for their liberation and against the structures of oppression. We cannot let those who support the structures of oppression define what theology is. On this point, black theologians identify with the way Malcolm X expressed it: "Don't let anybody who is oppressing us ever lay the ground rules. Don't go by their game, don't play the game by their rules. Let them know that this is a new game, and we've got new rules."[15]

The dominant theologians of Europe and North America want the same theological rules to be observed because they made them, and their rules will help to keep the world as it is—with whites controlling blacks, men dominating women, and the rich nations keeping the poor nations dependent. But what most European and North American whites find difficult to understand is that we are living in a new world situation, and this requires a new way of making theology. Again, I like the way Malcolm X put it:

The time that we're living in . . . and . . . are facing now is not an era where one who is oppressed is looking toward the oppressor to give him some system or form of logic or reason. What is logical to the oppressor isn't logical to the oppressed. And what is reason to the oppressor isn't reason to the oppressed. The black people in this country are beginning to realize that what sounds reasonable to those who exploit us doesn't sound reasonable to us. There just has to be a new system of reason and logic devised by us who are at the bottom, if we want to get some results in this struggle that is called "the Negro revolution."[16]

In EATWOT, black and Third World theologians have been attempting to develop together a new way of doing theology. In contrast to the dominant theologies of Europe and North America that are largely defined by their responses to the European Enlightenment and the problem of unbelief that arose from it, our theological enterprise focuses on the European and North American invasion of the continents of Africa, Asia, and Latin America, the slave trade, colonization, and neocolonialism.

Our primary theological question is not how can we believe in God in view of the modern, Western confidence in reason, science, and technology that seem to exclude the necessity for faith in God. Rather our theological problem arises from our encounter with God in the experience of the misery of the poor. How can we speak about Jesus' death on the cross without first speaking about the death of a people? How can the poor of our countries achieve worth as human beings in a world that has attempted to destroy our cultures and religions? The chief contradiction out of which our theologies achieve their distinctiveness is the problem of the nonperson. That is why our most important conversational partners are not philosophers of metaphysics and other socially disinterested intellectuals in universities; we are primarily interested in talking with social scientists and political activists who are engaged in the liberation of the poor.

Concern for the oppressed led black and Third World theologians to establish links with communities of the poor, and we experienced in their ecclesial life something more than a routine gathering of like-minded persons. In the religious life of the poor is revealed a knowledge of themselves that cannot be destroyed by the structures that oppress them. The liberating character of their spirituality can be seen in the way their faith in God evolves out of their cultural and political aspirations. It can be observed in the basic Christian communities of Latin America, the black and Hispanic churches of North America, the indigenous churches and traditional religions of Africa, and in the religious life of Asia. In their worship, the God of grace and judgment meets the poor and transforms their personhood from nobody to somebody, and bestows upon them the power and courage to struggle for justice.

Worship is not primarily an expression of the individual's private relationship with God. It is rather a community happening, an eschatological invasion of God into the gathered community of victims. With "the divine Spirit from on high," God empowers them "to keep on keeping on" even though the odds appear to be against them. In the collective presence of the poor at worship, God re-creates them as a liberated community that must bring freedom to the oppressed of the land. Black and Third World theologies are being created out of the ecclesial and religious life of the poor. They seek to interpret the God encountered in religio-cultural and political struggles to overcome Euro-American domination.

It has been within the context of the churches and the religions of the poor that black and Third World theologies have begun to reread the Bible. In this rereading many of us began to speak of the "hermeneutical privilege of the poor" and of "God's bias toward the poor." Although Latin theologians have done more exegetical work than others have to demonstrate the biblical option for the poor,[17] a similar concern is shared by most Third World theologians. Suh Nam-Dong, an interpreter of the minjung theology of South Korea, may be quoted as an example:

> Theological activities do not end with the exposition of biblical texts on salvation or liberation of people by God. In the Bible, the exodus, the activities of the prophets, and the event of the cross offer new insights, but these texts ought to be rediscovered and reinterpreted in the context of the human struggle for historical and political liberation today.[18]

Granting that the distinctiveness of black and Third World theologies is primarily defined by their particular contexts, their theological methodology may nonetheless be summarized in the following emphases.

1) Black and Third World theologians do theology in complex religio-cultural contexts and with the political commitment to liberate the poor from

oppression. Theology, then, is reflection upon the meaning of God in solidarity with the poor who are struggling to overcome cultural and political domination. The acid test of any theological truth is found in whether it aids the victims in their struggle to overcome their victimization. There are no abstract, objective truths that are applicable for all times and situations. Truth is concrete, and it is inseparable from the oppressed who are struggling for freedom.

2) Because the liberation of our peoples is the central motivation for us to engage in the theological enterprise, the second element of our method is social analysis. Social analysis brings to light that which is hidden. It unmasks untruth so that truth can be seen in a clear light.

Black and Third World theologians do not believe that the work of theology can be done unless the truth is known about systems of domination. Racism, sexism, colonialism, capitalism, and militarism must be comprehensively analyzed so that these demons can be destroyed. We agree with Karl Marx's eleventh thesis on Feuerbach: "The philosophers have only *interpreted* the world, in various ways; the point, however, is to *change* it." In our use of the critical tools of the social sciences, as well as religio-cultural analyses, black and Third World theologians have been attempting to construct theologies of liberation rather than theologies of domestication.

3) Through a political commitment that is informed by social and cultural analyses, a new hermeneutical situation is created. The Bible is no longer merely an ancient document whose meaning can be uncovered only by the historical criticism of biblical experts. Political commitment, informed by social analysis, provides an angle of vision that enables us to reinterpret the scriptures and thus bring to light the message that European and North American biblical exegetes have covered up.

When the Bible is read in the community of the poor, it is not understood by them as a deposit of doctrines or of revealed truths about God. Rather it becomes a living book that tells the story of God's dealings with God's people. Its importance as a source for creating theology cannot be overstated for black and Third World theologians. Even feminist and South African theologians, who question its authority (largely because of its sexist and racist misuses), do not ignore the Bible.[19] They wrestle with it, refusing to allow an abstract biblical authority, controlled by white males, to negate the authority of their own experience. God, they insist, cannot be less than the human experience of liberation from oppression. We must not allow an abstract word of God to usurp God's word as Spirit who empowers human beings to be who they are—fully human in search of the highest beauty, love, and joy.

4) The meaning of the gospel that is derived from our rereading of the Bible cannot be communicated with old European and white North American theological concepts. The truth derived from our peoples' struggles must be communicated through the histories and cultures of our people. Truth is embedded in the stories, songs, dances, sermons, paintings, and sayings of our peoples. Because many of us have learned how to do theology in Euro-

pean and North American universities and seminaries, we have had to be converted to a radically new way of doing theology.

How do we make theology by using the history and culture of our people? What method is appropriate for these sources? The answer to this question is not clear to many of us, and that is why several EATWOT members wish to spend the next three to five years working on this methodological problem.

Because black and Third World theologians have been doing theology for a short tim and doing it together for even a shorter time, we do not have a fully developea method for making theology.

These points represent my attempt to listen to what we have been saying to each other in our search to build a Third World theology that is derived from the religio-cultural and political struggles of our peoples to overcome Euro-American domination.

NOTES

1. For an account of black theology in South Africa, see Basil Moore, ed., *Black Theology: The South African Voice* (London: C. Hurst & Co., 1973; Allan Boesak, *Farewell to Innocence: A Socio-Ethical Study on Black Theology and Power* (Maryknoll, N.Y.: Orbis, 1976).

2. For an account of this boycott, see Martin Luther King, Jr., *Stride Toward Freedom* (New York: Harper, 1958).

3. The best general history of the black church is that by Gayraud S. Wilmore, *Black Religion and Black Radicalism* (Maryknoll, N.Y.: Orbis, rev. ed., 1983). See also Vincent Harding, *There is a River: The Black Struggle of Freedom in America* (New York: Harcourt Brace Jovanovich, 1981).

4. *Black Religion* (Boston: Beacon, 1964), pp. 142–43.

5. The best source for an introduction to Malcolm X's nationalist views is his *Autobiography* (New York: Grove, 1964).

6. The best analysis of black power is that by Stokely Carmichael and Charles V. Hamilton, *Black Power: The Politics of Liberation in America* (New York: Random House, 1967).

7. Cited in Gayraud S. Wilmore and James H. Cone, eds., *Black Theology: A Documentary History, 1966-1979* (Maryknoll, N.Y.: Orbis, 1979).

8. *A Black Theology of Liberation* (Philadelphia: Lippincott, 1970), p. 17.

9. See especially Jacquelyn Grant, "Black Theology and Black Women," and Pauli Murray, "Black Theology and Feminist Theology: A Comparative View" in Wilmore and Cone, *Black Theology: A Documentary History,* pp. 418–33 and 398–417. See also the important essay by Theressa Hoover, "Black Women and the Black Churches: Triple Jeopardy," in the same anthology, pp. 377–88.

10. An important account of black theology in contact with Third World theologies is found in Wilmore and Cone, *Black Theology: A Documentary History,* pp. 445–608. Black theologians have been involved in the EATWOT dialogues since their inception in Tanzania (1976). For an interpretation of black theology in

dialogue with African, Asian, and Latin American theologies, see my "A Black American Perspective on the Future of African Theology," in Kofi Appiah-Kubi and Sergio Torres, eds., *African Theology En Route* (Maryknoll, N.Y.: Orbis, 1979), pp. 176-95; idem, "A Black American Perspective on the Asian Search for Full Humanity," in Virginia Fabella, ed., *Asia's Struggle for Full Humanity* (Orbis, 1980), pp. 177-90; idem, "From Geneva to São Paulo: A Dialogue between Black Theology and Latin American Liberation Theology," in Sergio Torres and John Eagleson, eds., *The Challenge of Basic Christian Communities* (Orbis, 1981), pp. 265-81; idem, "Reflections from the Perspective of U.S. Blacks," in Virginia Fabella and Sergio Torres, eds., *Irruption of the Third World* (Orbis, 1983), pp. 235-45.

11. Our first efforts to transcend the particularities of our respective continents and to create a Third World theology of liberation occurred at the New Delhi conference (1981). See especially Fabella and Torres, *Irruption of the Third World.*

12. The classic description of this methodological point is that by Gustavo Gutiérrez: "Theology is reflection, a critical attitude. Theology *follows;* it is a second step. . . . The pastoral activity of the Church does not flow as a conclusion from theological premises. Theology does not produce pastoral activity; rather it reflects upon it" (*A Theology of Liberation* [Maryknoll, N.Y.: Orbis, 1973], p. 11).

13. Black theology emerged as a reflection *upon* the civil rights and black power movements. The origin of African liberation theology can be dated as early as 1950 and it was inseparable from the movement toward nationhood on that continent. A similar happening occurred earlier on the continent of Asia. A similar observation can be made about feminist and other forms of liberation theologies as well. The distinctiveness of Latin American theology is its careful formulation of this methodological point with the use of Marx's philosophy.

14. Again Latin Americans have been the most articulate in the formulation of this point regarding orthopraxis. See Gutiérrez, *A Theology of Liberation,* p. 10.

15. Malcolm X, *By Any Means Necessary,* George Breitman, ed. (New York: Pathfinder Press, 1970), p. 155.

16. In Archie Epps, ed., *The Speeches of Malcolm X at Harvard* (New York: William Morrow, 1968), p. 133.

17. See esp. José Miranda, *Marx and the Bible: A Critique of the Philosophy of Oppression* (Maryknoll, N.Y.: Orbis, 1974); idem, *Being and the Messiah: The Message of St. John* (Orbis, 1977); Elsa Tamez, *Bible of the Oppressed* (Orbis, 1982).

18. "Towards a Theology of Han," in Kim Yong Bock, ed., *Minjung Theology: People as the Subjects of History* (Singapore: Commission on Theological Concerns of the Christian Conference of Asia, 1981; Maryknoll, N.Y.: Orbis, 1983), pp. 53-54. A further explication of this point is made by Cyris Hee Suk Moon, "An Old Testament Understanding of Minjung," and Ahn Byung Mu, "Jesus and the Minjung in the Gospel of Mark," in the same anthology. On the use of the Bible in black theology, see my *God of the Oppressed* (New York: Seabury, 1975), especially chapters 4-7. For African theologians' view of the Bible, see Kwesi Dickson and Paul Ellingworth, eds., *Biblical Revelation and African Beliefs* (Maryknoll, N.Y.: Orbis, 1969).

19. Questioning of the authority of the Bible was sharply expressed by several South African and feminist theologians at the EATWOT Geneva conference (January 1983). The attitudes of many feminist theologians are well known, but the biblical questioning of South African theologians was new to me. Some North American feminists reject the Bible and Christianity as incurably sexist. For a variety of perspectives on white North American feminist theology, see Carol P. Christ and

Judith Plaskow, eds., *Womanspirit Rising: A Feminist Reader in Religion* (New York: Harper & Row, 1979). It is important to note that many Third World women theologians do not like the term "feminist" as a description of their theological work. They view it as Western and thus not fully accountable to their cultural and political aspirations. They do, however, affirm the importance of women's experience in making theology. See especially Amba Oduyoye, "Reflections from a Third World Woman's Perspective: Women's Experience and Liberation Theologies," in Fabella and Torres, *Irruption of the Third World,* pp. 193-200. Black North American women do not reject the term "feminist," nor are they as negative in their attitude toward the Bible and Jesus as are many white feminists.

16

Georges Casalis

Methodology for a West European Theology of Liberation

Methodology is not something that should be discussed in the abstract—as if manner were more important than content, or theory more basic than the passage to act.[1] Thus we reverse these categories in our theological undertaking: the point of departure is practice, which becomes the principle of epistemological rupture at the basis of our systematic development. Theoretical reflection is thus founded on practice, and in turn illuminates, explains, and corrects practice. There is a back-and-forth movement between the two, a movement of incessant exchange and reciprocation, which makes practice the *conditio sine qua non* of theological formulation, and makes theology one of the critical instruments for a "reading" of practice, along with its perspective and its meaning.

We have the classic definitions of Gustavo Gutiérrez and Pablo Richard: theology is the "second act of evangelical interpretation of a liberation praxis" (Gutiérrez); "critical reflection on the faith from a point of departure in praxis" (Richard). These definitions are definitive. We are not reciting formulas, then, or seeking to reproduce analyses rooted in some other geopolitical and ecclesial context. Our approach is to take up and assume this movement and follow this method, which together define an original theological finality. It is not a matter of classic theology with a new content. This is a theology that is radically *other*.

I should like to define the methodology of a theology of liberation in the west European context in terms parallel with the historical reality of my own life. Hence the following data, whose very order is meaningful.

106

I am male, white, European, occidental. I was born into a middle-class family, thanks to which fact I have become a scholar and a theologian.

I am a Protestant, in the employ of church institutions for forty-two years now.

I have never really had to worry about material things.

The woman whose husband I am is also a middle-class scholar, and a social worker in charge of an ecumenical service that receives political refugees from all over the world. Our four children are also scholars.

I consider this social conditioning and these indubitable privileges, these radications and existential bonds, not as accidents of fate, but as so many motives for accepting political, civic, and international responsibility.

I belong to a country of the North—or of the "center," in the imperialistic configuration of the world—a country that is a partner in European imperialism, a liberal democracy that for more than twenty years now has been engaged in an ineffective, ruinous, and dangerous nuclear policy. France is the leading arms vendor of the world, if you count by quantity of arms sold per capita population. The 1981 elections, which were a great popular victory, did not call these traits into question any more than they did the neocolonial orientations of French politics. France is still the prisoner of Northern imperialist capitalism, still under the thumb of the multinationals, and still infiltrated by the "national security" ideology propagated by the military-industrial complex so solidly implanted in our country.

The challenge to me, then, is: What will be my *practice* in this context? Or, better, *our* practice, for I cannot imagine a true practice that could remain individual. We know, with Marx (eleventh thesis on Feuerbach), that we are not about the business of explaining the world, but of transforming it.

As to the evolution of my social practice, I shall speak in a very personal way, in the hope of encouraging others. I might characterize it as a passage from *resistance for* the *real* France (under the occupation, 1940–44, where I have nothing to be specially proud of, but "if it had to be done again, I would take the same road"—Aragon!), to *resistance against* the *legal* France (during *our* Vietnam war and the Algerian war, 1946–54 and 1954–62, respectively). I know that this distinction, which I borrow from Maurrasian categories, is not self-evident. But all the same, the legality of the Vichy government, very docile as to the orders of the occupying power, was less evident, much more open to challenge, than that of the Fourth or Fifth Republics. And the "real" France was clandestine then, whereas after 1945 it could show itself openly in the midst of, first, a democratic opposition, then a democratic majority.

More decisive for me than my entry into the Resistance movement—beginning on June 18, 1940 (I was running a newspaper at the time)—were the repeated shocks of the colonial wars waged by France, on the very morrow of its own liberation, against the Vietnamese and Algerian peoples. I have written elsewhere about my first personal experience of class hatred:

It was in December 1957. I was at the Ouchaia wadi, a horrible shanty-town in Algeria where men, women, and children were subsisting in an indescribable subhuman state. Suddenly, in a particularly filthy hut where I was helping distribute flour, I was overcome by an irresistible wave of class hatred. It was an experience all the more disturbing because, until that time, nothing had prepared me for it. The liberation of the area and the colonial fight for independence appealed to other motives. Here the evidence was overpowering—nothing at all could justify such misery, which was the direct result, the legitimate offspring of our conquest and occupation of that country. I can still hear one of my companions muttering, "After a hundred and thirty years of French presence. . . ."

I know that at that moment I would have been capable of any kind of "terrorist" act, no matter what, against a system that had not only tolerated but engendered the slow and violent death of "underdeveloped" multitudes. Yet at the same time I knew that my class hatred was self-hatred, hatred of myself as a beneficiary and an accomplice of the colonial system as well as a product and an exported expression of the capitalist order. Middle-class persons who undergo such an experience, if they do not make their escape through the distractions at their disposal, cannot help hating themselves. Surely it is not by chance that the Gospel of St. Luke, the gospel of the poor, speaks of *hating* one's family and one's life as the first condition for becoming a disciple of Jesus (Luke 14:25–26).

There are only two solutions: suicide or conversion. Conversion itself is a form of death, a severance from a previous way of life, rebirth into a struggle for the present and future of humankind.[2]

It was not merely the evidence of the ultimate consequences of oppression and exploitation, nor even, above and beyond the terrible reality of this misery, the discovery of an "official, generalized system of torture" of which the procurator general of the French Republic in Algeria told me—it is the immediate confrontation with the true face of class struggles (here, those of the dominators against the dominated!) that for me is the universal manifestation of capitalism and its highest form, imperialism. Racism and sexism, ethnocide and genocide, are part and parcel of class struggles. They cannot be reduced to these struggles, but neither can they be separated from them.

I wish to make it very clear that what we are about is not a matter of sector-based struggle, or of reduction of all forms of oppression to a single principle. No, each form has its own specificity, and at the same time all are interdependent. If we merely speak of class struggles, without entering upon an analysis of concrete situations, as Marx invites us, we run an ideological steamroller over the reality of the domination and discrimination serving as the basis for the maintenance of minorities in power over dispossessed majorities.

The first sentence in the 1848 Manifesto—"the history of all hitherto exist-ing society is the history of class struggles"[3]—is not an ideological statement, but a scientific observation. To deny it is to be a "political illiterate," as Paulo Freire would say. And here I have mighty succor in our efforts to raise our revolutionary consciousness: I have Gustavo Gutiérrez's challenge to do theology *only* in the context of liberation struggles; I have the militant profes-sional praxis of Dorothée, whose husband I am, in her daily solidarity with political refugees; and especially, we had the presence among us, for several years, of Pablo Richard who, in his exile, was for us not only a marvelous companion, but also, and even more so, an inestimable pedagogue who tire-lessly helped us along the road of "theological conversion."

Has Richard not doggedly called on us to face the question of the "social credibility" (measured by the yardstick of the poor) of our ecclesial life and our theological discourse? Has he not asked us at every moment to become aware of our social roles and impact, to make no social or ecclesial "institu-tional analysis" without calling ourselves into question personally, no longer leaving any space for pharisaism or "spectator justice"? In a word, through him, as through others, we have been mightily evangelized, so well did this foreigner teach us in his own person to drop the mask and recognize our own faces.

Our self-conscientization leads us to an appreciation of the impossibility of remaining neutral. On a practical level, it corresponds to the passage from a *class situation*—inherited, attaching to our person by the sole fact of our birth, education, and social status—to a *class position,* something freely cho-sen, in solidarity with those who are the victims of institutionalized violence. It means entering *with* them into the class struggles being waged from below, entering into the counterviolence that is necessary, or at least inevitable in most cases, to put an end to arbitrary and abusive power.

One thing is clear above all else: it is *here at home first* that we must face up to imperialism, militarism, capitalism, oppression in all its forms, and the ideology and practice of materialist abundance (for those who benefit from it!—are we not faced with accelerating poverty and misery right in our own "rich countries"?). It is *here at home first* that we must confront the ideology and practice of all forms of exploitation, and all the idolatries they foster. It is *here at home first* that we must struggle against the arms race, that murderous folly that each year, without open war, occasions the death of millions by starvation, that emasculates and ravages the economies of the First, Second, and Third worlds together, and causes us who are rich to lose the meaning of life, and suffer instead a permanent, all-pervading anxiety.

This being said, I am not proud of my praxis, but I am willing to be judged by it, and I hope that each of you will have the same willingness.

Let me add that, in this area as in all others, it is *no shame to be an intellec-tual,* and it has been a long time since I have had a bad conscience in this respect. What is important is this: At whose orders, in whose service, does one stand? On whose side are we? Gramsci tells us that intellectuals are always "organic"—always in league with one or another sector of society. The poor simply ask us: "Whose side are you on?" If they discover that it is their side, they are ready to receive us into their battles and their friendship.

It is an extraordinary thing to experience the forgiveness and the confidence the poor bestow on those who join their battlefront. And although it is surely they who are the subjects of history, and the true producers of the theologies of liberation, it is no less true that they have need of the competence and the knowledge of scholars to assist them to formulate and to deepen the lessons of their hard life.

In contact with them, a decisive process gets under way—namely, the passage from the motto *vita mea mors tua,* symbolizing the predatory life, to the dynamic of *vita tua mors mea,* characteristic of life in solidarity with others. It becomes clear that conversion means dying as an individual in order to rise again within a revitalized humankind.

CRITIQUE OF TRADITIONAL THEOLOGY

The practice of militant solidarity leads us to a process of the rereading of reality.[4] Such practice is inseparable from a search for all possible elements of information, and all possible aspects of the employment of adequate instruments of analysis. It is here that the social sciences come in—history, statistics, sociology, and the rest—as an integral part of theological methodology. There is no theology of liberation that is not rooted in them, illuminated by them, de-idealized, and brought to earth by them. Here is where Marxist methodology comes in, which seems to me to be indispensable for deciphering reality. Let us say, at all events, that a "practical conversion" to the poor, the willingness and the humility to undertake a concrete life of costly, dangerous solidarity with them, is the epistemological principle of an exact reading of the real.[5] Or, if you prefer, only a clear praxis of engagement, commitment, on the battlefronts of class struggles, empowers one to decipher the history of the world in its diachronic (development and evolution) and synchronic (current situation) dimensions. The national and international situation can be understood only "from the bottom up." The measure of the state of the world, here and afar, is the humiliated human being, *wherever and whenever this human being is to be found.* Anyone ignoring that human being, and failing to keep close to him and her in the moment of agony, will be unable to have any experience whatever of Christ crucified, or consequently of Christ risen.

It is under these conditions, and in this new *life,* that two important elements of the theological methodology of liberation occur: (1) the critique of the conditions of production of the classic theological discourse, and (2) the critique of the socio-political role of traditional theologies and theologians.

Charles Davis, cited by John A. T. Robinson,[6] speaks of four productional sites of the classic theological discourse: the diocese, the monastery, the university, and the seminary—loci of hierarchical power, frequently linked to the authoritarian presence of celibate males, concentration points of capital and of the alienation of theologians by the guarantee of a salary attached to the license to teach, places of the organization—via ideological entrenchment—of the reproduction of a socio-political system of "established disorder." And for the second half of the twentieth century Davis hopes for and prophesies theologies that will translate the needs, hopes, and militancies of the *laos,* lay persons engaged in the various struggles for the upbuilding of a new world. The security, the protected and comfortable—sometimes opulent—lifestyle of specialists in theology explains the sclerosis in their productivity.

Consequently it is not surprising that traditional theology became the religious dimension of the dominant ideology, that of domination. Power accords it this role, and expects this function to be strictly carried out. I recall Napoleon Bonaparte's cynical observation:

> As far as I am concerned, what I see in religion is not the mystery of the incarnation but a mystery of the social order: it prevents the rich from being massacred by the poor by relegating the idea of equality to heaven.
>
> Religion is also a sort of inoculation or vaccine which, while satisfying our love for the marvelous, protects us from charlatans and sorcerers; priests are worth more than Kant and all the German dreamers put together.
>
> Without religion, how could we have order in the state? Society cannot continue to exist without inequalities in personal fortunes; for inequalities to continue we must have religion. When someone is dying of hunger and someone else nearby has everything, it would be impossible for the starving man to acquiesce to such disparity if there were no authority to tell him: God wills it so; in this world there must be rich and poor but in the hereafter for all eternity, fortunes will be reversed.[7]

The unsettling thing about this passage is that it reflects characteristics of *contemporary* religious reality. We could hardly have a better account of the religious mentality, naive or artful, still underlying the conduct of a number of religious institutions and their representatives.

Gramsci is correct in saying that the institutions that produce theology are part of the "state ideological apparatus," having the function of effectuating the consent of the oppressed to their situation of oppression, and of causing them to interiorize its justifications. Thus, for example, theology is assigned the task of representing the de facto social order—and its manifold injustices—as the natural, the normal, configuration of the human condition. Such theology does not at all stand up to a genuine practice of liberating solidarity, and this is why the "theologies of liberation," quite deliberately, though minority theologies, are also countertheologies—calling into question both the social role and the discourse of the classic theologies.

Rereading the Bible

All this makes a rereading of the biblical texts an absolute necessity. Bonhoeffer speaks of an *areligious* interpretation of the traditional elements of Christian doctrine. In light of his praxis as a member of the July 20, 1944, conspiracy to assassinate Adolph Hitler, he calls for a political hermeneutic, which, far from being separated from subversive practice, is totally immersed in it. In Bonhoeffer's eyes, religion is still serving as a means of escape from political reality. Indeed this is one of its primordial functions.

Fernando Belo, for his part, has initiated us into a *materialist* reading,[8] one that should permit a "confrontation between a political practice seeking to be revolutionary, and a Christian practice no longer seeking to be religious."

In our Western situations and categories, such readings correspond to those of theologians of liberation in the Third World. Obviously they are not a matter of the recitation of formulas, or of conclusions worked out elsewhere. They are original efforts, still embryonic and still very minoritarian, and probably doomed to remain such for a long time to come.

However this may be, the biblical texts, redacted in the course of the centuries are documents representing a wide range of values, to be sure, and originating with various authorities—but documents having this in common: that they all sprang from the bosom of various social conflicts that marked the Near East between 1000 B.C. and A.D. 150—and the rest of the planet since that time. They are contradictory in themselves: they bear the mark of successive dominant ideologies, but also that of movements of protest and resistance that, over the centuries, have opposed the established ecclesiastical and political powers. There is, right here and now in the First World, a whole body of research on this subject, thanks to which we can read the ensemble of this literature as a series of "reports" on practices of oppression and liberation. They are composite texts, then, among which we can discern those that are "open," hence that challenge us, criticize us, reorientate us, and bring us face to face with the God of the poor, the Servant who slays our selfishness and our will to power, and raises us up, within his people, at the heart of popular struggles.

A Hermeneutic of Risk and Promise

This is the hermeneutical risk and promise: an undertaking, a step, that is in no way reductionist with respect to the uniqueness of the word of God, but which, quite to the contrary, bestows upon that word its full meaning. For the word does not come to us as texts, but through texts as a living person, the one who died and rose again, Jesus of Nazareth, yesterday in Galilee and Jerusalem, today in the infinite diversity of our geopolitical situations, and the same forever, as the one in whom faith salutes the limits of individual destiny and of world history. It is he, then, who, by his liberating practice, issues his call and challenge to every human being—and in a special way to those involved in the tensions that characterize the desire to be at once militant socialists and disciples of the gospel. His critical judgment—but his promise, too—bear, with all their force, on the social structures, historical junctures, political and ecclesiastical institutions, and our personal roles that are at the heart of our collective becoming, at the heart of our inextricably intertwined commitments and involvements both here and afar. For the particular is never really to be found apart from a world perspective, just as the universal is never really to be found apart from an earnest acceptance of immediate and local responsibilities.

The reading grid, the interpretation grid, that this hermeneutic yields is the dialectic of exodus-and-resurrection: the eschatological meaning and significance of all historical liberations, with their dynamic of political risk, courage, and hope that is inscribed in the existence of the disciples of the living subversive, Jesus of Nazareth.

Self-Interrogation for Western Europe

Without attempting to be exhaustive, I shall present a few of the points of reference for the definition of our activity and the clarification of our commitments in western Europe, France especially.

What is the concrete and basic meaning of our *rejection of the capitalist system?* We must come to know this system, not in a traditional, abstract fashion, but precisely in its current forms, and arrive at precise notions of the types of actions we can carry on against it. We cannot pretend that we are going to leave it and go elsewhere, so the question for us becomes, How can we destroy it from the inside? In particular, our policies of financial investment in the Third World, our participation in the policies of the multinationals, our arms sales, and so many other expressions of our neocolonialism and our subimperialism—all this must be studied, understood, and denounced, to the end that we may arrive at certain decisions: for example, in the area of food consumption, by reducing consumption of products obtained by plunder (pork and soy beans), by participating in boycotts, by proposing appropriate, collective refusal to pay taxes used for warmongering.

What is our participation in the defense of peace and the struggle for disarmament? We know that the imbalance between the nations of the center and those of the periphery is largely the result of the senseless expenditures of the arms race, and we know that the latter, to boot, can lead to universal catastrophe. What conclusions do we draw from this, and how does it come about that France is one of the countries of Europe where peace movements are least active? Is it not because we are so concerned with redefining our Christian identity *a priori* that we forget "the time in which we are living" (Rom. 13:11)? Is it not true that we are what Albert Camus called "false comrades," those who desert the battlefronts where the concrete fate of the multitudes is being decided today? In this perspective, the question of the reconversion of the arms industries seems to me to be a test of our political earnestness, and *thus* of our spiritual and theological earnestness. All the palaver of governments—in particular that of the socialist government of France!—on the necessity of arms sales for economic equilibrium is simply unacceptable. But it is our responsibility to study and popularize credible alternatives.

This goes hand in hand with serious commitments to peace, and thereby to *détente by disarmament.* But the current tendency is precisely in the opposite direction, and we see U.S. imperialism exerting pressure on all the economies of East *and* West to overarm, thereby ruining them and obliging them to submit to the conditions dictated by Washington. Profiting from the mistakes and difficulties of the "socialist" regimes, Washington threatens all these regimes constantly, both from without (by blockades, encirclement, surveillance by air, and so on) and from within (by infiltrating resistance movements and protest currents), with the intent of forcing them to retreat— that is, with the intent of overthrowing them. Whatever its shortcomings, the Yalta Agreement has made a certain equilibrium possible between East and West since 1945. Now this equilibrium is endangered by U.S. aggression, as well as by brutal countermeasures on the part of the Soviet Union (Afghanistan, Poland, after Hungary and Czechoslovakia, and so on), and the equilibrium teeters precariously. The threat of a world conflict grows apace. Hence the necessity of "keeping our cool" and not yielding to all the passionately anticommunist movements sweeping across western Europe, including those of leftist political parties and Christian circles (those claiming that a justifiable solidarity with "Solidarnost" has its limits).

What type of *growth,* and consequently what *models of development,* do we support, submit to, and make others submit to? How can we overturn, reverse, the generalized system of unequal exchange, and thus arrive at an equitable, new, world economic order? Is there any possibility of putting an end to the systematic murder of fifty million human beings a year? How are we involved in campaigns against hunger, or against murderous regimes that use torture as a means of governing underdeveloped and terrorized masses? How may we work concretely to upset, to reverse, the diabolical, vicious circle whereby the rich grow ever richer, and the poor ever poorer?

Obviously we are going to have to be active at home ourselves on the battlefronts drawn up against the existence of the Fourth World—that of the marginalized, the hospital and prison worlds, the migrant workers, and ethnic minorities. Campaign promises in these areas must not be allowed to encourage us to passivity, but on the contrary, to vigilance, and incessant demands.

Once more, I have not attempted a complete enumeration. I have sought only to list a few examples of choices and practices that could make of us, here and beyond our borders, "believable believers" (Abbé Pierre). But we must figure out and implement, on these points as on others, *breaches* in the system of international colonialism in which we are encased. By such personal acts—or better, community acts!—of rupture, of treason to the established order, the gospel can make its irruption anew, into us and through us.

TOWARD A SPIRITUAL AND THEOLOGICAL RESURRECTION

The practice of modest but meaningful struggles bears within it implicit and explicit elements of a global conception of the history of the world and of the *meaning of life*. It has a utopian value, and this is what gives it the strength to penetrate mentalities and structures. This is also what causes "poets" and "prophets of meaning" to be attacked and denounced as "subversive." Here as elsewhere, fidelity to the human being, the one from Nazareth and every other, is inseparable from the price to be paid. How may we include this in our family, social, and professional perspectives and ethics, without any "nostalgia of success," or self-pity, but as one of the components of our daily life? The first Christians—and a great many others today— were and are "blessed" to suffer for the sake of the gospel (Acts 5:41). How may we incorporate such a dimension—by no means woebegone—in our ideology, our piety, our psychological "health" (if this is the word to use)?

The present time is characterized by the rediscovery of the profound nature and positive elements of *folk religions*. At the same time, we are becoming aware of how much they contain of the heteroclite and the retrograde. Are we capable of distinguishing between what Engels called their "Constantinian" and "apocalyptic" faces—between their sacralizing pole and their "profaning effect"—and renounce our scholarly (not rigor but) pride enough to be humbly inscribed among those who share the solidarity and religious hopes of the poor? The May 1968 dream in Paris was reconciliation and unity of action between students and workers. In Brazil, a most dynamic encounter is underway between intellectuals, laborers, and the rural poor. Christians in all three component groups are playing a decisive catalytic role.

It seems to me of capital importance for any renaissance of Western "Christianity" that we learn, not to renounce our own identity and specificity, but to encounter others without dominating pretensions or contempt. We ought to come to the point where we can go beyond labels, and to welcome among ourselves, as allies on the battlefronts of the class struggles, as companions in solidarity, brothers and sisters who are different, but who are called to toil for the same Father who is none other than the Liberator of humankind (and be rid of a superficial Freudian—if indeed it is authentically Freudian—critique of the fatherhood of God!).

Our great difficulty is that the gospel is *good news originally addressed to the poor* living in a civilization of destitution, of misery—and we try to read it and live it in our affluent neighborhoods with their materialistic comforts. Surely the only way to reunderstand that gospel will be to open our ears to the poor, which we shall be able to do only by being in unlimited solidarity with them in their denunciations, their hopes, and their struggles. "The rich are ignorant," says Abbé Pierre, "when it comes to anything not strictly concerned with the defense of their material interests." The God of the poor grants intelligence to those who become converted to those whose side God has taken once and for all. Only effective communion and solidarity with the poor can open our eyes, can give us the sense of the human being, can open us to present reality and future horizons that we have never known, can set us on our feet (that is, make us Christians, as Bonhoeffer said!).

Our new formulation of the faith will be inscribed in an irreducible conflict between all the gods of death, and the living God who is the Liberator—the "rehumanizer," if you prefer, the one who restores to all human beings their lost humanity: restores it to the poor by delivering them from poverty and allowing them to live in a more just, less imbalanced, more peaceable society of sisters and brothers; restores it to the well-off (like myself!) by allowing them to place all their instruments of domination at the service of the poor— by despoiling them of their privileges, and delivering them from the will to power. The "spoliation" dynamic of Jesus of Nazareth—who was born on the lowest fringe of the middle class and who became the companion of the miserable of his time, of slaves, day workers, landless peasants, and other marginalized or exploited persons—can become not only the rule, but the motivating, driving force of our life. It is the *resurrection,* then, that is the strength and force that makes me stand up as a new human being, without fear or covetousness, and transcend myself, go out beyond myself toward an existence whose center of gravity is no longer the search for personal satisfaction, but the happiness of the other, of all the others.

In the mid-1960s "secularization" was being discovered, and debates were held on Harvey Cox's *The Secular City.* I was very much interested in Cox's analysis of the triple biblical secularization: the "disenchantment" of nature, the desacralization of politics, and the profanation of accepted values. But I was struck by the total absence in Cox of any critique of the power invested in the secularized metropolis. Yet it is in the secular order, and the powers that maintain it, that the sacred is "reinvested." And it is becoming more and more clear that, for anyone encountering the meaning of life in the living person and word of Jesus, there is a radical incompatibility between the *sacralizations* everywhere operative today—disguised as secularization or not—and *sanctification*—that is, the liberating activity of God in history.

Sacralization—of the instances of power, especially—is a procedure whereby the "secularized" (= "autonomous") human being attributes an absolute value to structures, functions, and persons. Under Christian or "national security" regimes, this is sometimes done in the name of "Christianity." It always means a freeze in social progress and the maintenance of a people in submission. Ideologically, it finds expression in a claim to be guarding and defending "Christian civilization" against the threats of "militant atheism." *Sanctification,* by contrast—a sustained activity by which God permits us access to the fullness of our being—necessarily leads to the profanation of all idols of the sacred. Thus the first Christians were accounted "atheists" because they refused to venerate the gods of the Pantheon and their function as forces in the service of the imperial order.

Everywhere in the world today, the Christian undertaking consists first of all in the denunciation and profanation of idols, and, consequently, in the recognition and manifestation of the fact that "atheists" are the natural allies of those inscribed in the lists of the dynamics of sanctification. The exhortation of the first Johannine Letter to "be on your guard against idols" (5:21) takes on a startling meaningfulness today. Our idols must be discovered and unmasked, for they sacralize and kill, whereas the God of life liberates—for fellowship, joint creativity, and the future.

Christian institutions are more often to be found on the side of sacralization than on that of sanctification. Thus they should not be accorded unconditional confidence, or just any random infallibility you please. But neither have we any intention of allowing ourselves to be hypnotized by them and go looking for how to be "counterinstitutional" without falling into "antiinstitutional" anarchism. No, according to the situation, Christian freedom can be manifested sometimes within church institutions and functions, sometimes on their margin. Here as elsewhere, a genuine ecclesiality will manifest itself in its solidarity with struggles against all instances of power that exploit, oppress, and alienate. This conformity to the style of Jesus may be either recognized or rejected by the institution, but in no case does it allow itself to be dazzled or discouraged by religious powers.

A contemporary Dutch theologian, Hans Hoekendijk, a specialist in missiology, once declared: "Have a responsible concern for the world, and the incarnate love of Christ and the church will be given to you for good measure." Niemöller says the same thing in his own way when he asserts: "The church *is* not, the church springs up." It is important for us to be ever disposed for this birth-resurrection of the confessing community, in the hope that is inseparable from the cause of the people.

The *"spiritual tone,"* then, that should characterize this praxis, these practices of liberation, in western Europe, will be one of tranquil resolve, a spirit of determination neither bitter nor negative, but joyful, positive, and solidly utopian. To march and struggle from act of faith to act of faith is to walk in the direction of history. Indeed it is to make history go in the right direction, despite all the obstacles and roadblocks. It is to build the human future.

The Search for Spiritual Identity

As an example of the new formulations of the faith, and celebrations, toward which we are moving, "from beginning to beginning, by beginnings that never have an end," I shall quote a text presented for reflection in an ecumenical Christian group that was seeking an authentic spiritual identity in and for the present time. The speaker is a woman:

> I declare that I am bound to Jesus of Nazareth—
> Who for a number of years walked the length and breadth of Palestine, a region in turmoil by reason of violent political shocks, conflicts of rival powers, and foreign occupation—the pawn of huge economic interests, and the victim of pitiless class exploitation, under the aegis of dominative ideologies and religions.

He walked, he spoke, he recounted, he disturbed, he pacified, he consoled, he attacked, he touched, he disconcerted, he gathered together and divided the throngs of the poor, throughout *Galilee*—he a Galilean himself, condemned and spurned by the mighty of Judea.

He confronted the mighty authority of the Temple, of jurisdiction, of doctrine, of Zealot insurgents, at *Jerusalem,* where he finally died and rose again—telling the women [!] that Easter morning: "I go before you to Galilee" (see Matt. 28:7, 10).

He is *before* us, today, in the history we are living, a history whose scenarios are not all that different from his, save that we know their planetary dimensions a little better.

It is this history of Jesus, and our history, that I want to continue to read and decipher, together with other men and women of our time. Neither the Bible nor history are closed texts: there is a Future. I want to perceive the movement, the change, the signs of the kingdom of justice, and take part in them—and that is the *meaning* of the reading I wish to undertake with my fellow human beings.

After every step—every advance or defeat—there is another, new, step to take, for this God claimed by Jesus of Nazareth is and has been the God of the living ever since Abraham, down through the entire history of the people of Israel and of humanity itself.

It is the history of nonpower (not the same thing as nonviolence), the history of being-with-the-oppressed, that forever leaps back up again and gives hope its strength.

History is not the history of the great, of the tyrants, but of the people—of each nameless one who is nonetheless an essential "factor" in history (Rosa Luxemburg)—of those who are capable of giving their lives for others instead of snatching life from others by destroying them.

This strength is the secret of history, and its leaven. We have only to reread the parables! It is by this strength that all history, personal and collective, has meaning.

West European Liberation Theologies

We have begun to be affected by the irruption of the Third World. We have begun to hear the cry of the poor and the voiceless. The first elements of a new theology emerge in the context of a socio-political conversion. Theology is no longer the affair of specialists, but of a whole community on the way to becoming, a community in which the true makers of theology are the ones most dangerously engaged in the struggles for the transformation of our European societies and their relationships with the rest of the world. It is *there,* and only *in these new practices,* that we begin better to understand and live the word and will of the living God, the Liberator.

The development of a "theology of liberation for western Europe" thus stands in close relationship with liberation movements throughout the world. To mention only a few examples, apart from the pioneer work of Latin America, with its various components, there are "second acts of gospel re-readings of liberating practices" in Korea (minjung theology), Vietnam (in a framework of resistance to successive colonialisms), Africa, Madagascar, and elsewhere. It is not for us to parrot Third World liberation theology, but to make an effort to take account of our "demicontinental" reality, marked as it is by the proximity of the Second World with its positive achievements, its failures, and its faults. For a number of us, working out a theology will involve a considerable amount of common praxis and critical dialogue with communist organizations and socialist countries.

This is the context, then, in which we pursue an effort of theoretical scholarship and development that is destined to see a happy issue only to the extent that it be genuinely articulated upon practices of militant lay persons, in whose service it is—and is to be—elaborated. This necessarily implies fragmentary and "inductive" theological elements—with all due apologies for the ambiguity of the term, by which I mean a movement, a process, prompted by faith, to be sure, but becoming theological only in relationship to a social practice whose theological status is at once that of an epistemological grid and that of the object of constant challenge by the irreducibility of the word of God (precisely what is rejected by those who attack this inductive approach). Clearly, it is a matter of countertheological movements that will radicalize the class conflicts now penetrating the warp and woof of ecclesiastical institutions—which means that a goodly number of us are destined to experience conflict, marginalization, and minority status.

The elaboration of west European liberation theologies is in its very first beginnings. It is well for us to think, whatever our age be, that we are opening a new path on this old continent, excavating in the deserts of our mindless, senseless wealth the highways the prophets opened up—in the past and in the present—for the advent of the Liberator we await—we too, in our history.

I should like to conclude by reading a brief passage from the works of a well-known "deductive" theologian—a passage more prophetic than methodological, to be sure, but one that shows the extraordinary parallelism of his line of thought to what I have propounded above. Indeed, by very reason of his unconditional resistance to clerical oppression, he was a political refugee for thirty years. (Evidently, in the absence of a praxis tending to the institutional marginalization of the practitioner, the gospel remains obscure.) John Calvin wrote:

> Will not the Lord say, "Why have you allowed so many needy to die of hunger? Surely you had gold with which to minister sustenance. Why were so many prisoners carried off and not ransomed? Why were so many killed by the enemy? It were better for you to preserve vessels of living men than of metals." To these you cannot give reply for what

would you say? "I was afraid lest the temple of God lack ornament."
He would reply: "The sacraments do not require gold, nor do those
things please with gold that are not bought with gold. The ornament of
the sacraments is the ransom of prisoners."[9]

APPENDIX
RESISTANCE AND SUBVERSION: LIBERATION FOR PEACE

*The document that follows is the final statement of an international theologi-
cal seminar held in Paris, May 28–31, 1982, organized by West German university student communities. It is presented here as a representative example
of what I have advocated in my own address to the EATWOT conference in
Geneva.*

We are some two hundred Christians of Austria, West Germany, East Germany, France, Spain, Portugal, Norway, Poland, Switzerland, Luxem-
bourg, the Netherlands, Great Britain, and Italy, engaged in various
capacities in struggles for liberation. We have come together to reflect on the
demands of our faith in the present situation in the world and in our own
lives.

Among the different problems facing humanity today, that of war and
peace seems to us to be the most urgent. In spite of a daily broadening awareness of the danger represented by the current arms race, we observe that
disarmament fails to materialize. On the contrary, the arms race, unleashed
by capitalist imperialism, with the participation notably of the strike forces
of France and Great Britain, is provoking a corresponding phenomenon in
the countries of the Warsaw Pact. This process is engendering, in western
and eastern Europe, an accumulation of might in the form of military apparatus.

At this very moment European powers are in a state of war. The conflict
over the Malvinas (Falkland Islands) has exposed the imperialist character of
the United Kingdom. The nations of the European Common Market lent it
their support by decreeing an export embargo, a measure that hurt the Argen-
tine people. This is but one more demonstration of the fact that our governments find it impossible to break with economic and political imperialism
whenever the interests of the countries of the northern hemisphere are at
stake. We deem, nevertheless, that this situation fails to justify the nationalism and tyranny of the military junta in control of Argentina.

To be sure, our views on these questions are very diversified, especially if
one compares the peace movements of western Europe and eastern Europe.
Nevertheless, we are all convinced that the current arms race represents a
threat to the future of humanity; and we all pursue the same final objective,
that of a world where arms and violence will have been proscribed.

It is especially from a point of view of west Europeans that we here seek to work out certain lines of action and research. We are convinced that the struggle for peace in our respective countries represents our major contribution to understanding and collaboration between East and West.

1) *We observe at this moment the mobilizing power of the peace theme* in each of our countries. It is a theme that transcends political, ideological, and religious differences. We consider, nevertheless, that it is necessary to go beyond a certain unanimity of declarations and appeals, and to denounce the relationship between militarism and the capitalist economic model. Founded as it is on the exploitation and domination of human being by human being, unbridled capitalism inevitably appeals to violence, and to ever more lethal weaponry. Thus economic logic joins hands with military logic, and their conjunction begets a fearful praxis of death.

In these conditions, our commitment to peace must be a struggle against all forms of exploitation and domination, at the national and international levels alike. Work for a world of peace cannot be separated from the radical transformation of the economic and social order.

2) *The arms race affects primarily the peoples of the Third World,* and becomes one of the most decisive factors of their oppression. This oppression is maintained and supported by the industrialized countries in order to ensure their control of raw material and markets, and to defend their political and economic interests. The orientation of an economy in the direction of arms production prevents that economy from devoting itself to the production of the basic necessities of life. Thus production is orientated primarily to dealing with death rather than to promoting life.

Further, the nations of the First World become accomplices of the oppression of the peoples of the Third World by the sale of arms and advanced technology to military regimes.

Our solidarity with the countries of the Third World, then, necessarily involves a challenge to the production of and traffic in weapons by our countries, which in turn implies a challenge to the basic economic options of our countries.

3) *War has its roots not only in the structural, but in the cultural* as well. The dominating cultures of our nations are war cultures. They fashion the conscience of our peoples, and give their education its orientation: first by the systemic justification of war and weaponry that they inculcate—in the national-security theory, the bloc-balance theory, the communist-threat theory, and the like; but it is especially the culture imposed by the capitalist system—the law of "might makes right," an interpretation of history centered on the First World, and so on—that is in its deepest inspiration a culture of war and death.

The struggle for peace, then, requires a corresponding transformation of consciences in depth—the development of a culture of peace. Such a culture will entail a systematic demystification of the various justifications of war and the arms race, a making public of the real cost and threat represented by the militarization of the economy, and conscientization with respect to the essential relationship between war and the capitalist economic model. But the culture of peace must be an alternative culture in all areas, capable of generating new forms of life and of the organization of the world. A culture of peace is not a culture of resignation, then, but one of resistance and liberation. It can be developed only by groups and peoples who are willing to fight for their own emancipation.

4) *As Christians, we must answer for our role in this combat.* If we try to propose the gospel today as a message of love and peace, history gives us the lie. Recourse to the gospel has only too often and too flagrantly served to justify wars. There have even been holy wars, crusades, holy alliances, and so on. The churches have blessed the weapons of all the powers to which they have been allied. Nor is this a phenomenon of past history alone.

In our days the discourse of the institutional churches is marked by an evident discrepancy between declarations of principle—for peace—and a compliant silence on the structural causes of war. This abandonment of the spirit of their origins is occasioned by the alliances maintained by these churches, in the past as in the present, with economic and political powers.

The result has been that the preaching and the proselytism of the churches have become elements of a culture of war, to the point where war and oppression have actually become necessary in order to sustain, impose, or defend "Western Christian civilization."

Christian communities today are called upon to bear witness to peace by resisting militarism—by adopting a subversive attitude vis-à-vis the economy and culture of war, which express a will for death, and are thus contrary to the will of God, who has called us to "choose life" (Deut. 30:19).

5) *It is therefore urgent that all the historical weight of the gospel be thrown on the side of peace and life.* This presupposes that Christians recognize and denounce their compromises with war; that they analyze without quarter the economic and political conditioning that has deflected the proclamation of the gospel in the direction of war; and that they find the courage to break with the logic of domination and death in which they have become involved. Only Christians and churches capable of questioning themselves will have the necessary credibility to question the logic of war.

We call for a church that will be capable of renouncing, as Christ renounced, a life lived for oneself—a church capable of entering into solidarity with the victims of the imperialist praxis of domination, a church capable of taking an unambiguous position, cost what it may, wherever the poor are, in Europe and throughout the world.

Militancy for peace implies concrete involvement with the various liberation movements of urban and rural workers, the unemployed, women, youth, and so on. It is through these instances of resistance and these practices of liberation that the Kingdom of God appears in our world. It is by these praxes of solidarity that the church can become a genuine factor for peace and for life.

—Translated by Robert R. Barr

NOTES

1. What follows is a revision of the material I hurriedly gathered for my last-minute presentation at the Geneva EATWOT conference in place of the speaker designated by the Coordinating Committee for Western Europe, who was unable to attend.

2. Georges Casalis, *Correct Ideas Don't Fall from the Skies: Elements for an Inductive Theology* (Maryknoll, N.Y.: Orbis, 1984), pp. 3–4.

3. Karl Marx and Friedrich Engels, *Manifesto of the Communist Party,* Great Books of the Western World, 50 (Chicago, London, and Toronto: Britannica, 1952), p. 419.

4. Here I refer the reader to the material I have published in collaboration with Pablo Richard and Pierre Goldberger: *Libération et religion: Défis des théologies de la libération* (Paris: INADEP, 1981), esp. the article "L'Evangile des pauvres." Various bibliographical references given throughout that publication support the position maintained here.

5. The dangers, threats, and reprisals that I have had to face and from which, to my surprise, I have emerged unscathed are of little importance, of course. But I should like to point out that the consequences of certain actions are sometimes paid by another generation: thus one of my sons was refused a Brazilian visa for the sole reason—*official*—that he bears his father's name!

6. *The New Reformation* (London: SCM Press, 1965), pp. 60–63; this text is also quoted in my *Correct Ideas,* pp. 11–14.

7. Adrien Dansette, ed., *Napoléon, pensées politiques et sociales* (Paris: Flammarion, 1969), p. 146; Engl. trans. taken from Casalis, *Correct Ideas,* p. 40.

8. *A Materialist Reading of the Gospel of Mark* (Maryknoll, N.Y.: Orbis, 1981).

9. John T. McNeill, ed., *Calvin: Institutes of the Christian Religion,* Library of Christian Classics, 21–22 (Philadelphia: Westminster, 1960), 21:1076.

17

Samuel Rayan

Reconceiving Theology in the Asian Context

The process of reconceiving theology and reexpressing it in Asia is already underway. Theologies that appear to be academic hobbies or exercises in conceptual abstractions are being rejected. Rejected also are colonialist theologies that have been party to imperialism and have connived at or collaborated with world domination and world plunder. Theologies that have been silent about the oppression of our peoples and the global holocaust of many centuries are cast aside as enemies of life and of the living God.

We want theology to be a service to life and to human wholeness. It should be service to life at all levels—from the tiny blade of grass to the singing bird, to the growing baby, to the heights of rigorous thought and warm friendships, to the depths of mystic joy and divine darkness. We want a theology that will be at the service of life with its many needs and spiraling possibilities as well as its transcendence and its endlessly expanding quest and onward thrust. Our theology will be at the service of those who work, suffer, and hope, those who struggle for justice and human dignity for all women and men.

A theology capable of serving the wholeness of life will be ever springing forth at the meeting point of faith and the reality of Asia. The experience of faith and the experience of human existence meet in tension, love, and suffering; they illumine each other's depths, question and challenge each other, and enable each other to new self-understanding, to fresh interpretations of human hope, to committed action and profounder silence.

Obviously, it is not possible, nor is it perhaps necessary, to give here a complete picture of the Asian reality. This reality has been extensively dealt with in the third and the fifth EATWOT conferences held in Wennapuwa, 1979, and in New Delhi, 1981, respectively. There are, besides, books and articles, too numerous to list here, on various aspects of life in Asia.[1] Here we need only refresh our memory on the more salient points that confront the faith with particularly sharp challenges. After that we shall take stock of our chief resources for reconceiving theology; and finally indicate some of the lines along which Asian theology is beginning to move.

THE CHALLENGES

The Teeming Millions

Before and above all else, Asia is persons. That is the most important fact about the continent and its most significant challenge. Of the world population of 4,584 million (as of 1982), 2,671 million live in Asia. Even without counting the Asian peoples in the U.S.S.R., Asia is the home of more than five-ninths of the world population.[2]

More significant than numbers is the fact that in Asia persons belong, persons matter. The old are cared for, the young are cherished, and relationships are strong. Some of these beautiful features of Asian life have suffered down the ages from feudal oppression, caste oppression, and most of all from colonial oppression and capitalist exploitation. Nontheless, the sense of the human is deep. It manifests itself in a thousand small ways. Time, for instance, is not money but persons. Punctuality is not a point in a chronometer but an area of relationship. Hospitality is a way of life, and a guest is one who comes unannounced, like God. The guest is *atithi*; someone who makes no appointment but is welcome, like God.

This sea of persons that is Asia represents numerous peoples, colors, and cultural traditions, most of which count thousands of years of unbroken history. That gives them a sense of rootedness, of history, and of being heir to an ancient heritage. This perhaps is one of the factors that make for the quiet rhythm and the unhurried pace of Asian life. Characteristic Asian compassion and undogmatic broadness of mind are born in part of its long acquaintance with life and the vicissitudes, limitations, and sufferings of life.

Asians, these teeming millions, ask: Could there be an Asian theology without us? What is our part in the shaping of this theology, in choosing its focus, determining its method, and guiding its future? Where do we come in? What role will our simple, ordinary experience of life play in the processing of theology. And what contribution is theology going to make to our life and our history, which we are determined to mold with our own hands?

Then there is the challenge of the religious sense of Asian peoples, and of the many and ancient religions of the continent. The Asian sense of the sacred, of the transcendent, of depth, meaning, and mystery, of communion, of tragedy and of hope, has found expression in a vast body of religious, spiritual, and secular literature abounding in stories, prayers, songs, myths, theologies, criticism, and humor. It has also found expression in renunciation, worship, and ritual with flower, water, fire, food, word, and fragrance, and in every form of art and creative activity, as well as in the organizing and structuring of life around, and in view of, the central values of life, culminating in liberation-salvation. The Indian conception of life as structured in terms of the four *asram*s and the four *purusharta*s is a case in point.[3]

It is in Asia that all the great scripture religions of the world were born. Some of them originated in western Asia, others in southern Asia, and the rest in eastern Asia, but most of them have gone out of the region of their birth and spread to other parts of Asia and of the world. All of them are marked with deep mysticism, but each religion has an accent of its own, the differences bearing the imprint of the geography of the birthplace of each. In western Asia arose the Semitic group of religions (Judaism, Christianity, Islam) with strong monotheistic and ethical features and militant prophetism. Theirs is a mysticism of future-oriented transcendence and struggle. The southern Asian group of religions (Hinduism, Buddhism-Jainism, and Zoroastrianism) range from personal theism through polytheism and pantheism to atheism. But they all exhibit a mysticism of interiority and unity. The religious traditions of eastern Asia (Confucianism, Taoism, Shinto) bear a this-worldly social emphasis and their mysticism is one of action.

Aloysius Pieris has noted that Asian religiousness ranges from metatheistic conceptions of divinity to monotheistic, polytheistic, and nontheistic, and includes explicit atheism: "The common thrust, however, remains *soteriological*, the concern of most religions being *liberation* (vimukti, moksa, nirvana) rather than speculation about a hypothetical liberator."[4] Despite the differences, the diverse religious sensitivities converge in a quest for human wholeness, including communion, and enabling persons to experience it and create communities: "These have so much hold on the hearts of men and women in Asia that the personal, communal, and social life of the people is deeply rooted in . . . socio-religious and cultural-spiritual traditions of communion."[5] But Asian religiousness is ambiguous. It has aspects that liberate and aspects that enslave. It has sometimes collaborated with feudalism, sometimes conspired against it. It has connived at caste oppression and bartered away its credibility. Still several of the religions, more ancient than Christianity, have given orientation, meaning, and hope to many more millions of persons over a longer period of time than has Christianity.

The challenge of theology comes from the depth and persistence of this religiousness as well as from its varying emphases and its disconcertingly diverse symbol systems and the unclarity of the social role it has played in history. Asian religiousness and spiritual traditions ask: What account will you take of us in your theological striving, and what role are we expected to play? Are you really convinced at last that without us no meaningful word about God can be spoken in Asia and no undertakings for liberation envisioned?

Material Poverty

A third challenge to theology comes from the poverty of the peoples of Asia, from the destitution, misery, and squalor in which the Asian masses are forced to live and die. Slums such as those of Calcutta and Bombay, widespread malnutrition, the high rate of infant mortality, low labor power, low resistance to diseases, the existence of bonded labor, the migration of the poor from villages without drinking water to cities where they become victims of multiple economic and moral exploitation, the despair of the unemployed whose numbers grow even as industrialization progresses, the plight of women exploited by tourism and organized "flesh trade," extensive child labor— these are some of the signs and standards of oppression and wretchedness rampant on the continent, side by side with extravagant wealth and cloying affluence. To take but one example: of the 713 million inhabitants of the Indian subcontinent, some 600 million live below or just above the poverty line as defined by scholars or the government; about 85 million are well-to-do; the rest are rich or superrich. They possess the major means of production, hold the reins of power, live in luxury, and control the economic and political life of the country. To retain their privileges they make it a policy to set one group against another, to keep the masses divided on the basis of caste, prestige, religion, and language.

What we must keep in mind is the sharp contrast between the crushing poverty of the masses and the great wealth of the elite, as also the steady growth of the gap between these classes, and the nature of the system that causes "a continuous and unabated flow of resources from the masses to the minority elite."[6]

Poverty is not new to Asia. Asian life has continued for centuries on a subsistence-level economy. But it was once a self-sufficient economy: the community used its resources for its own well-being; the various factors and forces of economic and social life were integrated; life was based on a balance of agriculture and artisan industry, as well as of rights and duties. Asian village communities of long ago had a three-tier social organization with inbuilt mechanisms for the exploitation of the lower classes as well as inbuilt checks and balances to prevent escalation of poverty. Full-fledged members of the community had limited land-holding rights. In India these were and are the higher castes. Then came the cultivators and artisans, and last of all the hired-wage laborers. But Asia was not all agricultural. Some Asian countries had manufacture and export economies, with a vast network of maritime trade with the Middle East, eastern Africa, and southern and southeastern Asia. They had thus accumulated considerable merchant capital. Economically, then, Asian lands are rich in resources. They have a history of development and prosperity. They also have a history of oppression.

With the coming of colonialism and its all-out drive for gain, all checks and balances and mitigating factors in the Asian system were removed, the entire fabric of the age-old way of life was disrupted, and new, refined structures of oppression were introduced. The deep changes effected by colonialists in modes of production and the system of land holding, the introduction of land revenue, the inhuman ways of exacting taxes, the extraction of surplus in cash, the sale of surplus collected in kind, the inadequate supply of money in circulation, the high-handed restrictions on indigenous industry in favor of the conquerors' commodities, and a host of other factors—all contributed to a thoroughgoing distortion and alienation of Asian life, paved the way to a market economy, to a shift from food production to production of cash crops, and to exploitation by moneylenders. Colonialism thwarted and radically destroyed the further evolution, perhaps an industrial revolution, of advanced Asian countries.[7] The present economies of Asian lands are tied, like carts, to the powerful trucks of the capitalist economies of former colonial masters. They have to go where they are pulled, serving foreign interests. They have little to offer by way of hope to the poor of Asia.

The enforced poverty of the Asian masses poses questions to every theological undertaking. Will this plight of the people be a central source and locus of God-talk, or will the God of the oppressed continue to be ignored? Will there be a clear break with theological traditions that legitimized slavery and conquests, and with the European program of the deindustrialization and underdevelopment of Asian lands, or will they carry on under a different guise? Will the theology that grows within the cry of the poor be helped to birth or will it be smothered to death with cunning upper-class jargon?

Religious Poverty

Asia has a history not only of religion and material poverty but of religious poverty as well. Both religion and poverty have a positive pole as well as a negative one; both can be liberating or enslaving. Aloysius Pieris has been insisting on synchronizing the "positive poles of poverty" with the "positive poles of Asian religiosity." He finds the two poles meeting in the ancient tradition of Asian religious socialism, which has two distinct versions: one is the primitive form practiced by clan societies of Asian peasants whose religiousness is cosmic: the other is the sophisticated form represented by monastic communities of Buddhist, Hindu, or Taoist origin, founded on metacosmic religiousness and associated with feudalism. The two belong to different social systems, and there are contradictions between them. Nevertheless both witness to a search to evoke in persons a desire to renounce the ego, to purify the self of its propensity for acquisitiveness, to abandon the worship of mammon, and experience interior liberation from greed.

In addition, there are regions in Asia where the contradiction between the two types of socialism has been overcome, where monks are supported by villages "in the framework of a religious socialism which knows no cultural or economic gap between the monastic community and the village community," and where religion is not made to justify class division. There "the earth is everybody's property and nobody's monopoly," and one is satisfied with what one really needs but gives all one can to the community. Voluntary poverty is a spiritual antidote against mammon. It works psychologically; it can also be organized to work socially and politically in the battle against organized greed or mammon's principalities and powers." Voluntary poverty can be a protest against imposed poverty, a rejection of obsession with cosmic needs, and the promotion of a new vision of society in which wealth is made to serve human needs and never allowed to enslave human hearts. Pieris points to Mahatma Gandhi as "the most outstanding example of voluntary poverty with both its psychological and sociological implications."[8]

This tradition too challenges us and asks: Will your theology take a clear and firm stand for socialism? Will it bring to light the socialist dimensions of the gospel faith and sacramental practice that now lie submerged beneath bourgeois interpretations and feudal cultural forms? Will it institute a searching critique of capitalist social order and the concrete geopolitics of the churches? Or will it succumb to European economic and ecclesiastical pressures and choose to continue to be vague about the social and political demands of the faith while supporting capitalist models of development and quietly legitimizing egoistic acquisitiveness and the idolatry of avarice?

Aftermath of Colonization

Most Asian countries are former colonies. Their souls bear deep scars from their colonial past. They have been uprooted from their history and culturally distorted. It is as if they had been hijacked and forcibly taken to some strange land and left, stripped and broken, in a wilderness from which there is no egress. The rhythm of their life and growth has been shattered, their self-image distorted, their creativity blocked, their self-confidence undermined, their imagination violated and annexed, their history raped and fettered. This profound spiritual breakdown wrought by colonial terrorism, this invasion of souls, is far more disastrous and fatal than the brutal massacres, the planned genocide, and the total plunder practiced by the system.

It is important to note at this point how noncolonized nations (e.g., Japan) and those only partially colonized (e.g., China) have retained their creative élan and spiritual resilience. They are able to take their history into their own hands.

Spiritual and cultural factors have consequences for economics, politics, and every aspect of human growth. Aid and trade alone cannot rescue the former colonies, nor can a generous injection of capital alone. These often worsen the malaise. The need now is for the peoples to rebuild their pride, to find their atman—their innermost self—to discover their own power, to dream new dreams and see fresh social visions, and to act.

It is here that theology must make a contribution. How culturally free will theology itself need to be in order to do this? And which culture, in a classed society, will theology make its own?

Political Background

The political realities of Asia represent a different set of challenges. The former colonies of Asia started their independent existence as formal democracies modeled on Western parliamentary systems. But soon the system broke down in one country after another, giving way to military regimes, martial law governments, dictatorships, authoritarianism, and severe repression of the people, with the support, almost always, of Western "democracies," especially of the United States of America, their armies, their advice, their weapons, and their money. Behind this noteworthy phenomenon stand the contradictions of the economic and cultural system as bequeathed by retreating imperial powers. Behind it stands also the disillusionment of the masses at the policies of the elite class whom the former colonial lords trained, empowered, and left behind as their permanent presence and penetration, and whose economic and cultural interests are integrated with the interests of the former metropolises.

Will our theology be of service to the people and life, and will it therefore naturally assume a critical, prophetic role with regard to the ruling classes and to political processes set afoot by them? Or will it play safe and claim to be apolitical, and thus indirectly support the status quo and its rulers?

Social Background

The challenge of the social situation is no less pressing. Social evolution and the gathering forces of revolution in Asia were blocked by colonial domination. Later, the transfer of power took place without social revolution and cultural change. Power was handed over to elitist groups culturally assimilated into the retiring masters' class. They had been their collaborators in carrying on colonial rules, and came to form a privileged group apart. These ruling elites found it to their advantage to keep intact the entire imperial system with all its institutions, attitudes, values, and reactions. The result is that on most Asian scenes there are societies in which the poor are dishonored, despised, and used; women are marginalized, humiliated, and exploited in many ways; caste and class represent great social gulfs that cannot be forded. And there are in this ancient society numerous taboos, fears, and superstitions that keep society fragmented, keep the individual too much submerged in the collectivity, and block new steps in thought and social practice. But the masses also want to change what they have experienced as oppressive and dehumanizing.

Will theology come to discover the liberative presence and action of God in the people, and make that discovery a summons to the oppressed to stand by God and struggle for liberty? Will theology dare to take sides, to think in terms of class as Jesus did, and to explore the implications of "the good news to the poor"?

Socialism

There is finally the challenge of the socialist countries of Asia. A little below half the population of Asia are in these countries. The revolution in China, the liberation of the land, the transformation of this ancient society, the new sense of dignity and burgeoning of hope among the masses as well as the victory of Vietnam over the mighty United States have become a sign and a promise to the oppressed masses of Asia. They inspire, give strength, and build up confidence. The masses have taken note of the fact that (with the exception of the 1905 defeat of Russia by Japan), it is only the peoples and groups inspired by Marxism that have in Asia (Africa and Latin America) successfully fought and driven out Western imperialist forces and their local allies.

But the masses are also aware of the nonsocialist behavior of these countries and of their quarrels among themselves. The nonsocialist countries remember the Japanese role in World War II and see in it the disclosure of the imperialist character and expansionist instincts of capitalism. No less are they concerned with the expansionism of U.S. capitalism as represented by its international imperialism of money and its military presence in the Pacific, in the Indian Ocean, in western Asia, and in other parts of the world.

Will theology explore the place of these events in God's providence, and their significance for the kingdom of God? Is it ready to pursue the religious and spiritual meaning of the unbelief and atheism that accompany the political realization of the Marxist dream? Or will it conform to the rabid anticommunism of ecclesiastical politics and ignore this loudest of questions God is posing?

Such is the situation, such are the challenges. We want theology to be able to relate to them in depth, and to discern God's presence in them and God's summons from within them. We want a theology that can shed light on reality, arouse consciousness, denounce all that is dehumanizing and unjust, and announce prophetically the freedom, the dignity, and the human rights that the kingdom of God enshrines—a theology that can lead persons to commitment, illumine their struggles, enable them to self-critical reflection against the wider horizons of meaning opened up by the faith, and unflinchingly sustain their hope.

RESOURCES

What are the resources relevant to our effort to reconceive theology in Asia? The resources common to Christians the world over (the faith, the Judeo-Christian scriptures, the historical experience of the churches) are presupposed and will not be commented upon here. Our specific resources are our people, the sacred writings of the other Asian religions, the spiritual history of the people, and the liberative potential of their traditions.

The People

Asians themselves, their experience of life and their rich humanness, are the main source of an Asian theology. The courage and the strength that have enabled Asians to survive, despite material destitution and great physical and mental suffering, in the midst of death; their readiness to share with and to care for one another as long as they remain uninfected by urban-industrial bourgeois civilization with its individualism and competitiveness; their struggles; the hope that sustains them and the hope that they sustain—these are theological loci. Our common experiences, our daily existence, are loci of revelation and of grace. Because the incarnation signals God's involvement with humankind, "all of life is caught up into the holiness of God, all is blessed, all is locus for revelation, ground for salvation."[9] The peoples themselves are then a revelation, and from them we learn and by them we are saved.

John Dijkstra writes about the poor of Asia:

> They have faith in their fellow poor, a rare value in nonpoor individuals who isolate themselves from one another. . . . They thirst for justice because they feel themselves treated unjustly. . . . They strengthen their mutual dependence and use their gracious human values to serve their community beyond individualistic desires and needs. Those who want to live egotistically among the poor cannot last long in these communities. . . . The poor who are more defenseless, vulnerable . . . are more cared for and served. . . . They enjoy together any good that comes to their fellow poor. . . . They know one another thoroughly. . . . Their human potentials are allowed to be used together for their common good. . . . The Asian poor have faith not only in their fellow poor but also in their caring God and Lord whom they name according to the religion they follow. . . . [God] loves them creatively and this love cannot be ineffective. God's ongoing creative love shows itself in [God's] people, whatever their religion or nonreligion may be.[10]

There is therefore, an implicit, unspoken theology in human lives and relationships. The tribals of Chotanagpur are reported to have said of Lievens as he struggled to win back their lost land: "If he gives us land, he is a prophet of the true God." They knew in what relationship God stood to the land, and they knew in what historical concerns and actions God appeared. Much indeed of the life of the poor is theopraxis—the matrix of all theology. There is an implicit theology in their will to change, in their vision and dream, however vague, of a just society and their readiness to achieve it and to pay the price. It is the peoples, the illiterate peoples who created our languages, who are laying the foundations of a new theology.

I must emphasize here the Asian view that religion is commitment and faith is a matter of praxis. No great emphasis is laid on definitions and dogmas. Truth is historical and concrete. The truth of spiritual experiences cannot be adequately expressed in words, much less can it be defined. Nor is spiritual truth exhausted by the experience of any one age, culture, tradition, or religion. Hence the refusal of Asian religions to set up tribunals to pass judgment on truth, to dogmatize, to use dogmas as weapons, or to separate religious authority from spiritual experience, ethical practice, and competence born of service.

There is among the Asian peoples a unity of experience, action, and word. There is also a unity among the varieties of spiritual experiences, a complementarity of diverse spiritual perceptions and religious symbol systems. Most Asian religions refuse to demand or impose change of religious affiliation. This has its basis in the strong conviction of Asians that God relates to all women and men everywhere: God's self-giving revelation and saving grace are universal. Every historical situation is seen as adequately provided for salvation and for free, life-transforming human activity, but as imperfect too and called, therefore, to reach out to the other and the more, and remain open.

We realize at once that the horizon and the reference point of a theology of the people will be not the church but the kingdom of God, not any particular history but the history of humankind, not redemption as contradistinguished from creation but creation as the beginning of salvation and the first grace. Here the church will be called upon to be a symbolic reality, a light in the house, a city on the hill, the fragrance of Christ broadcasting the experience of God. And mission will, in this context, have a meaning, purpose, and function other than anxious proselytism.

Other Asian Scriptures

Asian non-Christian scriptures—Hindu, Buddhist, Taoist in origin—will be sacred to us too and form part of the resources at our disposal for reconceiving and reexpressing theology. For centuries they have been the word of God for Asian peoples; they have guided and nourished life and sustained hope in a hopeless world. As written records they may not be accessible to the illiterate masses of Asia, but they represent the experience of these same illiterate masses. They are their creation under God, just as all the languages of Asia and of the world are creations of ordinary preliterate peoples. We are heirs to a much larger body of holy scriptures than are the peoples of other continents.

The vast world of spiritual experience and vision symbolized in these writings forms part of the spiritual grounds of Asian existence from which we refuse to be uprooted. There we must stand if we are to receive the further word that comes from God, and speak it for the liberation of life and the humanization of the world.[11]

Rereading Asian Scriptures and Folklore

Among our resources is the liberation potential of the traditional religions with their numberless stories and myths. The general impression among Christians seems to be that religions such as Hinduism and Buddhism have little or nothing to contribute to the process of human liberation in history. Books such as *Why Is the Third World Poor?* by Pierro Gheddo[12] suggest that these religions are the main cause of the underdevelopment of Asian peoples. Such ideas betray a lack of understanding of these religions and a tendency to overlook the history of how Europe underdeveloped Asia.

I suspect that a great many stories of the people have been lost: stories of popular protests and struggles that were later co-opted by ruling classes, re-molded and distorted, and used to threaten and to subjugate. It is necessary to retrieve such stories for the people, explore afresh their liberation potential, and release their revolutionary power.

This work has already begun. The story, for instance, of Rāmāyana, one of the two great epics of India, has been reinterpreted in recent times to serve the cause of women's liberation and the conscientization of villagers and peasants. It is the story of the exile of Prince Rāma and his wife Sitā, the abduction of Sitā by King Rāvana, and her rescue by Rāma who kills Rāvana in battle with the help of devoted tribes. Traditionally the story was used to inculcate womanly obedience, wifely fidelity, and feminine patience. In more recent times the personality of Sitā has been reinterpreted as that of a woman with a will of her own, who registers firm and well-argued protests against the ways and values of her husband, subjects him to searching criticism, and condemns his ambiguous attitude to court intrigue, to which both of them had fallen victims.[13]

Closer still to our times, the story has inspired a social film *Nisānt*, ["the end of the night"]. The film presents the revolt of an entire rural population against a landlord and his family who had been cruelly oppressing them for years. The revolt is provoked by the memory of Rāma, the object of popular devotion, who had waged war aginst the organized forces of oppression. "What did Rāma do when his wife was abducted?" asks the temple priest whose social consciousness had been awakened by the rural schoolmaster whose wife had been kidnapped by the landlord's brothers. "Rāma fought and did away with the abductor," replied the villagers. "And what do you do when your wives and fields are taken away?" The villagers begin to see the significance for the here and now of the religious story. The insight is forthwith translated into action, and they set themselves free.

The *Bhagavad Gita*, a philosophico-religious poem embedded in the epic *Mahabharata*, would constitute a call to the oppressed to struggle for libera-tion. A hundred royal brothers join to oppress their five cousins. The numbers are symbolic of oppressive power and oppressed powerlessness. The five brothers, after many trials and long endurance, decide to resist and fight it out. God, in the person of Krishna, is presented as involved in the struggle on the side of the oppressed five. At the last minute, in the battlefield, with the lines drawn up, one of the five, the most skilled of warriors, refuses to fight on various personal, religious, and social grounds. He is challenged by Krishna, instructed by him, given a new perspective on life, and urged to shed his lethargy. He must stand up and struggle for the redemption of freedom and dignity from the forces of heartless injustice.

The whole poem is cast in the form of a dialogue between God and humankind that is liberationally significant. Humans may question, object to, debate with God and only thus, critically and creatively, move toward faith and obedience. The dialogue is framed within a doctrine of avatar, the descent of the divine into history every time that justice has been overthrown and injustice has taken over. God is with us amid the struggles of life and not only or principally in the solitude and quiet of forests and caves and monastic peace. It is there that we are guided by God, the charioteer of our lives. It is there we enter into the deepest mystical experience and the overjoying, terrifying vision of the Lord. In this poem speculation and ritual are transcended, the path of devotion is opened up and made known to all regardless of caste, and salvation is offered to all. Work, action, historical involvement are emphasized, not for selfish purposes but for the sake of the well-being of all creation. Self-regarding action alienates; socially meaningful action liberates. During the struggle of India for political liberation, this poem became a source of inspiration to the nation. It is not without significance that some half dozen of the leaders of the struggle wrote commentaries on this text.

Sadhu Mohan offers us a sample of the way in which the ancient stories of India are being radically reread today in terms of popular struggles:

What did Krishna stand for? According to the Chandogya Upanishad, he received instruction from the sage Angirasa, to the effect that sacrifices can be performed without rituals, that true sacrifice consists in practicing liberality and righteousness. The Puranas present him as in conflict with Brahmanic institutions. . . . The Vishnu Purana contains a vindication of his character and of the tribal way of life. What Krishna preached was cosmic consciousness. . . . He attacked the caste system and repudiated sacrificial ritualism. . . . In the land of Krishna no sacrifice was performed, no Brahmins were to be found, and people were not allowed to read the Vedas and the Sastras. All this shows that Krishna resisted his people being integrated into the caste system. Which, of course, the leaders of Brahmanism could not tolerate. So they modified the Krishna tradition. . . . Krishna of the extant Gita is probably of later interpretation. If D.D. Kosambi is right, the priestly class rewrote the Mahabharata and the Gita between 200 B.C. and 200 A.D.[14]

Eqbal Ahmed, a Pakistani scholar, has urged us to note that "the Khomeini episode is the *eighth* major battle that the Muslim nation [Iran] em-
barked on to defend its sovereignty against mercantile and military exploiters
from the West. . . . Religious clerics were in the thick of the struggle." Between 1872 and 1905 there were three revolts against concessions to the West
to the detriment of national interests. The constitutional government that
came into being in 1906 was overthrown by Czarist Russia and Britain in
1911. Popular revolts occurred in 1919 against Lord Curzon's Anglo-Persian
Treaty, in 1941 against the dictator Reza Khan installed by the British, and in
1950 when nationalists succeeded in forcing elections and establishing the
Mossadegh government, which was overthrown in 1953 in a CIA-organized
coup d'etat that initiated the murderous regime of the shah. Then Iranian
Muslim masses fought not simply the shah but "the superpower which forced
him to be its gendarme in the Persian Gulf, sold him $19 million worth of
weapons and supported his repressions until the last murderous days of his
regime."[15] But the religious concern of Islam for the defense of national integrity, freedom, and honor is well known and needs no proof.

Buddhism is commonly associated in our minds with compassion and
peace, and rarely, if ever, with revolution. It is a fact, nevertheless, that Buddhist scriptures demand radical social change, and "even orthodox Buddhism has to its credit a theory and praxis of rebellion." Aloysius Pieris
recalls the Burmese Buddhist resurgence that was messianically political and
directed first against Burmese kings, then against their British successors:
"There must have been about twenty revolts from 1838 to 1928—all inspired
by the Maitreya cult, the eschatological expectation of a just social order to
be ushered in with the appearance of Maitreya, the future Buddha." The
Burmese independent movement belongs to this line of Buddhist rebellion.
Similar patterns may be discerned in Sri Lanka and Indochina. Vietnamese
history reflects a militant political Buddhism that is as strong today as in the
past. It was two rural movements of 1919 and 1939, of distinctly Buddhist
inspiration, that finally challenged and fought French colonialism and defeated it in 1954.

China offers a series of examples of revolutionary praxis of great radicalism in the fringes of Buddhist institution. Some ten armed rebellions were
organized by monks between A.D. 402 and A.D.515: "These monastic rebellions were directed against both the state and the official religious establishment. Since then there have been many messianic sects that had a popular
base."[16] The conclusion is that the great religions of Asia have shown themselves sensitive and flexible enough to respond to contemporary moods and
needs, and to reinterpret their scriptures and stories and hopes even when this
meant armed struggle and costly revolution.

Spiritual History

The spiritual history of Asians as the history of a relentless quest for truth,
meaning, and freedom is one of the basic resources we have for the shaping of

a relevant Asian theology. I shall illustrate this only from the history of India. The pre-Buddhist secular history of India is practically undocumented, although records of its religious history are abundant. They take us back to about 1000 B.C. and present us with the story of a spiritual journey with clear stages and new discoveries.

In the first stage, the Vedic period, up to 1000 B.C., sacrifice holds the center of the stage with life and nature orbiting around it. In it gods and humans meet and transact the affairs of life on equal terms, to the advantage of both sides. The gods reflect nature as well as the anxieties and struggles of human life, and the world is a world of elaborately organized and expensive sacrifices and abundant sacrificial songs.

The next stage, the age of the Brahmans, around 1000 B.C., is marked by ritualism as well as the creation of significant stories. Worship becomes an endlessly complicated mechanism of rites and chants that only professionals can master. Because sacrifice was the hub of life, those skilled in the technology of sacrifice—namely, the priests—become spiritually and socially dominant and oppressive.

Discontent with the entire sacrificial system, with the meaning it offered and the whole shape of things characterizes the third stage. It is at this point that the history of an independent and relentless quest begins. Spiritual freedom is from now on a secure acquisition. It is remarkable that reaction and criticism came from priests themselves, though not exclusively. They stood to lose, but passion for the truth and its pressure upon the heart won the day.

The fourth stage, dating perhaps from the eighth century B.C., witnesses a withdrawal from externalism and the mechanics of religion, and the setting out on a journey inward in search of the meaning of life and the ultimate reality of the world. Through disciplined concentration and intense meditation, the discovery is made of the Atman, the self, and of the Brahma, the Self of every self, the ground, source, and support of all that is real, the abiding center of everything that is. The discovery is marked by surprise, joy, and wonder; and there is a sense of having arrived, having realized, and having been liberated and completed. Brahma is *saccidananda*—being, consciousness, and bliss. Brahma is joy, joy, joy.

The journey inward brings the questing spirit not only to one's own atman but to the atman of the universe of reality and hence to the reality of the universe, the self-expression of Brahma. The sense of the unity of the interior and the exterior, of atman and Brahma, of the personal and the structural, of the individual and the social, will never be lost again. Did not something similar happen to and at Vatican II? An honest concern for internal reform of the church leads the church outside itself, to other churches, to other religions, and to the vast secular world with its multiple concerns. To Asia religion is the whole of life to be lived Godward, and not a department of life or one function of life.

The exit of the inward journey into the outer world meant a new search for the concrete significance of it all for the daily life and social existence of the people, for the economic, political, and cultural activity of the people. Here two roads opened up and two great movements came into existence. These were the Buddha's path and the Bhakti *marga*. Living in a time of crisis and transition, a time of conflict between egalitarian tribal traditions on the one hand and emerging empire-building powers on the other, Gautama the Buddha saw concrete existence as alienated and suffering, due to the deeper alienation of individualistic greed. His message was to renounce greed and radically reorient life in terms of truthfulness and compassion, total and measureless. The whole of society was to be recast, the monk being to the lay community a mirror, a reminder, a challenge, and an encouragement.

By a radical questioning of the orthodoxy derived from the Vedas, the Buddha rejected the mediation of priests, the usefulness of sacrifice, the authority of scriptures, and the caste system. He insisted on the corporate reality of the human and on community existence. He rejected as idle all God-talk untouched by the strivings and tears of human beings. From religious mechanisms and abstractions he called people back to history, to the real problems of life, to concern with real men and women, to the building of new human relationships. Through a radical criticism and fidelity to historical existence, the Buddha brought about a profound religious and social revolution in the sixth century B.C.

By the third century B.C. the Bhakti movement surfaced, and found its first theological expression in the *Bhagavad Gita*, grew luxuriantly in southern India in the hands of the Alvars from the fourth century A.D. onward, came to a culmination in the Bhagavata Purana around the tenth century and received new theological undergirding and development from Ramanuja in the eleventh century. In succeeding centuries the movement spread to western India (Maharashtra), northern India (Uttar Pradesh), and eastern India (Bengal). Bhakti, then, has been the religion and spirituality of the Indian masses for over two thousand years. Hence its importance for a theology that hopes to be of service to life and humanization.

There are in fact two streams of Bhakti: one centered on Vishnu and his avatars, especially his avatar as Krishna, the revealer of the path of Bhakti in the *Gita*; the other centered on Shiva with whom no doctrine of avatar is associated. Both streams are probably non-Aryan in origin and nature. They are certainly nonconformist vis-à-vis classic Brahmanism. The figures of Shiva and Krishna and the stories told of them bespeak nonconformism, unconventionality, and protest, and the determination to walk a different path from the one prescribed by orthodoxy. Brahmanism sought to co-opt and reinterpret these native traditions precisely because they are traditions of the people, and precisely for that reason it could never fully succeed.

Robert Miller has suggested that Bhakti is a tradition that grew up separate from and opposed to the great tradition of the upper castes. He finds such a separate tradition among the untouchable Mahars of Maharashtra. In it "equality is opposed to inequality; individual ability is opposed to merger of the individual in the group; emotionalism is opposed to ritualism; escape from the system is opposed to movement within the system.'' Miller thinks such a great culture, counter to the other great culture, has always existed in India. Bhakti and militance should be seen "not as a variant of the system, but as an entirely different system in itself."[17]

The Bhakti traditions are rich in liberation potential. They have been described as "the most creative upsurge of the Indian mind," which has inspired "several social and political revolts . . . from Shivaji's rebellion in the seventeenth century to Mahatma Gandhi's in the twentieth."[18] This religious current has helped many low castes to bear their social status with courage or to seek release from it. It is imbued with the protest of downtrodden social groups and remarkable for signs of revolt. The inclusion of untouchables, other low caste persons, and women among the Bhakti saints, such as the Alvars, Chakradhar (13th century A.D.), Chokhamela (14th century), Kabir (16th century), is a form of protest, a declaration of freedom, and a word of promise. These traits are present in the *Gita*, which for all practical purposes rejected almost everything that the Buddha had rejected and with the Buddha turned to real human conflictual history and committed action. But Bhakti does this within the clear faith in a personal God to worship whom is to work for the well-being of all creation even as God works.

The movement of Asian spiritual history as illustrated in this brief survey of the religious history of India lies in the direction of a profounder and wider freedom in a noncaste, nonhierarchical, egalitarian community in which the within of persons and the within of society are held together in creative, dialectical tension for commitment to the concrete history of the people with whom God lives and works. This perspective is vital for rethinking and restructuring our theology.

PROSPECTS

Asian theology will be a process of discovering and joining God as God lives and works with Asian peoples. Asian peoples are poor and oppressed. They resist oppression and struggle in many ways to defend their dignity, win back their rights, and establish justice, freedom, and a human community. It is in these poor and their struggles that theology will have to seek and find the living God. For God identifies with the poor and the oppressed, hears their cry, and acts in history to liberate them and put them in charge of the future of the earth (Exod. 3:7-10; Ps. 103:6; Matt. 25:31-46, 14:13-21; John 5). Any god, however mighty and splendid it might seem to be, is but a dead thing and an idol if it has eyes only for great temples and magnificent liturgies and not for the affliction of the people; if it has ears only for fulsome praises and not for the cry of the oppressed; if it has feet only to walk marble floors and velvet hallways and not to walk the squalid slums of Asia and the wretched villages of our people; if, in brief, it is on the side of the pharaohs, presidents, and generals and not with the powerless and the downtrodden (Pss. 82, 115). It is to the poor that God gives the good news, and to the simple and children that God discloses the saving truth and grace that are withheld from the learned and the clever (Matt. 11:2-6, 25-27). The poor have the experience of the word and of the Speaker of the word, and of striving for freedom and wholeness; it is from this experience that theology comes to birth.

The poor of Asia are mainly non-Christian. To meet God in the poor is to meet God in the non-Christian poor, to meet God in their beliefs, hopes, and symbols, in their traditions and in their religiousness. Here is a new agenda that the Asian Christian churches have to take in hand with imagination and courage. The resultant theology will be different.

God is with the poor in their history. God is deeply and passionately involved in their life and its concerns. God is not neutral, abstract, atemporal, unaffected by the joys, wounds, and tears of the lonely. The divine transcendence does not consist in the immutability and eternity of a Platonic substance but in loving and doing justice unconditionally, and unconditionally demanding justice and love. God is not to be conceived as absolute and impassible, but as responsive in fidelity and sympathy. The divine unchangeability lies in the inexhaustibility of God's love, the steadfastness of God's purpose, and God's utter dependability and faithfulness. God is therefore known and experienced in the practice of love and justice (Jer. 22:16). It is such experience that theology seeks to register and transmit back to the community to help consolidate and deepen its practice. God is discovered in the process of committed action to build history, the struggle of a people for justice and freedom.

Is it true that God approaches us only at the limits of our despair, when we are on the point of committing suicide? Care must be taken lest we present God as someone who, like a feudal lord or a military general, builds a throne on our humiliation and our ruins. No, God approaches us at the height of responsible initiative on our part, in the thick of struggle and revolt. We must wrestle with God and be invincible before God can bless us and give us a new name (Gen. 32:23-33). We must challenge God as Job did (Job 9:2-4, 11-35), and question God as the psalmist did (Ps. 44:18-26) and as Jesus did (Mark 34), before God can raise us from the grave. Theology will have to reflect upon the God who summons us to freedom and liberative action and the building of history and the co-creating of the earth.

Theology will have to pay far more attention to the subversive dimensions of God's interventions. Too often and for too long we have pictured God as the guarantor of the establishment and the guardian of law and order. It is time to fix our attention on the God who takes the rejected stone and makes it the keystone of the building; who raises to life and to the leadership of history the rejected and crucified Jesus, in defiance of death-dealing powers; the God who overthrows the thrones of the mighty and uplifts the lowly. How is this God to be worshiped and followed except by standing with the downtrodden with whom God works to upset established powers and transform the earth? Theology will have to be converted from, and reject, the god of the conquerors and killers and slave owners, the god of the shahs, the Batistas, the generals, and the transnational corporations, the god of zamindars and moneylenders and warmongers.

From such gods our theology will be converted to the God who identifies with women, the landless, the untouchables, the unemployed, the bonded, the half-starved, and all the broken and humiliated of the vast Asian continent—the God who comes to reign on our earth and restore justice to the poor, dignity to the despised, and sufficient food for all, in a community of equals. This is the God who speaks to all peoples and not only to Christians, and whose grace reaches out to all and encompasses the universe—the God who is revealed both in creation and in history, and who is disclosed not in the churches only but in secular events of human history, and whose revelation is about this concrete historical world, not about the churched part of it only.

Theology will speak of and be in touch with the God who reveals a word that includes the world that is addressed. Hence the vicissitudes of the revealing word are bound up with the vicissitudes of the world and its human population. God is included in the destiny of the world. God's future depends on our response, on what we make of history, and what we thereby become. Theology will remain open, for God is known only in the measure in which the kingdom of God comes and we become it.

NOTES

1. See Virginia Fabella, ed., *Asia's Struggle for Full Humanity* (Maryknoll, N.Y.: Orbis, 1980); Virginia Fabella and Sergio Torres, eds., *Irruption of the Third World* (Orbis, 1983); "Select Bibliography on India," prepared by I.S.I. Documentation Center, Bangalore, 1981.

2. *Asia 1983 Year Book (Far Eastern Economic Review),* p. 43, quoting United Nations statistics.

3. The four *asram*s or stages of life are *brahmacarya*, celibate studentship; *garhasthya*, householdership; *vanaprastha*, state of retirement to the forest; and *sanayasa*, state of the wandering ascetic sage at the service of the people. The four *purushartha*s or goals of life are: *dharma*, religion and duty; *artha*, wealth and economic activity; *kama*, enjoyment and celebration; and *moksha*, final liberation and wholeness.

4. Aloysius Pieris, "The Place of Non-Christian Religions and Cultures in the Evolution of Third World Theology" (address given at the fifth conference of the Ecumenical Association of Third World Theologians, New Delhi, Aug. 1981), *CTC Bulletin* (Christian Conference of Asia), 3/2 (Aug. 1982), p. 57; also in Fabella and Torres, *Irruption*, p. 133.

5. D.S. Amalorpavadass, *The Church as a Community of Faith in the Asian Context* (paper prepared for the third plenary assembly of FABC, Oct. 1982), FABC Papers no. 30, p.2.

6. Ibid., p.4.

7. See Gladys D'Souza, *British Rule* (Bangalore: CSA Publ.) and the books referred to there, such as *Indian Economic Development* by A.I. Chicherov

(1971); *Modern India* by Bipin Chandra (1971); *The Economic History of India* by R.C. Dutt; *The Crippled Tree* by Han Suyin, etc.

8. Aloysius Pieris, "Mission of the Local Church in Relation to Other Major Religious Traditions," *Witness*, II/4 (fourth quarter 1982) 66–71, 61.

9. Juliana Casey, "Emmanuel: A Reflection," in *Starting Points*, Lora Ann Quinonez, ed. (Washington, D.C.: Leadership Conference of Women Religious, 1980), pp. 2–3, 11.

10. John Dijkstra, "The Poor of Asia," *Info on Human Development*, 8/9 (Sept. 1981) 8–9.

11. See D.S. Amalorpavadass, ed., *Research Seminar on Extra-Biblical Scriptures* (Bangalore, 1975).

12. Maryknoll, N.Y., Orbis, 1973.

13. Kumaran Asan, *Cintavistayaya Sita* ["Sita in a reflective mood"], *A Malayalam Poem* (Thonnackal, 1920).

14. Sadhu Mohan, "The Radical Krishna," *Negations*, 1 (Jan. 1982) 30–32.

15. Aloysius Pieris, "Place of Non-Christian Religions," *CTC Bulletin*, pp. 53–54 (*Irruption*, p. 129), where he quotes from a manuscript version of a lecture given by Dr. Eqbal Ahmed at the Riverside Church in New York City, Jan. 20, 1980.

16. Ibid., *CTC Bulletin*, pp. 55–56; *Irruption*, p. 132.

17. Robert Miller, "Great Traditions, Little Traditions, Whose Tradition?" in *Anthropological Quarterly*, 39 (1966) 26–42, referred to in Siddhartha, "Bhakti as Social Protest," *Negations*, 6 (1983) 7–8.

18. Balachandra Namade, "The Revolt of the Underprivileged," *Journal of Asian and African Studies*, 15, 1–2 (1980) 113, quoted by Pieris, "Place of Non-Christian Religions," *CTC Bulletin*, p. 54; *Irruption*, p. 130.

18

Mercy Amba Oduyoye

Who Does Theology?
Reflections on the Subject of Theology

Not reading and speculation, but living, dying, and being condemned make a real theologian.

—Martin Luther

I have been asked to reflect on the subject of theology, a request phrased variously as "Who is doing theology today?", "What does the theological task consist of?", "What makes a real theologian?" Faithfulness to the issues that surfaced in the subgroup I participated in prevents me from ending my assignment with an amended version of the quotation above. The group, deliberating on the relationship of social analysis to theology, brought out what Martin Luther crystalized for us, but maintained that "reading" and "speculation" are also part of doing theology.

A THIRD WAY

Our "dialogue" turned out to be a conversation among persons I have chosen to call "third way theologians." Not that there are identifiable schools of theology designated first, second, and third, but that from all over the world had come theologians who in their various contexts are attempting to offer fresh ways of doing Christian theology. Conspicuously absent were those who, in the face of contemporary challenges, continue to state Christian theology in the language of nineteenth-century pietistic Christianity. Absent too were those who, in spite of critical historical scholarship, continue to write exposés of the Christian faith as if nothing had changed. Present but

143

somewhat subdued were theologians who call us to a reassessment and re-statement of the cardinal tenets of the faith in relationship to the momentous issues of our times. The first two ways may be grouped together and called "traditional theology," "the first way."

In whatever part of the world you find critical theologians, one thing stands out; they take the contemporary world seriously, whether in the area of scholarship, politics, economics, or religion. They take seriously the primary contexts in which traditional Christian symbols were formulated, including the worldviews and philosophies that informed them. With such an orientation, they then do the same for the expression of the faith vis-à-vis their own contemporaries. Ordinarily, such theologians are found in universities and other academic institutions, but that is not to say that they are not found elsewhere. They serve on theological commissions of various churches and are quoted as "authorities" in their specialized fields. Critical theologians deal with the problematics of the faith at a professional (academic/specialized) level and their findings tend to stay within their own circles, become new dogma, or are decried as new heresy. In either case this exploratory edge of theology only very slowly penetrates to the Christian grass roots to effect any change in the way that religion is conceived and lived. This could be designated "the second way."

The theologians who met in Geneva must be described differently. They are critical, they face contemporary issues, but in addition they are a marginalized group who are attempting to free theology not only from the *academic* but also from the *ecclesia*, so that the Christian grass roots may reappropriate the faith and express in their own media and in their own lives. These "third way" theologians belong to the academic world and to the church, and they take the world seriously enough to lay themselves open to hearing the word of God in contemporary events. But the results of their studies are always qualified in one way or another—political theology, feminist theology, black theology, liberation theology, as if they were something less than traditional and critical theology. The question is often raised, "Are they theologians or sociologists and social anthropologists?" The inclusion in their ranks of some persons with no formal theological training raises eyebrows. Who then is doing theology today?

The Theologian

If I could state precisely what a theologian is, I might say that "a theologian is one who is competent in writing, analyzing, evaluating, and criticizing theological works," just as a historian is one who specializes in historical scholarship, or a philosopher in philosophical studies, or even a novelist who writes novels, or the literary critic who evaluates them. But theology has proved singularly difficult to define, for theologians interpret history, they promote philosophies of life, they even compose or unravel stories— "myths" that suggest how God is to be apprehended. They tell stories from the premise that "God is the foundational factor in human life and experience."

Rather than attempt to refine this definition, I propose in this reflection to bear in mind persons who are in fact designated theologians, using as my point of departure the description of the theological task proposed by Maurice Wiles: "a critical reevaluattion of the Christian tradition we have received on the basis of the best knowledge available to us from all sources."[1]

Once, in a period of two weeks, I was involved in three meetings that had to do with theology and theologians. By the end of it all, I was thoroughly at sea. Who indeed is doing theology? They are called theologians who are engaged in scholarly, philosophical, and detailed analysis of our language about God. Or they are those who construct expositions of the Christian faith directed at conserving the faith once and for all delivered, or who produce and teach well-reasoned statements aimed at building the Church and winning converts. Or they are those who are engaged in taking seriously the "Christ-event," but do so in the context of the events that bear directly on the lives of women and men of today. These theologians often call for a reorientation and reordering of prevailing structures and relationships. Indeed it is in the attempt to do so that they theologize.

Even if one confines to the scholarly world the actual craft of hammering out the expressions appropriate to the Christian faith-experience, these and other theologians will be represented. They are all doing theology.

The most persistent criticism of "third way theology" has been that it is sociology, not theology, and because it pursues a particular ideology—a partiality for the poor, oppressed, and marginalized—it has nothing to say to those who are imprisoned in a style and view of life that creates the oppressive situations that burden the poor. Sometimes these theologians are charged with being representatives of a Christianity that has lost its nerve and is now seeing God at work in other religions—Islam, Hinduism, Buddhism. They are said to have lost their nerve vis-à-vis the traditional Christian condemnation of the culture of peoples who are not at the power centers of the world—Africans, Asiatics, minority Americans, Pacific Ocean islanders. I find these criticisms too short-sighted to deserve countercriticism. If one grants that the study of humanity contributes in good measure to the study of God, then it is the whole of humanity that should be under review.

The Voice of God

At the center of this criticism is the problem of the "study of God." Can we comprehend God outside events in human life? Can we find God apart from our human experience? Where do we encounter the objective truth about God? Some criticism suggests that we could do theology outside the events of our times, that there is a metaphysical, revealed knowledge available to us in sacred scripture, quite apart from anything that historical criticism can lead us to believe about the nature of what we have in the Bible and in the articles of faith formulated in the formative age of the church.

The option that third way theologians have made is the "we cannot hear the word of God apart from an event." Hence the importance of social analysis for their theology. Social analysis has been described (by an EATWOT study group) as "a comprehensive analysis including the total dynamics of social, cultural, economic, religious, and political manifestations of the human community. It is not just descriptive but transformative." Social analysis and theology are seen as being together when they both make an option for the poor and oppressed. These theologians place action and experience before analysis and theory.

Viewed from Martin Luther's perspective, the option for the poor is an option to be with those who daily theologize from the pain of marginalization. Therefore third way theologians include in their ranks not only official and academic theologians, professionals, but also lay theologians from the grass roots of the church. This theological trend has highlighted once more a fundamental biblical perspective that the poor constitute "a theological locus where Jesus can be found." An EATWOT participant from North America, an Evangelical, put it this way: "When we break fellowship with the poor, we break fellowship with Christ. . . . [for this reason] the Evangelical faith is slowly becoming uncivil to the American way of life."

There are many doing theology today, but the ones I find relevant are those who have their feet firmly planted on this earth even when they claim to be standing in the council of God. The scholarship of the scholarly should enable all who call on the name of Christ to cope with the problems of life and live according to the demands of the Christian faith. The 4-year-old son of a friend of mine asked his mother, "Are Jesus and God the same person?" This was part of a conversation that began with "Where do Jesus and his mother live?" (this is a boy from a one-parent family), and ended with the response, "Ask your Sunday school teacher." The boy's greatest immediate concern, however, was protection from violence: "If Jesus does not kill people, how can he save me when a burglar comes into my room?" Theology is expected to answer the ultimate questions of life and those that only children dare voice. And it is expected to enable persons to interpret real-life situations in the light of the Christian faith. It is here that the academic theologian's skill, if informed by an awareness of and involvement in the community, becomes an asset.

A New Approach

This new approach to theology involves interdisciplinary effort, because of the social analysis involved. The *theologian* provides input from the perspective of God's presence in and involvement with the world. Others look to theologians to provide a well thought-out "framework of belief by which their lives can be sustained and directed at the deepest level of their being."[2]

Issues that are of the deepest personal concern as well as those having to do with the well-being of the whole community are what have led to the chain of theologians around the world, especially in the Third World, who are working on a third way. They are seeking to do theology in a way that does not shy away from being prescriptive, and they are actively involved in bringing about new communities and lifestyles that come close to their vision of what the world would look like if God were allowed to rule absolutely.

In the dialogue at Geneva, these theologians shared experiences, theological methods and priorities, and told of their personal struggles. They saw their theological task as a search for a way for the church to preach and live the Christian faith more effectively.

The new approach demands the skills of academic theologians. Not all Christians can dedicate their lives to the study of the whole Christ-event. Most grassroots theologians concentrate on what is preserved in the Bible, and even that is done without an adequate critical hermeneutic. As for the events that shaped early Christianity, most of them know only a few stories about the martyrs. To get the full benefit of the Christian experience demands the utilization of our total history.

The academic theologian can also cooperate with those who daily spend their lives in a living dialogue with persons of other faiths. The challenge to the Christian God-talk by adherents of other religions is totally ignored when Christian theologians continue to treat those religions as devoid of that which speaks of God. In this enterprise, too, we can expect academic theologians to provide linguistic and other tools for understanding these other sources of theology.

Criteria for a New Approach

Cross-fertilization of the academic and the popular is one of the marks of the new approach. In the classic academic theology, for instance, one is not supposed to introduce personal experience. Classic academic theology assumes that its culture and history are the epitome of the universal, and it produces conclusions and abstractions that are supposed to apply worldwide. This universalization of theological perspective has been questioned by the new approach.

Women's reading of the Bible and of Christian history has raised questions that even their male counterparts in the same geographical and ecclesiastical contexts had not seen. It has thus been found mandatory to take seriously the fact that popular theologians and other grassroots Christians are an integral part of the *community of interpretation* out of which Christian theology grows. Theology becomes a task that demands "all hands on deck," but recognizes that some participants have expertise that others lack. It is a communal labor of the church, to keep its structures and relationships healthy. The contention of the new approach is that this task may at several points be rendered more meaningful if Christian theologians relate to those of other communities of interpretation. No single context can be *the* source from which the whole of Christian theology emanates.

In such an enterprise tension between the various emphases is inevitable. Dialectical tension between the professional theologian and grassroots communities may be reduced, but not eliminated. Their joint presence on the worksite and their contributions have differing levels of meaning. The new approach results from the recognition that no one can stand isolated *and* claim or hope to be effective. Even those whose theology one disagrees with perform the beneficial function of making one reexamine one's foundations. They all belong to the same worksite who use as their tools the criteria of justice and the tenets of the kingdom of God.

In this respect the dynamics of social analysis have been a great asset in Latin America and in Europe, whereas in Africa and Asia the religio-cultural background continues to provide immense resources for the task of doing theology.

As a result of the renewed attention paid to what it means to believe in God incarnate, the new theologians take into account the whole of humanness—intellect, emotion, physical strength. They make their commitment to fidelity to Christ out of the hurt and pain of the whole community. Their thoughts are embodied in carefully constructed logical statements, but more and more theology begins to be expressed in poetry, song, dance, and drama. When the option for the marginalized has been made, and nonacademics have been recognized as "lay theologians," more gifts are brought to the service of doing theology. Their participation has already called us back to the springs of doing theology—faith, experience, action.[3] New energy is also released as the tension between the academic and the pastoral takes on more positive dimensions and removes from the academic the stigma of being "the destroyer of the faith." In the resultant communal effort, the language of theology ceases to be obscure and mystifying, for it is a construct of the people, not an attempt to understand some classic theoretical formulation of the faith.

FURTHER EXPLORATIONS

Inasmuch as this effort is only at its beginning, there is of course a whole future that cannot be charted. Theologians must be flexible and innovative. It is clear, however, that even now there is a need to explore better ways of expressing theology as life and art that can communicate as well as reflect the option for the poor. There is also need to work harder at discovering how to relate to other religious faiths, especially those that have different perspectives on humanity and God. It seems to me also that we have to find how to deepen the work of social analysis by including feminist analysis in the overall task of theology.

Our spirituality as religious persons cannot be divorced from our theological task, in fact our zeal for theology arises from the joy, suffering, pain, and hope in our relationship to the Ultimate Source of our humanity. Spirituality is an integral part of our theological enterprise. The reintegration of the whole people of God in the doing of theology has underlined this factor. Indeed once more God has used the "foolishness" of this world to put to shame the wisdom of the wise. The focus of the third way is to be found in what an EATWOT participant said: "Action in contemplation of God is the beginning of theology." Wherever that is found, theology is being done.

NOTES

1. Maurice Wiles, *Explorations in Theology* (London: SCM Press, 1979), p. 38.
2. Ibid., p. 2.
3. See Ernesto Cardenal, *The Gospel in Solentiname*, 4 vols. (Maryknoll, N.Y.: Orbis, 4 vols., 1976–82).

19

Jim Wallis

Spirituality of Liberation

An underlying theme of our gathering in Geneva was the quest for a new spirituality, a spirituality of liberation. Although the conference was not planned to have major papers or sessions to focus on the topic of spirituality, it was nonetheless a part of personal conversations and group discussions. Some participants expressed frustration and even a certain alienation from the conference because of the inadequate amount of time for prayer, worship, and sharing of faith.

By the same token, however, most participants would probably agree that the high points of the conference were the moments in which we shared in music, told stories, read poetry, offered prayers, created art, and worshiped together. The closing liturgy was especially moving to all present. Tears welled up in many eyes as stories of faith, struggle, and hope were lifted up in the context of our worship. It is true that we experienced divisions among ourselves, reflecting the painful and violent divisions in the world in which we live. But it was at the point of worship, more than at the point of analysis, that our unity was most revealed and felt.

Even the word "spirituality" conjures up many problems and old images. We were all very painfully aware of the otherworldly spiritualities that have plagued our lives and the life of the church. We have had enough of the kind of spirituality that denies the world, denigrates the physical things of life, escapes from the realities of history, and distracts attention from economic and political oppression. Western spirituality in particular has been so frequently privatized, individualized, nationalized, and subjected to ideological manipulation. Indeed, many have suffered greatly from a spirituality that seems to give religious justification for the domination of the rich over the poor, of whites over persons of color, and of men over women.

In our rejection of false and destructive spiritualities, however, another danger lurks: that those who flee the bankrupt and unsatisfactory forms of piety and spirituality will emerge with little or no spirituality at all. In the absence of alternatives, the rejection of false piety can result in an emptiness of personal faith.

It has become painfully evident to many of us that in the struggle for justice, persons easily dry up. In both the First and the Third worlds, we have witnessed what the consequences of involvement in intense political struggle can be. Persons begin to feel drained and utterly exhausted. The consequences of suffering and injustice may even become so overwhelming that some succumb to bitterness, cynicism, or despair.

In Geneva, participants in our small-group discussion on spirituality told stories of how the pressure and weariness of political struggle can cause activists to feel unable to relate to one another, and to sustain relationships. We shared sad stories together about the breakup of marriages, the disintegration of families, the rupture of friendship, the dissolution of community, and a loss of the centrality of faith.

It is abundantly clear that historical struggle requires deep roots and resources, especially in view of the inevitable suffering that the struggle will bring. A deep and vital spirituality must undergird the struggle for justice. The freedom and strength that comes to us through worship and prayer, confession and celebration, can provide a foundation for liberation.

The starting point of theology is not analysis, but faith. At conferences such as the one we shared in Geneva there is a natural tendency toward what Martin Luther King, Jr., called the "paralysis of analysis." As vital a tool as social justice has been to our elaboration of theology, an overemphasis on analysis can only move us in the direction of secularization. This paralysis is a result of the old First World method that values the rational, cognitive, and verbal over the nonrational, intuitive, creative, and nonverbal.

In the First World we experience a false secularization on the one hand and a religious triviality on the other hand. Both are signs of a lost faith. Millions of North Americans have forgotten how to pray, whereas others say prayers for parking places at shopping malls.

In contrast, biblical spirituality has to do with faith in God in the midst of the world and all of its struggles. Biblical spirituality does not deny the world, but embraces it. It does not denigrate the physical things in life, but gives them sacred value. It does not try to escape the agonies of human history, but incarnates the love of God in the midst of that history. It does not distract attention from injustice and oppression, but rather brings God's purposes of justice and reconciliation into history with an explosive force.

Biblical spirituality is rooted in the unshakable hope that structures of injustice, the arrogance of dominant elites, and the sufferings of the present will not have the last word. Biblical spirituality trusts in the power of the word of God and knows that victory over death is already assured. This assurance comes with the knowledge that there is a God who rules, and it is God who shall have the last word.

The most powerful spirituality ever produced by North American churches has been that of the black church. In contrast to white and affluent Christians in America, for whom spirituality has usually been associated with feeling strong and being in control, black spirituality reflects the experience of a people who turned to God in its distress and pain, in hope for deliverance and freedom. Instead of making faith a measure of success, black spirituality comes out of the faith of poor persons who knew they needed God.

For impoverished, oppressed blacks, spirituality comes from the experience of feeling weak, tired, discouraged, downtrodden, and tempted to just give up. It is spirituality born of struggle, and it results in finding the strength and experiencing the power to sustain the struggle for freedom and liberation.

The North American black theology articulated by James Cone and Jacqueline Grant at our gathering in Geneva was firmly rooted in black spirituality. Black spirituality, more than any other in North American churches, points the way in our common search for a new spirituality and faith radically engaged in our historical situation.

We are on the path of that new spirituality. Just as there is a false spirituality of domination, so there is also a true spirituality of liberation. We are engaged in the process of finding the language and forms to express that new spirituality. Every indication seems to show that it will be a spirituality of the cross.

The New Testament makes clear that to participate in the joy of Christ, we must be willing to enter into the sufferings of Christ. To try to avoid the sufferings of Christ is to prevent the experience of joy that comes from depending upon God for our lives. We can already see the vivid contrast between the "complacent Christianity" of the captive First World church and the joyful faith of a suffering church in the Third World.

In the New Testament, the cross signifies a moral clash with the principalities and powers of this world. The cross reveals the inevitable confrontation between the world system of domination and the kingdom of God — a confrontation that is good news to the poor and the oppressed. It is out of that confrontation that a new spirituality is emerging. This spirituality is rooted in the resurrection, in the confidence that the power of God will triumph over the principalities and powers of this world. We must realize that our own efforts, analysis, imagination, and energy are not enough. Instead we must depend upon the power of God working through us and among us, multiplying our gifts, energies, and resources like loaves and fishes.

At the heart of Christian resistance in the United States is the recovery of the Bible. We are beginning to see the Bible set free from theological methods that robbed the word of God of its power to change our lives and our history. For evangelicals the Bible has often been reduced to doctrine. For liberals it has frequently become merely the object of academic scrutiny, dispassionate intellectual inquiry, and critical methodology. Both practices have served to rob the biblical word of its power. Now we are learning to read the Bible from the perspective and experience of the poor and in the context of our own history. The question for us is no longer, What do we believe about the Bible? but rather, How is the word of God changing our lives and our history?

Biblical spirituality is rooted in conversion. Conversion is the very heart of biblical spirituality. Intellectual inquiry, social analysis, and political action are in themselves inadequate responses to the historical crisis we face. The times in which we live cry out for our conversion. True spirituality in our day requires that we break the shackles of social conformity and passive acceptance of injustice and evil that leads to moral death. With the grace of God we turn again to Jesus Christ who is the source and ground of our liberation.

The Greek word *metanoia* refers to the process of conversion or transformation, the radical turnabout, that forever alters our present course and sets our feet on the path to the kingdom of God. Biblical conversion never occurs in a vacuum, apart from the events, issues, and struggles that challenge the lives of men and women. In the Bible, conversion is always historically specific. It is never abstract, metaphysical, or theoretical.

In a world perilously divided by race, class, and sex, conversion places us on the side of the poor and the oppressed. In a world enduring the agony of violence, a world on the edge of nuclear holocaust, conversion makes us ministers of justice and reconciliation. True spirituality for these times will always be good news to the poor. True spirituality in our day will enable us to be the makers of peace in risky and violent circumstances. The question is not, What do you believe about Jesus? but rather, Are you willing to forsake all and follow Jesus?

Historically, conversion has always been at the heart of the most powerful expressions of Christian witness against tyranny and violence. When we are willing to trust God with the whole of our lives, and abandon ourselves to the gospel to the point of sacrifice and even death, the powers and principalities of this world take notice. They consider those of us who are genuinely converted to be a threat to their power.

Conversion is always personal, but it is never private. Conversion is the spiritual transformation by which we enter into active solidarity with the purposes of the kingdom of God in history. It is this personal transformation that brings our lives forever into the public arena.

PART VI

WORD AND SONG

20

Don Prange

Liturgies in Geneva

It is significant that many EATWOT conference participants felt that some of our more important time together in Geneva came during moments of *worship* and *liturgy*. Perhaps that was true because liturgies, especially relevant ones, are action-filled, centering around the deeds of God and the people of God in history. In one of many private conversations (which were also some of our "more important" moments together), Carlito Gaspar put it this way: "Liturgy is the instrument of maintaining the collective memory of the community in celebrating and strategizing its struggle for liberation."

What made the liturgical elements of our dialogue meaningful was that they *celebrated* the *struggle* for liberation. The poetry, the prayers, the reflections, the songs, the symbols—all were rooted in concrete experiences we brought to Geneva from our different contexts of struggle. And we did affirm, after all, that *doing theology* can emerge only out of the particularities of our various struggles.

I reproduce here excerpts from three of our liturgical services. The concluding liturgy was felt to be the most important of all. It brought together not only the celebration of those diverse struggles going on throughout the world wherever oppression is being named and resisted; it also reflected our own corporate struggle, *with* each other and *for* each other, as we went about the task of *doing* theology in a divided world. Divisions, were, at times, all too apparent. But by the grace of God we were helped to transcend our differences in celebrating the unity of our struggle.

We discovered that *liturgy* (from the Greek *leitourgeia, laos + ergon*) is indeed the "work" of the "people," just as is theology. We stopped playing the game of trying to be "theologians" at those liturgical moments and got

157

down to the *work* of being the *people of God*: we were a community celebrating and strategizing the struggle for liberation.

MONDAY, JANUARY 10:
"GOD AND IDOLS"

Psalm 16: A Prayer of Confidence; Reading by Audrey Shilling

> Protect me, O God; I trust in you for safety.
> I say to the Lord, "You are my Lord;
> all the good things I have come from you."
> How excellent are the Lord's faithful people!
> My greatest pleasure is to be with them.
> Those who rush to other gods
> bring many troubles on themselves.
> I will not take part in their sacrifices;
> I will not worship their gods.
> You, Lord, are all I have,
> and you give me all I need;
> my future is in your hands.
> How wonderful are your gifts to me;
> how good they are!
> I praise the Lord, because he guides me,
> and in the night my conscience warns me.
> I am always aware of the Lord's presence;
> he is near, and nothing can shake me.
> And so I am thankful and glad,
> and I feel completely secure,
> because you protect me from the power of death
> and the one you love you will not abandon
> to the world of the dead.
> You will show me the path that leads to life;
> your presence fills me with joy
> and brings me pleasure forever.

Reflection, by Per Frostin

Our whole life should be a worship of the true God. We want to celebrate God's presence in all the facets of our daily lives: politics, manual work, sexuality, etc. But our worship is often disturbed and destroyed by idols.

There are many powerful idols in our societies: capital (money), sexist and racist pride, national security.

If we set our hearts on the idols, we shall betray the kingdom of God and its justice. Thus, the idols isolate us. They separate us from our brothers and sisters, they separate us from God, they separate us from our own inner being and destiny.

Theology is the doctrine of God. The basic task of the theologian is to distinguish between God and the idols.

Benediction, by Per Frostin

> God, the creator and source of our life,
> Jesus Christ our brother, and
> our sister the Holy Spirit,
> bless all of us.

TUESDAY, JANUARY 11:
DIVISIONS IN A THEOLOGICAL WORLD

Reflection, by Don Prange

We have come here to *do theology in a divided world*—divided because of a world system of domination. In the context of that reality, we have also spoken of the "religion of domination." In a variety of ways it has been described as a force serving the interests of a spirit of power and competition—and in that context we have heard it spoken of as a "religion of idolatry." But there are the words of our Lord in Matthew 6:24:

> No one can be the slave of two masters: he will either hate the first and
> love the second, or treat the first with respect and the second with scorn.

With those words in mind, to say *a religion of idolatry* may not be strong enough. We may need to speak of *the religion of God-hating*. Part of the insidious nature of such a religion is that it appropriates and incorporates the symbols and liturgies of what we call *church*. We have, therefore, had to recognize the criticism of some of our sisters and brothers who have said that, in the context of their oppression, the church and Christianity itself are problematic realities.

We have spoken of the richness of a theology that we discern in seeing God at work in history and within the variety of cultural experiences we represent. There is also, nevertheless, a richness in our own Christian tradition—if we turn to the dialectical hermeneutics of being open and listen to other traditions and cultures (even listen to each other).

So there are some of us who resist the captivity of our symbols and liturgies by the dominative aspects of our Christian tradition, and have set out to recapture and rediscover the depth of the liberation content inherent in those symbols and liturgies.

I should, therefore, like to share two illustrations of how this might be

done. The first is a parody on the song of Mary in Luke 1:46–55; it manifests
the content of a "God-hating religion":

The Magnificat of the Church for Capitalism
>   Our soul proclaims the greatness of capitalism
>   and our spirit exults in capitalism—and in America,
>   the greatest of all the capitalist nations,
>   because it has looked with favor on
>   its servant:
>   the church.
>   Yes, from this day forward all generations will
>   call us blessed—
>   for the almighty powers of capitalism
>   have done great things for us:
>   they have given us tax exemptions and
>   let us pray at their meetings and conventions, and
>   given us the great privilege to go on preaching
>   a gospel of greatness and pride.
>   Holy is its name:
>   and its benefits reach from age to age
>   for those who stand in awe of all
>   that capitalist development has achieved,
>   It shows the power of its arms:
>   look how it routs the humble peasants
>   of the world who turn to "atheistic communism."
>   It pulls down elected leaders from
>   their seats of governing,
>   and has exalted those who were only
>   lowly mercenaries to be
>   dictators over the rebellious masses.
>   Those who are hungry for status
>   and wealth and power
>   are filled with all sorts of good things;
>   and the poor go on their way empty.
>   It has come to the aid of its servant, the church,
>   and given it recognition, mindful of its benefits
>   —according to the promises it makes
>   for hard work and diligence—
>   of its benefits to Adam Smith
>   and his descendents forever.

The second illustration comes from a reflection on the traditional lessons
for Maundy Thursday and deals with the theme of Discipleship as the Body
of Christ. Because there are times when we have also manifested symptoms of
the religion of domination—and have found ourselves, even here in Geneva,

forging divisions in a theological world—this may be an appropriate word for us.

Discipleship (and Doing Theology) as the Body of Christ
(Exod. 12:1–14; 1 Cor. 11:23–32; John 13:1–15; Luke 22:14–30)

How is the proclamation of the Lord's death "until he comes" to be lived out by the churches where signs of oppression are so clearly evident? For one thing, it is imperative that *the Lord's death* not be dwelt on apart from its social, economic, political context. His death was demanded by those who were offended by his concern for social outcasts and the oppressed, by those whose economics were challenged by his teachings (Matt. 6:19–34), by those whose political power was threatened by the signs he performed, reassuring the oppressed that God was on their side in a struggle for genuine liberation.

The red flag of national security (cf. John 18:14) was invoked to protect the interests of a ruling minority—and so he had to die!

Even those closest to Jesus were victimized by the spirit of power and competition. In the middle of the *freedom meal* commemorating the passover, a dispute broke out among them concerning which one of them would be "the greatest." The answer Jesus gave that night was clear (John 13:4–15): God becomes the servant of the world, in love, to give new life, to call us into a discipleship (and a way of doing theology) in which a radical understanding of *servanthood* is paramount.

Hence *proclaiming the Lord's death until he comes* wherever oppression is being suffered is to be the Body of Christ, *broken* for the oppressed, *broken* in the breaking down of systems that exploit humankind and the land, *broken* in a commitment to a new covenant, a new arrangement, a new way of doing things—including a *new way of doing economics*, a new way that will do justice both to the liberating God of history and to the people.

THURSDAY, JANUARY 13: WORSHIP IS JUSTICE

The Moment before God: Confession
(from the evaluation questionnaire: "What aspects of the dialogue disappointed you most?")

1) The design and general procedure of the conference, which still hamper communication between grassroots representatives and professional theologians.

2) Third World theologians seemed to be uninterested in the problems of European theologians, although they preferred to dialogue with well-known professional theologians from the First World.

3) There was little poverty in our behavior. We wear fashionable clothing, and we complain about the food! We seem to have enough money. Do we really start from *praxis*?

Praise and Celebration

(from the evaluation questionnaire: "What are the most important things you have learned in the dialogue?")

1) The diversity of our experiences and the inventory of factors of oppression in different contexts. The convergence of theological positions within these contexts. The importance of the spiritual life.

2) That we can learn from each other's struggles and cultures, and from the methodologies arising from them.

3) Faith and spirituality are crucial to how one relates to participation in struggle. Words should not be formulated in haste. There really needs to be an invitation from the oppressed; *then* we can "speak," in the sense of articulating a theology.

The Dance of the Seven Key Words of the Dialogue

Near the end of the dance seven quotations from the draft of the final conference statement were read by a member of the community. During the reading of each quotation one of the dancers moved to the front wall with a piece of a painting containing the key word of the quotation. The piece was affixed to the wall. When all the seven pieces of the painting were put together, they formed a circle, showing the seven key words with a cross in the center. The seven key words:

1) **Struggles of the Poor.** EATWOT has contributed to a new theological methodology. This methodological approach demands that theologians join in the suffering and the struggles of the poor. Only in this way are theologians enabled to understand God's revelation and to reread the Bible with the eyes of the poor with whom Jesus identified himself.

2) **Faith Experiences.** All Third World theologies are critical reflections on the faith experiences of Christians as they struggle toward political and cultural transformation and liberation. Theological reflection is therefore the second act that follows the prior act of commitment and praxis.

3) **God.** God is always the central object of our theology—the God who is lived and reflected upon internally in the world of the oppressed. The discovery of the true God of Jesus Christ demands the ending of the oppression that is the material base of idolatry. The question of God in the world of the oppressed is not the problem of knowing whether God exists or not, but rather knowing what side the God of Jesus Christ is on.

4) **The People.** The life of a people, its history and culture, its religious traditions and dialogues, its socio-political situation and spiritual experience—these constitute the fundamental context for doing theology.

5) **Human Life.** Only human life in all its fullness, dignity, and beauty constitutes the radical and highest imperative of authentic theology.

6) **The Cross.** The cross and the death of Jesus are being reread, starting

from the reality of the oppression and violent destruction of life in the world today.

7) **Resurrection.** Similarly, the resurrection of Jesus is understood as the definitive transcendence of death as seen in the beginning of a new humanity, the making of a new society, the new "heaven and earth." This is the foundation of the subversive hope of the poor.

PRAYERS OF INTERCESSION:
REFLECTIONS OF THE DEEDS OF GOD IN HISTORY

Earth—Reflections by Kofi Appiah-Kubi

> Oh, Mother Earth!
> We are fully dependent on you.
> It is you who received us
> with your open arms at birth
> when we were yet naked.
>   You supply our daily wants
> with your rich resources.
> Indeed you nurture us
> throughout our earthly life.
>   And when wicked death
> finally snatches us away
> you will still be there
> to open up your womb
> and receive us all back.
>   Yet, see what we have done
> to your loving kindness in return;
> we have in many ways
> raped, polluted, exploited,
> and wasted your rich gifts.
>   We have indeed treated you
> with greed and disrespect;
> we have monopolized all your gifts
> at the expense of millions of our brothers and sisters.
>   We have grasped
> the mystery of the atom bomb
> and ignored the Sermon
> on the Mount and the Golden Rule.
>   We have indeed become
> nuclear giants
> and ethical infants;
> we reach out to the moon
> while ignoring our earthly duties.

We have continually broken
our covenant with you,
the ethics of learning to live with nature
rather than conquer nature.
   Thus, our waters putrefy,
our environments stink,
our fish and animals die;
we are plagued with diseases.
The whole creation groans!
   Mountains irrupt
and swallow our homes and farms
like a roaring lion!
We are drowned by flooding
rivers and oceans.
   They elude our scientific knowledge.
We stand openmouthed
and repeatedly ask,
How long, how long,
how long—Oh, Mother Earth?
   We forget that
the use of your gifts
reflects our spiritual
and social well-being,
including our economic prosperity.
   Our spiritual health
is closely linked
to your health, Mother Earth,
and to that of the community,
in the use of your gifts.
   Unjust use of these gifts
brings about ecological disaster
accompanied by
spiritual and social decay.
   How do we expect
to do violence to ourselves
and to you, Mother Earth,
without precipitating
social, spiritual, and environmental chaos?
   Our constant plea therefore
is, Mother Earth,
forgive, forgive, forgive!
For the legs of the hen do not
kill the chicks.
Shalom, shalom, shalom!

Fire—Reflections by Samuel Rayan

The small fire burning timidly
on Delhi's sidewalks.
A kindly fire warming
   the pavement-dwellers in Delhi's winter
   and warming a thin rice porridge
     with which to stay
     the fire within them
     —the raging fire of hunger.
The fire of life is feeble and pale
unlike the fire of Francis,
strong, robust, and beautiful.
When this tiny fire of life is out,
the frail body is placed in the arms
   of sacred flames
     whose embrace conveys it to God.
The fire in God's heart
   warms the pavement-dwellers
   and their rice porridge.
The fire of love becomes a blaze of
   judgment and protest
   against all injustice.
Jesus Christ is
     fire from the heart of God
   lodged in the heart of the earth
   that the earth may live,
   and not die of frozen
   logic, mechanics, and
   market laws.
The fire of his spirit in our hearts
thaws us to one another
and girds us for action
   to protect the fragile fire
   stirring timidly
   on Delhi's sidewalk.

Water—Reflections by Marlène Tuininga

L'eau	*Water*
lave, transforme,	washes, transforms,
fait croître, donne la vie.	gives growth, gives life.
Jésus de Nazareth fut baptisé	Jesus of Nazareth was baptized
à l'âge de 30 ans. Il était pauvre.	at the age of 30. He was poor.

Moi aussi j'ai été baptisée à l'âge de 30 ans.	I too was baptized at the age of 30.

Moi aussi j'ai été baptisée à
l'âge de 30 ans.

J'étais pauvre et j'avais fait
un choix politiúe pour les
pauvres.

Mais par ce baptême ma vie a
été transformée; j'ai commencé
à croître dans la vie de Jésus
Christ.

I too was baptized at the
age of 30.

I was poor and I have made
a political choice in behalf
of the poor.

But through my baptism my life
has been transformed; I have
begun to grow in the life of
Jesus Christ.

SILENT EUCHARIST

Invitatory, by Elsa Tamez

Pronto! Pronto!
Come on!
Let us celebrate the supper of the Lord!
Let us make a huge loaf of bread
and let us bring abundant wine
as at the wedding of Cana.
Let the women not forget the salt.
Let the men bring along the yeast.
Let many guests come:
the lame, the blind, the crippled, the poor.
Come quickly!
Let us follow the recipe of the Lord;
all of us, let us knead the dough together
with our hands.
Let us see with joy
how the bread expands
because today
we celebrate
the meeting with the Lord;
today we renew our commitment
to the kingdom.
Nobody will stay hungry.

Consecration, led by Morar Murray-Hayes

Seven women come forward.
There are seven cups
seven baskets
and then,
amid all the words,
there is silence at the Lord's table.

The symbols are there:
earth and water
fire and incense
struggles and cross
behind us
bread and wine
before us.
Using universal symbols adapted from
the signs for the deaf
our own story is told.
COME JESUS
   touching the place of the stigmata
   on each hand.
THANK GOD, THANK GOD
   touching lips and hands
   and reaching for God.
THE BREAD
   lifted and turned
   to the African cross,
   to the struggle:
      the people
      God
      faith experience
      struggles of the poor.
      RESURRECTION.
THE BREAD
   broken at the cross
   offered to the people.
THE CUP
   lifted and turned
   to the cross
   receiving blood
   poured out of the struggle.
THE CUP
   filled with love and pain
   offered to the people.
The story of our faith.
JESUS
      touch stigmata
   BORN
      touch womb
   FOR US
      reach out in offering
JESUS
      touch stigmata

DIED
    sign of the cross
FOR US
    reach out cruciform
JESUS
    touch stigmata
LIVES!
    raise hands to life!
       silence
COME, HOLY SPIRIT
   one hand forms circle,
   the other hand lifts
   the spirit out of the circle
   then hands are placed over
   the elements
PEACE
   hands together as in prayer
   hands descend and separate
   in calming motion
   as if to touch the earth
   a reverse missile
   we exchange peace
BREAD AND WINE
   women share with each other
   women share with all
       silent waiting
   women return to the people

21

Sun Ai Park

The Wish

It is a season of splendor
when the creeks break free to run
and pussy willows bloom; the buds,
new greens, break through oppressing soil.
The flowers, delicate, paint scenes of joy and hope.
It was the same thirty some years ago
when, one day, in a glorious season,
I became a refugee, not knowing why.

Yes, we had thought that it was done
and that the time had come
that we could be ourselves,
the hosts of our own homes, in our own land.
But why have I become a refugee?
What crimes have I committed
that I have had to pack up like a thief
collecting someone else's belongings
in haste, perplexity, all hidden
from the neighbors' eyes,
abandoning my home, my heart,
to travel like a vagabond
loathing my luggage
in the tide of the evening darkness?

We went up to Wonsan for a boat.
There was no boat.

At least we had a truck we'd hired in Pyong-Yang.
We drove along the coast.
How beautiful the beaches of the land I left!
Myong Sa-Ship-Ri, the miles of white sand,
the matching miles of untainted sky and sea,
the smiling infant joy of innocence, the being
with the one, the changing and unchanging,
the sublime, with a being all its own.
How mystically serene, the far horizon
luring always far away
as if it were whispering "Come to me!"
and shouting "Stay!" at the same time.
We passed the pines, innumerable groves
Like parasols of green. They made my heart ache.
The pains of life were born in me, so young a child
who would normally play and laugh!

Then there was the magnitude and delicacy
of the mountains of Keum Kang.
How I wanted to jump from peak to peak
playing hide-and-seek on each, and standing proud.
I wanted to cry out to my heart's content,
to listen to the trails of my own echoes.
"I want to live like this!
I have the right to live like this!"

Bang, bang, bang!
It is a river in our own country
that we were forced to cross. Hoping for luck,
we rolled our skirts and pants up to our thighs.
We were desperate.
Some Russian soldiers fired at us. It was
our own river. It was a time of peace.
Who were they, these Russians?
They fought against the Japanese for several days
after Hiroshima. The Japanese defeat already
evident, they sided with another capitalist
in the fight of the bloody capitalists.
Then they were called the great army
that liberated us. And then they shot at us
unarmed and desolate
because we were crossing our own river
wanting only to be free.

Someone high up gave an order.
That order made a chain.

That chain bound them and us,
that chain bound him and me.
"Do I know him? Have we met?"
If only I had met him face-to-face
it might have been different.
We could have been friends . . . who knows?
We had no chance to try.
Even before we could question them,
They shot.
We were their targets.
Russians firing on Koreans.
It was absurd.
Was it a game? But how dangerous, and real.
And yet I didn't envy them their posts,
those soldiers dangling at the end of the chain.
And yet, at my endlessly vulnerable position,
I wept.

On the other side at last, we reached a hill.
Escaping narrowly
we fled, were refugees, not knowing why,
just sitting on a southern hill
just like a northern hill.
I could not laugh at the triumph of escape
but only weep again,
my laughter having been repressed
before I was born.

Help! Oh, help me and my people!
Someone said that all the refugees
should go to the camp—a sea of humanity.
I asked, "Is all of North Korea down here now?"
I saw Yankee soldiers for the first time in my life.
They all had shiny shoes,
clean, pressed uniforms.
They were clean themselves,
just out of the bath, perhaps.
They all chewed gum relentlessly.
They all held strange machines.
They were spraying us with powder, DDT, as if to say,
"We'll rid you of the bugs and germs
You are carrying from the north."
As if to say, as well, "This rite
will authorize you to live in the south,
like us, civilized and free."
Was this humanitarian benevolence?

We were made all white, baptized from head to toe,
all white as flour-packers or as homeless nomads
roaming in the dust. Weren't we the same,
once called the bourgeoisie
who have been pushed into this plight?
Some bourgeoisie! We whose very lives depend
on excess grain from the USA!
Do I thank them? Curse them?
I cannot distinguish friend from foe!

This is how my "freedom" and my "dignity" began.
This how my "politics" awoke in me.
As my knowledge grows, our plight seems more difficult.
As the dictators sing of "democracy,"
they call "communist" whoever speaks of
"rights," "justice," and "freedom."
And innocents are found, imprisoned, tortured, killed.
The schemes are devilish!
To reinforce their power
They lend us money,
making their pockets fat
with snow-balling interest,
and the weight of our country's debt
strangles the poor.
How dangerous this "anticommunism" is.
How mutable!

"Free the poor! Free the oppressed!
Free them from the grips of a thousand demons!
Jesus set the example: we are merely following
his steps." They say: "You are the reds.
You're communists, and dangerous."
The Christians exiled by the Kim regime
Are harassed by the Park/Chun regime.
Where can we turn now,
with the Red Sea and the desert before us?
Oh God, help our people to build a bridge
over the Red Sea and straighten the road in the desert,
to come out victorious from the hell
of hatred and division, to be led to the land
of love, unity, and peace!

Spring has returned again,
thirty-five springs since I crossed that wretched border,
the thirty-eighth parallel,

so arbitrary a division in the history
of Korea, where we each are born
with marks of death, indelible.
Yes, it is another spring, another hope.
My days are turning round and round, and I can see
the original point, but somehow cannot get to it.
My enemies are too many and too strong.
Oh, Korea! I suffer in my love for you!
Let the day come, let me see it all,
before my eyes, which have shed so many tears,
are finally closed.

22

Elsa Tamez

Letter to Job

Huampani
November 15, 1983

Dear Brother Job,

Your cries of suffering and protest have pierced our bones. We haven't been able to sleep. Blood flows from our ears.

Your hands move in all directions: they signal to us, they beat us, they inquire of us, they stroke us. Where are you taking us, Brother Job?

Your stench of death has penetrated our nostrils; we smell you everywhere. Your bony body goads us. Pieces of your wormy flesh cling to our own. We have become infected by you, Brother Job. You have infected us, our families and our people. Your eyes searching for justice and your breath saturated with fury have filled us with courage, tenderness, and hope.

How brave you are, Brother Job! How strong is your resistance! You are, like us, a ghost: sick, abandoned, rejected, oppressed. You are sickening. (Are *we* sickening?) Your friends Eliphaz, Bildad, and Zophar haven't ceased to torture you and give you bad advice.

They say that you should swallow your protests and stop defending your innocence. They say that God has punished you and that you need to repent. And you, Brother Job, in spite of everything, you haven't given up. Rather, your shouts have become louder. You don't believe them and you fight against them. What's more, you dare to argue and fight against Almighty God. You blame God for your sorrow and you blame God for being silent while you suffer. You fight against God. God, who was your friend, has now abandoned you. You don't understand why. You insist that you have been just and innocent. You have every right to defend yourself: you're human. It is the right of every man and woman to protest against unjust suffering.

174

Your friends have stopped being your friends because you have protested and because you have dared to touch the untouchable God. You have dared to touch the perfect God, the Totally Other who governs the world without error; the God who distributes justice left and right—but you don't see it. You see the suffering of the just and the innocent, and the joys and the pleasures of the unjust who pile up wealth. Your friends, with their beautiful speeches, affirm the contrary. But they should keep silent because you're the one who suffers injustice and experiences its consequences in your flesh and blood.

Let God talk! Let God explain the silence of God, that unbearable silence. God's absence invokes death. Our God, our God, why have you abandoned us?

Let God talk now and let your friends keep still because God can't be heard above their hubbub. Why don't your wise friends keep still? Their wisdom doesn't square with life. They deny with words the pain and suffering they see with their own eyes. Empty theology! A theology closed on itself! A theology that tries to defend God with incredible lies! (Job 13:7). They defend God at the expense of human beings, instead of defending human beings in obedience to God.

Let them be quiet! Let them go back to the trash heap with you and let them cry and tear their robes for another seven days and nights. Let them be in solidarity with you and share your pain without speaking a word. Maybe in this way they will come to understand why the innocent have a right to protest and to rebel. Maybe in this way they will be converted.

But let *us* be still as well, Job. Let *us* not complain any more. We have complained enough. Your wise words silenced the lips of the wise. They have no more arguments. There is no God who will back them up. Let's allow God to stand before us and explain God's silence.

God's silence is mysterious. Sometimes it fills us with fright and paralyzes us in the face of the legion of devils that squeeze out the life of innocent persons. But without this silence of God we can't become men and women. When God speaks all the time, human beings become deaf. They don't hear the cry of the poor and of those who suffer. They become dull; they no longer walk and hope. They don't dare to do anything. They no longer endure.

God remains silent so that men and women may speak, protest, and struggle. God remains silent so that we may become really ourselves. When God is silent and men and women cry, God cries in solidarity with them, but God doesn't intervene. God waits for the shouts of protest. Then God begins to speak again, but in dialogue with us.

God shows us how the mountain goat shakes off her young and they find their way on the rocks and don't return looking for her milk. God teaches us that the wild mule is free and that it laughs at the noise of the city. It doesn't hear the mule driver and looks for its own food. The buffalo refuses to spend its nights in a stable; the ostrich scoffs at the would-be rider who can't catch up with it; the horse neighs majestically and doesn't turn away from the swords of war; the eagle flies to the highest mountaintop and takes in all the world with one sweep of its eyes. It is God who gives all these their strength and freedom.

Let's arise, Brother Job, because you can't catch Leviathan with a fish-hook or the monster Behemoth with a smile. Only the strength of God in our strength can defeat them. The Lord is challenging us; let's respond.

Now, Brother Job, you have really come to know God. You will never be the same after this experience of suffering. You'll never be again that rich gentleman who had all his wants and needs taken care of and who gave of his surplus to those who had nothing. You've had the intimate experience of being wretched and no one can erase this experience from your personal history. Now you know God better.

You struggled with God until God blessed you and restored you. What will you do now? God restored you, but what of us?

Hoping to see you again here in the trash heap,

Elsa

PART VII

FINAL STATEMENT

23

Doing Theology in a Divided World:
Final Statement of the Sixth EATWOT
Conference

INTRODUCTION

(1) The sixth conference of the Ecumenical Association of Third World Theologians (EATWOT) was held in Geneva, Switzerland, January 5–13, 1983. This time the conference consisted of a dialogue between EATWOT members and First World Theologians, to reflect on the meaning of our Christian faith in a divided and conflictual world.

There were about eighty participants from the First and Third Worlds, as well as observers from the press, support agencies, and other ecumenical organizations.

We thank God for the testimonies we have heard about the presence of the Spirit of life and love in the struggles for justice underway throughout our world today. We are grateful that our coming together has enabled us to deepen our Christian commitment to total liberation for all peoples.

We want to share some reflections on our dialogue and how it has enriched us, the difficulties and obstacles we confronted, the convergences we discovered, the many questions left unanswered, and the hope and faith that sustain us in doing theology in a divided world.

The Participants and the Process

(2) Although we share a common commitment to interpret and respond faithfully to God's message for our times, we are aware of the many differences among us that reflect some of the real divisions that afflict our world. We come from rich and poor countries. We come from distinct cultures and races as well as from a variety of ethnic and religious backgrounds. There are also our differences as men and women. Furthermore, there is a

range of involvement among us: there are those working within the institutional framework of the churches, and others in marginalized Christian communities; there are grassroots activists, and academicians in seminaries and universities; there are some among us who are relatively young and new to the struggle for justice and liberation, and others who have lived a lifetime in it. All these differences have made our dialogue difficult at times, but they have also broadened our perspectives.

(3) Because the purpose of our dialogue was to determine how God is present in the struggle for human fulfillment, the Planning Committee of First and Third World members devised a process that would allow participants to share their own experiences of struggle and to draw theological conclusions from their stories. The process designed for Geneva had three phases: (a) story telling, (b) analysis, and (c) theological reformulation.

(4) Direct preparation for the dialogue began a year before the meeting itself. Each participant was asked to write a case history of personal involvement in a particular struggle, including the political and theological lessons learned from the experience. These stories formed the basis of both the analysis and theological reformulation. In addition, collective preparation was encouraged, and this typically took the form of small local or regional conferences. In many respects, then, our dialogue reflects the voices of many who were not actually present but had helped to shape the concerns, questions, and convictions that each of us brought to Geneva, and would later help us to understand the implications of our dialogue in the context of our struggles at home.

(5) The indirect preparation, however, started long before the process for Geneva was designed. In the Third World, EATWOT was launched after the first ecumenical dialogue of Third World theologians in Dar es Salaam, Tanzania, in 1976. The association was founded to provide a forum of exchange among Third World theologians about their reality of oppression and struggles for liberation, and the renewed theology arising from their situations and experiences. Subsequently, EATWOT organized other intercontinental dialogues: in Accra, Ghana, in 1977; in Wennappuwa, Sri Lanka, in 1979; in São Paulo, Brazil, in 1980; and in New Delhi, India, in 1981. It was at the Delhi meeting that the members decided to implement what was part of their long-range program and invite to a dialogue First World theologians, who in their own contexts were seeking new ways of doing theology in fidelity to the God of Jesus and the prophets who is revealed among the poor and oppressed.

(6) The indirect preparation in the United States even antedated EATWOT. In 1975, Theology in the Americas was formed to promote dialogue not only among feminists, blacks, native Americans, Hispanics, Asian Americans, and working-class and professional whites about oppression and liberation within their own country, but also with Latin American Christians who so often are adversely affected by U.S. foreign policies.

The situation in Europe and the challenge of EATWOT motivated European theologians and other Christians to look at their own theology again. A committee representing eleven European countries invited national delegations of involved Christians to a process of collective reflection that culminated in a symposium held in Woudschouten, Holland, in 1981.

In Canada there have been ecumenically supported interchurch projects around a variety of social justice issues within the country and extending to the Third World. It was primarily First World Christians involved in these various struggles for justice that responded to the EATWOT invitation to dialogue in Geneva.

Sharing Our Stories

(7) The starting point of our dialogue was storytelling about our experiences of involvement in struggles for liberation. Focusing on concrete experience helped us not only to get an overview of the range of involvement represented at the conference, but to get to know one another as persons.

In small groups we heard from a former missionary sister in Africa now a pastor to women in Holland; an Indian priest engaged in dialogue with Hindus on rereading their shared history and forging a new future; a socialist trade union leader from Sweden; a Sri Lankan bishop working with cultural renewal groups as well as with groups seeking political/economic change; an Irish mother of thirteen who is an advocate for battered wives and women in prison; a priest from Cameroon recapturing the vision of human life and destiny in traditional African religious through art; a lay woman scripture scholar from Costa Rica who is part of an interdisciplinary team of social scientists and theologians in the service of liberation movements; a black American woman teaching theology in a seminary in Atlanta fighting against racism and sexism.

(8) We heard stories about involvement with the landless poor in South Africa and with native peoples in Canada; the struggles of basic Christian communities in Brazil and fisher-folk in Asia; organized groups protesting the multinational corporations in Appalachia (U.S.A.) and trade zones in the Philippines. Among the First World participants especially, we heard about the growing peace movement which is succeeding in unmasking the world system which cannot feed the world's hungry but can waste resources on nuclear weapons; we heard about solidarity work with Third World causes which counters propaganda of Third World elites and pressures First World governments to change their policies with regard to the Third World. Christians with such commitments in the First World have been profoundly changed by their involvement and have paid a substantial price for their conversion.

(9) Sharing case histories in small groups elicited different reactions from the participants. Some preferred a more impersonal and abstract analysis of the structures of injustice to the more personal, concrete case study approach. But it must be admitted that the split between the two styles of collective theologizing did not always coincide with the division between the First

and Third Worlds. There were Third World theologians who resisted the case story approach and theologians from the First World who were at home in it, having used it for a long time.

NEED FOR A COMPREHENSIVE ANALYSIS

Analysis of Social Realities

(10) From the beginning of the history of EATWOT, we have underlined the role of social analysis as an important component of the theologizing process. We have said in all our past "final documents" that social analysis helps to uncover the causes of oppression and enables Christians to love their neighbors through strategies of change and structural reform. Many First World theologians involved in renewal also use analysis as an essential element in their effort. This time in Geneva, we took an important step forward through our dialogue with the First World. This progress was concretized in the inclusion of not only political and economic categories but also religious and cultural categories in a comprehensive analysis of reality.

(11) This happened in a moment of tension in the conference. The original plan called for an analysis of three major forms of oppression and their interrelatedness: racism, sexism, and classism. However, after the presentations and discussion, there was a feeling of uneasiness and dissatisfaction. Some expressed the need to go beyond a purely mechanical application of class analysis, bring in the role of culture in the structure of oppression, and discern the religious value of the symbols that support capitalism. The Third World women felt their particular perspective on the issue of sexism was not adequately represented. In short, many considered the social analysis done at the session too limited as a basis for our theological task. A comprehensive analysis should encompass all the major forms of oppression including religious and cultural domination. Although these oppressions cannot be subordinated one to another or merely listed serially, they are not separate, isolated issues but are linked in the working of a single world system of domination which involves a whole way of life.

Racism

(12) Racism is an institutionalized system of discrimination against other groups on the basis of skin color. In the past, racism became most obvious in the institution of slavery. Today, even with the legal abolition of slavery, blacks have remained objects of the most virulent racism, evident in apartheid in South Africa, and in discriminatory practices in the U.S.A. and elsewhere. But other persons of color—Asians, Africans, and indigenous peoples everywhere—have also suffered from segregation and marginalization.

(13) Racism has two aspects. The first and most evident is the dehumanization and subjugation of persons because of their color and physiognomy in

order to exploit their labor. But the second aspect goes beyond rational economic exploitation and takes the form of an odious ideology. Whites project phobic characteristics onto persons of color, dehumanizing themselves in the process. Racist ideology has penetrated the dominant theologies, which in turn have legitimized it. This ideology is reflected in segregated church life, denying the basic meaning of Christian fellowship. Any working toward a just world order must expose and combat the ideology and institution of racism. Otherwise, no authentic reconciliation in Jesus Christ is really possible.

Classism, Militarism, and Imperialism

(14) The complexity of the world economy did not allow for a full analysis, but our attention was called to the increasing gap between the rich and poor countries and to the immense debts of Third World countries to the international banks which are threatening the monetary system. The present workings of the world economy have impoverished large sectors in the Third World and invisible pockets in the First, while creating suffocating wealth for a small ruling elite. The powerful and opulent elites of the First World have their counterparts and collaborators in the Third World, who are closer to them culturally, politically, economically, and ideologically than to the majority of the persons in their own countries.

(15) The division of classes, due to economic and social differences, is a fact that exists both within and between nations, and is aggravated by racial and sexual divisions which are also turned into structures of labor exploitation. Though this division of classes was assumed by most participants, there were others who found the assumption simplistic. These others felt the need of a more thorough analysis of class oppression. Since global capitalism is much more complex now, capital-intense industrialization and new technology make the old exploitation of labor obsolete and the world faces growing unemployment. Furthermore, class analysis disregards the cultural and religious dimensions of social relations and does not account adequately for racism and sexism and their interstructural relationship with classism.

(16) Historically, the capitalist system has grown increasingly international and so takes the form of imperialist exploitation of the Third World. Since the beginning of European colonialism, the exploitation of labor and resources has been enforced by the military arm of colonial powers. But in the decades since World War II, the militarization of the world has become increasingly acute. For different reasons, not only the capitalist but also the socialist countries have become involved in the stockpiling of arms. Now there seems no rational way to stop the arms race, and the global system has become a tinderbox ready to explode at any moment and set off a conflagration that will consume all humanity and the earth itself.

(17) After we looked at the capitalist system which affects all the participants, we felt the need to have some kind of assessment of the situation in the socialist countries. Since there were no participants from the socialist coun-

tries, we hesitated to speak about them. But the interrelations between the two systems and the issues at stake forced us to express our opinion about them.

There are positive aspects in the socialist countries that should be acknowledged. In their plans for a better life for their peoples, socialist governments have confronted enormous obstacles, internally in the depressed economies they have inherited, and externally in the militant economic, political, ideological, religious, and military hostility from the centers of capitalist power. Despite these obstacles, they have made real gains in meeting basic human needs. In the historic struggles to create new societies, the sacrifices and heroism of many continue to inspire resistance to injustice throughout the world. It is also true that some of the socialist countries have given support to peoples elsewhere struggling against oppression.

(18) But we also have to recognize that existing socialisms have become a source of disillusion for many, for they have not accomplished what they have promised. In some places, new policies and institutions of oppression have emerged under the name of socialism, creating new forms of domination and exploitation of their own people and in relations with other nations. It seems that some socialist governments and movements have been infected with the same distorted values which undergird the capitalist system. These deficiencies represent a betrayal of the hope for liberation which inspired the original socialist struggle for a new society based on justice.

(19) Having looked at both the capitalist and socialist systems, we are convinced that the efforts to nurture new life must confront not only the economic dimension but also the issues of culture, anthropology, and spirituality which inform the development of institutions, structures, and technology of a new society. Liberation is never only a matter of political and economic transformation. It is also a matter of profound cultural and religious renewal. The aspirations of oppressed peoples everywhere for dignity and new life require that we examine more closely the values and visions which animate the efforts to create new societies.

Cultural and Religious Domination

(20) In previous EATWOT conferences, especially in New Delhi, the challenges to Christian theology from other cultural and religious traditions have been raised very strongly. As a result, Third World theologians, particularly the Latin Americans, have become more sensitive to this essential dimension of reality. In the context of the dialogue with First World theologians, this challenge had a real impact on the participants. Initially brought up by the Asians, the need to include religion and culture in the work of social analysis was later acknowledged by the whole assembly. In fact, sessions were rearranged to allow time for input from the Africans and Asians on this important dimension of personal and social life. The challenge was supported by many First World participants, especially women, who have been challenging their own First World theology to include this dimension of life.

(21) While admitting the disastrous effects that capitalism, imperialism, and neocolonialism have had on their continents, the Asians pointed out that they have suffered from internal domination long before the coming of the West. One prime example is the cultural oppression brought about by the caste system in India. Poverty and oppression in Asia thus cannot be understood simply in economic or political terms. The continent has had a protracted history of cultures and religions that have dominated and oppressed and a long heritage of acceptance of poverty and suffering. At the same time, it is undeniable that the Asian cultures and religious traditions have their humanizing elements and have stimulated resistance to economic and political domination. There are records of liberation movements which have been inspired and guided by the same traditions that have also oppressed.

(22) The Africans reiterated their stance which they had strongly expressed in New Delhi. While they recognize the reality of class domination and economic imperialism, what they consider to be the worst form of impoverishment is anthropological poverty. This is a serious form of oppression that despoils human beings not only of what they materially have but of everything that constitutes their being and essence. The root of this problem is the imposition on Third World peoples of Western anthropology which embodies a concept of human nature based on individualism, competition, and struggle for power. A radically different anthropology is called for in the African context that is drawn from and reflected in the customs and practices of their traditional religions and cultures. This anthropology will be based on community and cooperation, will include a sense of unity with nature, and avoid any dichotomy.

(23) The analysis of the role of culture is a necessary step in uncovering neocultural domination. In the past, cultural domination was the result of European expansion which enforced westernization and christianization. More recently, westernization has taken the form of the imposition of a technocratic and consumerist mentality that reduces all of reality to objects of use and exploitation. The meaning of human life is evaluated in terms of achievement in a competitive system in which the others are seen as enemies. Human life also becomes alienated from nature and from more poetic and contemplative forms of knowledge and self-expression.

(24) Thus the struggle against cultural imperialism is an intrinsic aspect of all liberation struggles. Asian, Africans, and the indigenous peoples of Latin America and elsewhere seek to recover values in their traditional religions and cultures denigrated by christianization and westernization. Feminists seek an alternative culture to those values defined by a masculine definition of normative humanity. Both of these struggles—to recover indigenous cultures and to create new ones—converge on a number of common themes. Both stress a need to place life and the cherishing of life at the center of human society. Ultimately the cultural aspect of liberation theology is a struggle for values that enhance rather than truncate human life. Christianity itself is renewed in the process, as it is rescued from its imprisonment in

death-producing forms of domination and restored as a message of liberation.

Oppression of Women

(25) Sexism, understood as the distinct structure of marginalization of women within the system of domination, became one of the major issues of the conference. It was clear from the start of the discussion that there was not a single view of sexism or a unified position against its detrimental effects on women and on society as a whole. Among the women themselves, those from the Third World were not always comfortable with First World feminists' definition of the issues and strategies for change. When sexism was discussed in small all-male and all-female groups, the reaction from the male groups ranged from dismissal of the issue as totally irrelevant, to a genuine self-examination of their own role in perpetuating a patriarchal system.

(26) The discussion on sexism, at times difficult and threatening, also proved to be enlightening and inspiring. Several important clarifications were made:

a. Sexism is not only a women's issue; it is a men's issue as well. It affects both women and men, for it concerns the basic fabric of human relationships in society. It forces both women and men to operate in narrow spheres, preventing them from using their full potential in the struggle to transform persons and structures. The patriarchal structures that reinforce sexism assert themselves over women and men alike and must be changed by both. Patriarchy is not only an economic and political reality but also a cultural one which has been imbedded in the psyches of all human beings.

(27) *b.* Sexism is found in all the traditional patriarchal cultures throughout the world which deny women their human and civil rights and divest them of power and influence. The oppression of women is a stark reality in the Third World where many cultures are strongly patriarchal. But to what extent this is an issue for Third World women is to be determined by the Third World women themselves. Neither Third World men nor First World women can determine the Third World women's agenda. Third World women maintain that sexism must not be addressed in isolation, but within the context of the total struggle for liberation in their countries. However, it must be addressed.

(28) *c.* In liberal capitalism, in Western Europe and North America, and increasingly in the Third World, there has been a relaxation of the restrictions against women from the point of view of civil rights. But industrialization and modernization have created new structures of oppression for women. They are expected to do the same work as a man, but they are still obliged to carry out the tasks of domestic service within the home. In the Third World, this double burden of women is further aggravated by the dehumanizing working conditions, the meager pay, and the threat of sexual exploitation in the work place.

(29) *d.* Feminism in the First World has often not taken seriously racism,

class exploitation, and imperialism, which it must do if it is to respond adequately to women's oppression in the Third World as well as in the First, where most women are not middle-class and many are not white. However, the contribution of First World feminism cannot be underestimated. Feminist analysis has contributed to the analysis of other forms of oppression through raising the question of power in a way it has not been raised before, thus exposing the dynamics which allow patriarchal structures to continue. Feminist theology has brought a heightened awareness of the need for a different and critical exegesis of scriptures and a new sensitivity to symbols, rituals, and community.

(30) *e.* Progressive men in both the First and Third Worlds have not taken sexism seriously. They may be progressive in their socio-political options but remain sexist in their attitudes and practices. They continue to regard women as inferior and incompetent. For example, in international conferences where women's participation is required, women are often invited because they are women and not because they are equally competent participants. Since men have had all the privileges, they are not eager to see change in this area.

(31) *f.* Unfortunately, the dependency and domination of women has been legitimated by Christian theology and expressed institutionally in the Christian churches through the denial of ministry to women and of their participation in the formation and teaching of theology. Any theology that claims to be liberational has a particular responsibility to rectify this sanctification of sexism by the churches.

Theological Analysis

(32) Our understanding of the global system of domination will not be complete without a specfically theological analysis. The capitalist system is using religious language and symbols to legitimize its policies to keep "peace," "order," and "democrary" according to its own terms. The system demands such a commitment and loyalty to the values it promotes that it is tantamount to worship. Its call for peace and security can be understood ultimately only in terms of idolatry, or allegiance to false gods. The idols have familiar names—"consumerism," "the free market," "national security." They promise wealth, power, security, freedom, peace, and fulfillment, and so they tempt multitudes. But they are recognized by their fruits; they lead only to death.

(33) Conflicts between oppressors and their victims have become spiritual battles. But without theological analysis, even religious persons fail to recognize that at the heart of the profound social conflicts which divide our world, there is a battle of the gods. The complexity of the conflicts makes it difficult to discern false gods which uphold the global system of domination from the true God who takes the side of the poor and oppressed (Ps. 69:32–33; 72:12–14, 82:1–4, 140:12–13).

Some religious movements that have arisen in recent years are at times actually promoting false gods. The widespread use of development strategies that have brought about greater starvation and poverty, militarism, the use of torture and covert action are manifestations of unswerving allegiance to idols.

(34) The present economic system, like an immense idol, the beast of the Apocalypse (Rev. 13), covers the earth with its cloak of unemployment and homelessness, hunger and nakedness, desolation and death. It destroys other ways of life and styles of work, which counter its own. It breeds pollution and hostility to nature. It imposes an alien culture on peoples it has conquered. In its infinite greed for wealth, it sacrifices persons, mostly of the Third World but also increasingly of the First, as a bloody holocaust to itself. The beast has become a raging monster armed to the teeth with tanks and cannons, nuclear bombs, warships with computerized missiles, radar systems, and satellites, bringing humanity to the brink of total and instantaneous death.

(35) But in the stuggles of the poor and the oppressed throughout the world against all forms of dehumanization, there is a sign of life and victory. There is faith and confidence in the God of life, in the Lamb who builds up, in the midst of this divided world, a new Jerusalem which comes down from heaven (Rev. 21:10), who gives hope of liberation from the domination of sin and death.

TOWARD A REFORMULATION OF THEOLOGY

Methods and Themes

(36) The need to develop a theological method has emerged as an important item on the EATWOT agenda. How do we develop a theology of the poor and oppressed that is different from a theology of the rich? Because EATWOT does not have a fully developed method for doing theology, our exchange with First World theologians has helped us to clarify our own direction, while First World theologians have been enabled to relook at their own emerging methodologies. In many instances we found ourselves in agreement on tentative principles involved in the new way that we are trying to do theology.

(37) In identifying the principles of a different theological method, it was commonly accepted that commitment is the first act and theology is the second. "By their fruits you shall know them" (Matt. 7:20). And so it is with us today. The doing of theology should arise out of a prior commitment in behalf of the victims of oppression struggling for their freedom. This understanding of methodology is determined by the revelation through the prophets and in Jesus Christ, recorded by biblical authors, of God's presence in the historical struggles of poor and oppressed peoples today. The criticism that liberation theologies have reduced theology to ideology is misplaced, because it camouflages the human character of all theology and the ideological option that critics have made for the rich and powerful. No theology can

be neutral. The enormity of the suffering of oppressed peoples demands that the theologian make an option for their liberation and against the unjust structures that keep them shackled. The option for the poor and oppressed is God's option, and thus it must be ours as well.

(38) Because commitment is the first act, theology is inseparably connected with the Christian community out of which it emerges and to which it is accountable. Theology partakes of the rhythm of action, contemplation, worship, and analysis that marks the life of the people of God. Thus the fundamental subject of theology is the Christian community in its witnessing to the restless presence of God in the history and culture of the oppressed. In this basic sense, all Christians are theologians. The rationale, the logic, the truth of theology is that which persons are actually living out in their everyday lives. "Love one another as I have loved you," Jesus said (John 13:34).

Integral human development, in its fullness, dignity, mutuality, and sensitive balance with the earth, constitutes the radical imperative of authentic theology rooted in the good news, the gospel. Our theologies, therefore, must flow out of the ecclesial life of Christian communities which attempt to give witness to a new way of life.

(42) No theological method is adequate apart from a critical analysis of all the major structures of oppression. How can theology participate in liberating the poor from poverty if it does not know its causes? Therefore comprehensive analysis becomes indispensable in the renewal of theology, an analysis which links the economic, political, social, cultural, and religious dimensions of our realities, which helps us to understand better our particular contexts, and which urges us to struggle more effectively for an alternative future.

(43) The practice of liberation is a basic element in the life of Christians: without it, no renewed theology can be born. There were different perceptions of liberating praxis in the conference, both among Third World and First World participants. Among those from the First World, many had difficulty in determining the real nature of social conflicts and human alienation behind the apparent success of scientific and technological rationality of social organization. An additional difficulty for some is their unawareness of how they benefit from the goods produced in the Third World and their indirect compliance with the unjust order. The educational background and concomitant advantages enjoyed by Third World participants sometimes blur their action for social transformation, and give rise at times to their being identified with the ruling elite rather than with the struggling masses of their own countries.

(44) Even though the reformulation of theological themes was a major goal of the conference, we were unable to accomplish this task in a systematic way. A new theological methodology and the liberation of the theologian and of theology must lead to the reformulation of traditional themes. This is not only a question of change of language, but of a new interpretation which comes from personal and social commitment to the practice of liberation.

Integral liberation from all structured oppression leads to a different way of thinking about God, Jesus, and the kingdom. This kingdom was inaugurated through the selfless life, the struggle against inhuman powers, and the death and resurrection of Jesus (Matt. 4:23; Rom. 1:4–5; Col. 1:13; 1 Pet. 1:3–5).

(45) A theology which emerges from the peoples' struggles rejects an abstract conceptualization of God made outside the historical practice of liberation. The discovery of the true God of Jesus Christ demands the destruction of the oppressions which are the material bases of idolatry. The question about God in the world of the oppressed is not knowing whether God exists or not, but knowing on which side God is. By idolatry is meant the deification of the ideologies used to sacralize the structures of oppression, culturally and sociologically, and to make them appear to reflect the will of God (Isa. 44:9, 17–20; Hab. 2:18; 1 Cor. 8:4–6).

(46) The perennial question of all theology about the presence and will of God in the world today has no easy answer. In Geneva the participants reaffirmed that the faith experience of the poor and oppressed involved in struggles for full humanity are a manifestation of the spirit of love and life. They manifest the continuing presence of the God who was revealed among the Israelite slaves in Egypt (Exod. 3:6–8), among the prophets when Israel abandoned the path of righteousness (Isa. 3:13–15, 44:22; Jer. 31:10–11; Mic. 7:18–19; Zech. 3:4) and in Jesus, who came to set captives free (Luke 4:18).

(47) We are witnessing in our time the same choice which confronted biblical peoples between allegiance to false gods and fidelity to the true God (Exod. 32:1–10; Ps. 78:52–64; Ezek. 6:3–7). In contrast to the gods of the global system, the true God is not revealed among those on the throne of power and affluence, but among the least valued according to the reigning canons of respectability—the victims, the voiceless, the powerless, those on the underside of history (Matt. 25).

(48) In the emerging theologies there is also a new understanding of christology. This new christology has recovered the practice of the historical Jesus as the model for discipleship in Christian life (Luke 14:27; John 12:26; Col. 2:6–7). This recovery has come through much suffering and pain. The present oppression and violent destruction of human life has forced Christians to reread the meaning of the cross and the death of Jesus. But it is not done without hope, because the cross leads to the resurrection. The resurrection of Jesus is reinterpreted as the definite transcendence of death, the beginning of a new humanity for men and women, the making of a new society, the "new heaven and new earth" (Rev. 21:1). And this reinterpretation becomes the foundation of the subversive hope and joy of the poor.

(49) The process of reinterpretation cannot be done without considering how the Bible has been read and used. In both the First World and the Third World, the Bible has been utilized as an instrument of oppression. Men in society and in the churches have justified the discrimination and marginalization of women through their patriarchal reading of the Bible (1 Cor.

14:34–35), while the whites in South Africa defend apartheid through a distortion of selective verses of the Bible (Gen. 9:25). In the United States, neoconservatives and fundamentalists point to the Bible as their inspiration for their campaigns against women's rights and against the political activities of progressive Christians.

(50) In emerging theologies there is a renewed way of reading the Bible, which consists in a dialectical interaction between current reality and the biblical story. The reality of oppression and the struggle for liberation call for a new interpretation of the Bible at the same time that the Bible helps in the understanding of reality in a deeper way. In the First World, especially in Europe, there have been efforts to reread the scriptures from the existential point of view, and recently, the materialist reading of the scripture has helped many Christians to understand the economic conditions which produced the Bible and to read it from the perspective of class struggle. In the U.S.A., feminist and black theologians converge in their criticism of the prevailing interpretation of the Bible. Feminists criticize the patriarchal character, while blacks focus on its racist nature. They diverge, however, in the interpretation of particular texts. The blacks turn to the exodus story as the paradigm for their own liberation; on the other hand, women have exposed and condemned the many exemplifications of patriarchy in biblical tradition.

(51) It has become clear in recent years that there are other sources of inspiration and revelation besides the Judeo-Christian scriptures. The other great religious traditions are also sources of revelation. Thus dialogue with other religious traditions is a necessity if theology is to be relevant for our times. This dialogue with the adherents of other faiths will help us to relativize our own traditions and will lead to a deepening of our Christian faith. For example, Hinduism and other traditions offer a holistic vision of life without dichotomies between the secular and the sacred, the spirit and the body, humanity and nature, society and the cosmos. It is precisely this kind of holistic perspective that will help to deepen one's faith in the midst of divisions and conflicts, and in articulating a vision of a different, gentler, and more peaceful future. It is true, however, that all religious traditions have been distorted to serve domination and oppression. So there can be no question of uncritical dialogue.

(52) Many of the participants reported the resurgence of new expressions of spirituality as a reaction to the spirituality developed in the capitalist world, and in response to the demands of the times. Spirituality developed under capitalism promotes aggressive individualism, acquisitiveness, hostility to the earth, ruthless competition, hierarchic discipline, and elitism. The emerging spirituality rooted in the person of Jesus celebrates the values of integral human development, openness to human needs, social responsibility toward the earth and its resources, harmonious cooperation, coordinated participation, and asceticism.

(53) In many countries in the Third World, Christians are facing persecu-

tion, torture, and death. They are being called to imitate Jesus literally (Mark 8:34-36, 13:9-13; John 15:18-20, 16:2). This is the context of a new spirituality which has sustained persons in their trials and sufferings and in the face of martyrdom. In First World countries Christians experience other contradictions in their quest for fidelity and discipleship. They refuse to be part of the consumer society and find ways of silence, worship, and community. Others resist the capitalist system and look to the Bible as the defense of the poor, and fight against the "principalities and powers" in their private and public life. In different ways, many witness to Christian faith in the triumph of life over death, and participate in the reign of God which will come to its fullness at the end of time (Rev. 21:22-27, 22:3-5).

Reviewing European Theology

(54) The conference took the time to look at the broad outlines of the development of European theology. The conference planners felt this was a necessary step in the process of reformulating theological method and traditional themes. We were reminded that for the past 150 years, European theology has in fact been a response of European elites to the challenges of the Enlightenment to Christian faith and to the subsequent cultural, religious, political, and economic developments in the emergence of capitalism that profoundly changed the role of the church and its place in society. Our brief study of this response, both from the Protestant and Catholic perspectives, pointed to the coming end of Eurocentric Christianity and the beginning of the influence of Third World Christian communities and theologies in both church and society.

(55) First World participants themselves recognized that most theology in the First World has not been sensitive to the suffering of oppressed peoples in the Third World. In fact, it has been used as a weapon against them, as, for instance, when it ignored slavery and legitimated colonialism. But neither has it been sensitive to the plight of the poor and working classes in the First World, to the internal colonization of blacks, native peoples, and immigrants, and to whites in depressed regions, nor to blatant situations of oppression, for example, in Northern Ireland. The theologies arising from these situations of pain and oppression are being ignored by many of the most influential theologians of Europe and North America.

(56) Recently, European theologians seeking genuine renewal are reacting against their own traditional theology. The irruption of the poor and oppressed everywhere and the impact of emerging Third World theologies have helped them in their effort to reformulate theology in their own contexts. But at the conference the First World theologians involved in this task did not come with a single voice, but spoke out of their different concrete contexts of oppression and struggle, while seeking to be in solidarity with the suffering peoples of the Third World. Feminist theology, theology of resistance, European theology of liberation, theology of conversion, theology of crisis, politi-

cal theology, and radical evangelical theology are some of the efforts expressing the fresh air of repentance and renewal in the First World. Proponents of these theologies want to be in dialogue with those doing theology in the Third World. This dialogue among First and Third World theologians was only initiated in Geneva, but it represents the presence of the Spirit of God in our divided world and the reason for hope for the future.

CONCLUSION

(57) We end our reflection on our dialogue with a sincere and humble expression of gratitude to God for this singular experience and with deep appreciation to all those who by their support and collaboration have made our coming together possible. In the end, it is not important whether the outside world considers this event a failure or a success. Although we did not say anything new, we learned to listen and to speak carefully and truthfully. Even if our differences and misunderstandings were not all resolved, our commitment to poor and oppressed peoples in search of freedom and justice has been reinforced, and we leave Geneva with new allies in the struggle.

(58) We are grateful not only for our conversations together but also for the deep spiritual experience that we shared. Our prayer and liturgies were life-giving and meaningful. We were especially moved by the final liturgy presided over by women, which gave us a foretaste of the new church where men and women are equal according to God's plan and where power and authority are at the service of the people.

(59) We are aware of the incomplete and all too fragmented nature of our meeting but the stories we exchanged will remain in our memories and on our tongues, reminding us of the lived experience of suffering and grace that brought us together in the first place. We look forward to future opportunities to continue what we began in Geneva. For many of us, our first dialogue between First and Third World theologians was a ray of hope in a dark and divided world.

PART VIII

ASSESSMENTS

24

Tissa Balasuriya

A Third World Perspective

From August 1976 (EATWOT, Dar es Salaam, Tanzania) to January 1983 (Geneva) is a short period of time, but a long distance in the evolution of Christian theology from the perspective of the peoples of the Third World. The twenty-two theologians who met in Dar es Salaam from the three southern continents hardly knew each other. They were unsure of the outcome of their meeting. It might have been just one more international conference—without issue. To be more free to be themselves the organizers had excluded theologians from Europe and white North America, for these even when benevolent tended to be stiflingly paternalistic. The Third World Christian thinkers had to discover themselves, discern their identities and commonalities, their differences and aspirations for the future.

In Dar es Salaam their togetherness was seen as primarily due to a common historical experience of Euro-North American oppression. The differences in accent in the evaluation of race, class, culture, and religion were strong and seemed even incompatible. The understanding of sexism was much less articulate. All were agreed that the dominant Euro-American theology was not only defective but also positively harmful to Third World peoples. A new theological thinking was essential. How was it to emerge? We were not sure of our role and path in this as a tricontinental ecumenical group. We sensed the inadequacies of the past and the needs of the future.

By the end of that week in August 1976 the participants had enough of a sense of togetherness to form themselves into an association, EATWOT. They planned continental sessions. These were held in Accra, Ghana, in December 1977, Colombo, Sri Lanka, in January 1979, and São Paulo, Brazil, in October 1980. A few from each continent met at these sessions and a larger

197

number assembled in New Delhi in August 1981. These sessions helped
EATWOT members to come to know each other and appreciate the differences in accents. It was altogether a long learning process, helped also by
the conference publications and critical evaluation by others.

When we met in Geneva in 1983 the Third World group had converged to
the extent of being sensitive to each others' positions. The differences of
background were always there, but the tricontinental dialogue had had its
impact. The feminist movement too had brought its challenges and contribution. James Cone noted all this at Geneva when he said that the Third World
theologians' movement had been vital for his theologizing. The black
theology born of his North American base had evolved to include an understanding of world capitalism in which the whole of North America was deeply
involved.

The thinking of EATWOT became more holistic in trying to appreciate the
intuitions of different races, sexes, cultures, religious backgrounds, and ideological positions. The forms of oppression were manifold; liberation struggles had to follow suit. The Third World was at the receiving end of most of
the oppression, whereas Europe and North America were its principal benefi-
ciaries. Dialogue included mutual questioning and self-criticism, which took
time to sink in and bear fruit in subsequent sessions.

The aim of EATWOT has been to influence all the major churches of the
world. It could therefore not exclude a dialogue or confrontation with traditional theological positions, especially those of Europe and North America.
By 1981 its members had enough confidence in their positions to propose a
dialogue between First and Third World theologians. They were no longer on
the defensive. In a sense they had a message to take to the other churches and
peoples of the world. They were looking for interlocutors and partners in a
common search.

The first to respond to this invitation were the Euro-American support
groups that had sustained EATWOT financially and morally from the first
stages of the enterprise. At Geneva these groups could share in the dialogue as
equals, not as patrons. They had performed a real function of mission in
helping to engender more authentic thought from among the churches. This
is a lesson for all of us on the dynamics of dialogue between oppressor and
oppressed.

METHOD OF THEOLOGY

One of the key perspectives of EATWOT is that serious commitment to
liberation from oppression is the first act of Christian faith. The life of Jesus
bears witness to this. Theology has to flow as a faith reflection from such
commitment to love of neighbor. This means that experience of the life of
faith in the difficult circumstances of our unjust world is an essential factor in
theologizing. The inductive method is therefore indispensable for theology.

This has to include social analysis and action for love and justice in a given conjuncture of events. Such an approach differed from the traditional theology that accentuated deduction from first principles known from scripture or an accepted philosophy.

EATWOT also proposed that the *subject*, the doer, of theology is primarily the whole Christian people living a genuine faith experience. This was different from the traditional view that professors and "professional" theologians were the main subject of theology. EATWOT argued that popular action for liberation, not the academic university or segregated seminary, is the primary place (locus) of theology.

The *object* of theology is not only sacred scripture but also the human reality through which God speaks and challenges us to build a new humanity in love and justice. This is the kingdom of God that is prior to the churches.

The Third World theologians expected a tough debate on these approaches from First World theologians. But those who came to Geneva from Europe and North America were generally in agreement with these perceptions. They had themselves moved in that direction due to their own experience. The absence of hard-core traditional theologians who dominate church thinking was a cause of some disappointment, for it diluted the debate. But the presence of committed partners was a source of encouragement to furthering the dialogue.

The Geneva consultation thus helped considerably to strengthen the convictions of the Third World theologians. Hard discussion and debate with traditional theologians of all the continents remains a matter of the future. The impact of the renewal of theology in Europe and North America and the very process of preparation for the Geneva dialogue helped to bring about this linkage. This preparation had been done through national and regional consultations. Some theologians from the Third World were also invited to them. I had the valuable experience of participating actively in such preparatory sessions in Britain and Ireland and other similar sessions in Australia and Sweden.

The Euro-American theologians were endeavoring to meet the problems that the less favored groups faced in their countries. The participation of Third World theologians as principal speakers meant that an active dialogue preceded the Geneva conference. This was a reversal of the usual direction of the flow of ideas among Christians—from the North to the South. The Euro-American theologians were reflecting from their own experience of the struggles for justice and peace due to problems within their countries and were also trying to relate to the problems in other countries. They were becoming aware that the roots of Third World problems lay partly in exploitation by First World groups. The Third World itself was presenting both the challenge the perspectives for a reorientation of Christianity in the Euro-American continents.

One of the principal accomplishments at Geneva was this realization by the participants that now there are persons and groups in almost all the churches of the First and Third World countries that are endeavoring to theologize in and through a commitment to love and justice. They are also almost everywhere marginal to the mainstream of the life of their churches. But they are not so isolated from the struggles of the majority of oppressed humanity. The women's movement brought a further universal dimension to understanding oppression and liberation. The remembrance of the martyrs of the contemporary church—Archbishop Oscar Romero of El Salvador and the many Christians killed or imprisoned because of their stand for justice in so many countries of the world[1]—added a sense of tragic realism to the intense optimism for the future.

The storytelling with which the Geneva conference began brought us evidence of much dedication from the four corners of the world. It helped build confidence among participants across the barriers of race, sex, and Christian denominations. When the stories of various forms of oppression and struggles for liberation were shared, it was realized that a unidimensional analysis would be inadequate. Social analysis was seen as essential, but also as requiring the complementarity of other approaches, relating to culture, religion, sex, and history. It was realized that different analytical approaches must be respected, given different experiences and epistemologies. This helped in the acceptance of a broader framework for the analysis of diverse situations and issues.

The global nature of the consultation made us realize the value of contextualizing our theological work so that it may be born from the lived experience of a people. At the same time it showed the inadequacy of any particular context for understanding the total human reality of our world. It helped us to see that each struggle for liberation has its own inner dynamic and justification. Struggles for racial and class equality, for women's rights, for peace and the environment—all have to be appreciated and respected for their own authentic nature and validity. They are correlated movements with independent centers. This is a valuable lesson that international meetings of groups engaged in different struggles can help to broadcast. At Geneva the lesson came strong and clear and had to be learned for the conference to be able to bear its fruits.

Different liberation struggles may at first seem counterproductive. It is necessary that they be in solidarity. This has a deep theological significance bearing on the need for localizing a particular group reflection *and* placing it within a global perspective. These are two essential dimensions of liberation theology. It is an approach in contrast to the former tendency of Eurocentric churches to universalize the theologies that arose from their particular contexts.

This realization of the diversity of forms of oppression and struggles for liberation will have an important consequence for the future evolution and understanding of theologies of liberation. The Latin American expression is one such articulation that has its value in its accent on social analysis relating to capitalist domination. It has much to learn concerning racist, sexist, and religious domination even in that continent. Other continents and groups have been developing their own theologies from their own backgrounds. A common element is the understanding of the Christian calling as one to full humanity freed from oppression. According to the type of oppression experienced, there are different struggles and accents in the search for liberation.

The Geneva conference showed that such searches have been taking place in all the continents of the world during the past decade. Many Christians all over the world have been going through a process of conversion or reconversion to understand their faith and call to holiness in their own context.

The irreducibility of all types of domination and struggle to one, such as that of class, also indicates a need to reexamine Marxism as to its tools of social analysis and its strategies of revolutionary praxis. The role of Marxism in the liberation process in the Third World was seen as significant in the recent experience of all three continents. But the inadequacies of the historical experience of socialist regimes has called for a critical approach to Marxism and historical socialism.

The contribution of the feminist movement was crucial in opening the First World to a realization of oppression within it and by it, and in making Third World males aware of their role as oppressors. The ambiguities faced by white women and Third World men as both oppressed and oppressor revealed the interlocking nature of dominating relationships and liberation struggles. Older white males and young Third World females seemed to be at the opposite poles of oppression/liberation in the contemporary world. International capitalism makes this situation worse when transnational corporations turn to young women of the Third World for various forms of the exploitation of class, race, culture, and sex.

One of the perceptions that emerged from the Geneva dialogue was the need to develop a new *internationalism* among Christians in and through their different local struggles, converging toward the building of a new humanity in the coming decades. This is a meaning of the catholicity of the church that can transcend the frontiers of denominationalism and the entrenchment of church organizations. It has to be a convergence of popular movements understood and supported by theological reflection. It can reduce the contradictions among different struggling groups and increase their reciprocity.

Ecumenism and internationalism—*eikoumene* and *oikoumene*—can be linked in the cause of integral human liberation. Otherwise there will be a balkanization of liberation movements, of benefit to oppressors who unite more readily for power and profit.

CONTENT OF THEOLOGY

In 1976 the EATWOT challenge to the traditional theology of the mainstream North Atlantic churches came mainly in relation to the history of

Western colonialism and the modern neocolonial capitalist exploitation of the poor. Since 1976 the Third World theologians' movement has grown in its understanding of cultural, religious, and sexual oppression. At Geneva this current was further deepened by the presence of representatives of the feminist movement from both First and Third World countries and the Euro-North American perspectives on liberation in their countries in response to militarism, unemployment, devastation of the environment, and the nuclear threat.

The convergence of critiques of established church policies, theologies, and spirituality has led to a search in which the reference to the religions and cultural traditions of Asia and Africa and the radical feminist critique of patriarchy were seen as essential dimensions of a broader approach to understanding oppression, liberation, and the work of God in the histories of the peoples of the world. In its momentum this is leading to perhaps the most radical questioning that Christian theology has ever experienced. The formulation of these issues found only brief expression at Geneva; their full articulation and impact will be experienced during the coming decades.

This questioning concerns not only the method and subject of theology but its very substance and content. Some of the issues raised are:

1) Can the concept of God that has been used by Christians for two thousand years to support the patriarchal exploitation of women, and for centuries to bolster white racism and capitalism, be truly of divine origin? Is such an understanding of God credible?

2) Can the self-understanding of churches that legitimized sexist, racist, classist, and religious oppression be theologically true? Do women need a male-dominated church for their sanctification and salvation? Do blacks need a white church? Does the proletariat need a bourgeois church? Do believers in other religions need the Christian churches to know God?

3) What, then, is salvation? What is mission? What is liberation? When do sacraments confer grace? When do they legitimize, at least implicitly, the different forms of oppression supported by white male-dominated churches and most Third World churches?

4) What is to be thought of the Bible and its interpretation when it has been so long utilized to justify dominative sexism, racism, classism, and myopic Christian chauvinism? Is scripture normative of faith? Who can interpret it correctly and how?

5) How are we to appreciate the historical Jesus whose life and message are being rediscovered in our times principally due to the reflections of those who suffer under oppression legitimized by churches?

6) How is Christ—the recapitulation of all persons and things—to be thought of in relation to the suppression of women, the poor, oppressed ethnic groupings, despised cultures, and marginalized religions? How can such a Christ—the life of the world—be the motivation of a church in relation to dictatorships, militarism, and nuclear armaments?

These are no longer questions of mere interchurch ecumenism or interreligious dialogue. They touch the very core of accepted beliefs within Christian churches. The future development of theology, encouraged by such encounters as the EATWOT conferences, will profoundly challenge the Christian churches to a much deeper and more transforming conversion than what Vatican II or WCC plenary assemblies have hitherto countenanced. These issues were brewing in different contextual theologies. At Geneva they converged like streams from different directions to form the headwaters of a mighty river that will eventually flow into the territories of the mainline churches.

The Geneva conference has the significance of giving a more global content and meaning to the questionings and new approaches that had begun among Third and First World theologians concerned with the struggles for human liberation. It became evident this thrust has now acquired a nearly universal relevance, though beginning from different backgrounds.

These Third World approaches have become challenging and creative points of theology in the First World also. Dorothee Sölle expressed this at the Geneva conference when she said that "the hope of European Christianity lies outside itself." This is true to some extent of all Christianity. Insofar as the gospel is a message of liberation and justice, it is those who suffer who can best manifest its radical demands. Most of those who suffer in the world are outside the churches, and particularly outside the dominant church establishments.

It is understandable that a particular conference as such cannot realize but a limited goal. International conferences are particularly hampered by their cultural plurality. And one week is hardly adequate for more than an exchange of views and a decision on the agenda for future work and cooperation. The whole atmosphere of such a conference does not permit deep, new theological elaborations, but it can ignite processes of reflection that will bear fruit over the years. In that sense Geneva marks a new stage in the intercontinental ecumenical dialogue begun in 1976 at Dar es Salaam.

We may say that with the Geneva conference the groping Third World theologians' search has entered a mainstream of theological discussion in the churches, especially around the World Council of Churches. Third World theologians contributed much to the many preparatory sessions prior to the WCC general assembly of Vancouver in July 1983. In fact theologians from the Third World have had important responsibilities in the WCC—for example, Dr. Philip Potter, its secretary general, who in his inaugural address graciously acknowledged:

Certainly we in the WCC have been greatly enriched by the work of EATWOT as we have endeavored to carry out our ecumenical mandate and as we prepare for the sixth WCC assembly in July 1983.

The WCC has fostered Third World theological thinking as far back as 1968 when it invited theologians from Latin America, Asia, and Africa to a session on theology and development. Many department heads of WCC have been from the Third World and have shared readily with EATWOT in our common concerns.

The Catholic Church is slower to accept initiatives from the base through its central Roman agencies. Here the influence of EATWOT is and will be felt more through local impact, especially at the level of lay movements, and religious congregations and groups of priests. It is the radicalization of local situations as in South Korea and the Philippines that induce large sections of a church to accept and live by the general orientations supported by a group such as EATWOT. Yet all over the Catholic world there are small but significant groups at all levels of the church seeking new theological approaches similar to what we have been discussing at Geneva. A slow germinating process is taking place. Should the church one day convoke another assembly like the Second Vatican Council, these groups will undoubtedly surface from the bosom of the local churches and represent another major wave in church renewal. Meanwhile steady step-by-step advance will have to continue.

The Geneva conference gave us an indication of the enormous challenges theology will meet in the coming decade in seeking to be the voice of the oppressed and to build a new world out of the present disorder and threat of universal destruction. From contextual theologies to an understanding of the operative world system in a pluricultural background is a task big enough for any one generation. To convert Christians and churches from being legitimizers of manifold exploitation to subverters of oppression and champions of liberation is a historic task that no generation of Christians has faced since the early centuries of the church. The Geneva conference moved in the direction of such a bold apostolic and spiritual venture.

During the coming years we should elaborate more clearly the evolution of theology that the Geneva dialogue stressed. The works of individual theologians, the publications in reviews, the influence on church agencies such as the conferences of bishops in Asia, Africa, and Latin America can further this process. If the African suggestion for an African ecumenical council is realized, there will doubtless be an enormous push in the evolution of relevant theology. The main impulse toward the actualization of these perspectives, however, will come from the Christian participation in popular movements for personal and societal liberation. As in the first centuries, the blood of martyrs will water the seedbed of Christian renewal.

The churches, especially the Catholic Church, are becoming increasingly a Third World body—not only in numbers of believers, but also in active participation in church life, and especially in martyrdom for justice and love, as in so many countries of Latin America, Asia, and Africa. These new insights of theology will be ultimately vindicated by the spirituality of self-sacrifice unto death for the cause of one's neighbor. It is such identification with Jesus who gave his life for others that will set the stamp of authenticity on these theologies of integral human liberation.

NOTE

1. See Martin Lange and Reinhold Iblacker, eds., *Witnesses of Hope: The Persecution of Christians in Latin America* (Maryknoll, N.Y.: Orbis, 1981).

25

Letty M. Russell

A First World Perspective

The most exciting thing about the Geneva dialogue between First and Third World theologians was the sense of shared participation in a common task. Coming after five international meetings attended only by members of the Ecumenical Association of Third World Theologians from Africa, Asia, and Latin America, the meeting could have been more of a confrontation than a dialogue. Yet the white participants from the First World of Europe, Canada, and the United States, and the participants from Third World countries and U.S. racial minorities were committed to action in behalf of the poor and oppressed, and to developing theologies from that perspective.

This was very exciting for the First World participants, in spite of the pain, frustration, and confusion that was bound to be part of such an international meeting. I know that many of them, like myself, work all the time in contexts where our interest in liberation theologies is barely tolerated. Even national and international theological and church meetings usually bring together only a handful of those committed to developing new styles of liberation theology. Although I am a frequent participant in such events, this is the first time I have felt the excitement of knowing that all around me there were persons engaged in the same sort of projects, sharing the same questions, and working to develop theologies of liberation in their own contexts.

As a white, middle-class woman from the United States, I could hardly expect to be welcomed with open arms by my sisters and brothers who struggle daily to overcome the results of U.S. economic and military exploitation, as well as the First World domination of church life and theological reflection. Yet that was not the beginning point of the dialogue. Those of us from the First World were guests of the Third World theologians. They set the agenda and decided how it would be carried out and interpreted. We were

206

included, not on our own terms, but on the terms of those who were willing to let us share in their work.

Perhaps I can communicate a little of this excitement of shared participation by pointing out ways the dialogue multiplied the energy and insight I can give to research already underway in my own First World context in the areas of liberation methodologies, sexism as systemic sin, and theology for oppressors.

LIBERATION METHODOLOGIES

The preparation, program, and follow-through of the Geneva dialogue was itself an exercise in orthopraxis. The planners and participants tried to *do* what they *teach*. Our First World preparation for the conference was rooted in our struggles against oppression in our own contexts, and the dialogue partners were drawn from faith communities of action for social change as well as academic settings.

Preparation for the EATWOT Dialogue

In each of the First World areas represented, groups were invited by EATWOT to develop their own process of preparation and selection. Linking the preparation to ongoing networks was important so that feedback from the conference could enrich the ongoing work for change in behalf of the oppressed. In the United States the link was made to Theology in the Americas and to its steering committee. With their approval, delegates were chosen from the various projects of Theology in the Americas (TIA) that include white women and men. There were representatives from the Labor and Religion Project and the Theologians' Task Force, as well as the Women's Project. TIA sponsored the U.S. preparatory conference: "Stories of Liberation," held in New York City December 17–18, 1982. This smaller meeting followed the methodology of the Geneva dialogue, beginning with case studies of struggles for liberation and proceeding to social and theological analysis and theological reformulation.[1]

A second link was made to the Working Group on Liberation Theology of the American Academy of Religion. This small group of professional theologians meets once a year for discussion and shares papers between meetings. It is currently involved in a three-year program on liberation and feminist hermeneutics. Both these U.S.-based groups will continue to provide a base for input from delegates and networking for those who wish to continue the dialogue between First and Third World theologies. It was noted in Geneva that the dialogue had *just begun*. The purpose of exploring how concrete struggles against all forms of oppression are interrelated, and studying the emergent theological methods and reformulations is something that needs continuing attention.

Participants in the Dialogue

A surprise of the Geneva dialogue was the makeup of the group gathered from the First World, representing a wide range of grassroots communities of struggle. Some participants had thought that the dialogue would be between First World theologians with their stress on questions of the *nonbeliever,* and Third World theologians with their stress on questions of the *nonperson.*[2] There was some feeling that the EATWOT theologians had developed their theologies and were now ready to meet with representatives of the white theological establishment. But the First World groups had been asked to send women and men who were rooted in the struggles for liberation. The participants included practitioners of social change through work in labor unions, feminist groups, rural poverty, and peace movements, as well as professional theologians involved in struggles for liberation. Dialogue developed around the common commitment to struggle against oppression as it is lived out in First and Third World contexts.

The tension that arose over the use of theological language was an important gift to the conference, for it prompted the professional theologians to examine their own use of language and to struggle against academic elitism. The First World delegations were able to include persons working at the base because they already knew at least one of the colonial languages used for interpretation at such meetings. But those participants brought a new ingredient to the dialogue: the search for common methods and language between professional theologians and the grassroots participants from the First World. The pain of the white, working persons at being left out of the theological discussion moved the participants to recognize the crucial importance of the liberation of theological method so that it is capable of communication through story, liturgy, and art forms that transcend class barriers. As we have often experienced in the development of feminist theology, the tools of research and reflection are an important gift for theological reformulation, but they are no longer the only gift when theology grows out of the life of communities of struggle.

SEXISM AS SYSTEMIC SIN

The basis of commonality among Third World participants was the same as that between First and Third World participants: commitment to do theology with and for the poor and oppressed. This common starting point made it appropriate that the groups should join EATWOT in what James Cone described as its exciting task of creating a Third World theology of liberation they could all support. The formulation of this task raises at least two questions for me as a First World feminist theologian. The first is the question of how much the participation and the concerns of women as the "marginated of the marginated" is included in this project of developing Third World theology of liberation. The second is how we support this autonomous effort of Third World theologies by developing a theology of liberation for oppressors in the First World context.

The Sin of Sexism

An important breakthrough in Geneva was the recognition that the sin of sexism is a universal system of marginalization of women that imposes further oppression on those already oppressed by poverty, race, and class in both First and Third Worlds. As Rosemary Ruether put it, there is gender oppression within the global context of oppression. In spite of personal reluctance and fear, the participants as a whole recognized that it is impossible to do adequate social or theological analysis without including sexism as part of the interlocking web of oppression and death that dominates our divided world.

After New Delhi, Mercy Amba Oduyoye called the process of feminine conscientization an "irruption within the irruption" of the voiceless majority of the world population. She called for the integration of the "study and exposure of sexism as a factor of oppression" into the work of EATWOT.[3]

At the Geneva meeting Third World women represented many different views on feminism, but they were united in the conviction that their struggle for a voice should be encouraged by EATWOT through support of dialogue among Third World women theologians. As Sun Ai Park put it, neither Third World men nor First World women are able to decide whether sexism is a Third World issue. Those suffering from this double oppression are the ones who must do their own analysis and reflection, and the women at EATWOT were prepared to work on that project in their own contexts.

First World Feminists

The role of First World women and men who were feminists was a difficult one. They were well aware that contextual theology would require advocacy of feminine equality and that the analysis of sexism would have to proceed as part of political, economic, social, and ecclesial analysis in each culture and situation. And they were painfully aware that feminism has emerged most strongly in a situation of Western white imperialism and reflects that oppressive context. Yet the professional feminist theologians from the First World can provide resources and tools for research that are lacking to women in the Third World because sexist structures have denied them access to professional theological education in the universities of both the First and Third Worlds. If women in the Third World are to do their own theology, they need equal access to the tools of theology and equal right to decide how to respond to the issues of sexism.

As a feminist theologian I was excited about two aspects of the Geneva discussion. One was the way that feminist critical analysis in the U.S.A. crossed over geographical boundaries at various points where it paralleled the agendas of different Third World theologies. For instance, the growing emphasis on cultural analysis and the use of Asian religious traditions is paralleled by much of the work that feminists are doing in the study of non-Christian religions. The concern voiced about the rejection of the Bible by Africans who see it used as an instrument of oppression is very much parallel to the concern of feminist hermeneutics in struggling with biblical texts that reflect patriarchal culture and provide divine reinforcement of sexist oppression in church and society.

The second area of particular interest for me was that the most fully developed theology of liberation in the First World appeared to be feminist theology. If one wants to speak of white liberation theology, there seems to be no other well developed network of scholars doing independent research out of a community of solidarity with the oppressed. For this reason there needs to be a great deal more attention paid to the methods, questions, and research that are being developed. The growing convergence in the recognition of the interlocking web of oppressions calls for convergence in dialogue about the responses.

THEOLOGY FOR OPPRESSORS

James Cone's statement about the EATWOT task of creating a Third World theology of liberation raises the question of how we develop a theology of liberation in a First World context that has the same common ground of doing theology in solidarity with persons struggling for liberation from different forms of oppression. To put it more sharply, Cone said liberation theologies are called by the names of those whom they advocate. What would we call white, affluent, male liberation theology?

Theology among the Fleshpots

Dorothee Sölle described this theology as a theology of resistance to the existing world disorder, built out of resistance groups within the "belly of the beast" working against apartheid and militarism for peace built on justice. It would seem that such theology is one of resistance, relinquishment, and betrayal of the economic and political system from which we benefit as members of the First World. I usually call this form of liberation theology *theology for oppressors,* meaning that it advocates the liberation of oppressors from being oppressors.[4] What we already have in establishment theology is "theology *of* oppressors," but we also have a marginal group of white men and women whose work is based in communities of struggle, represented by some of those who attended the EATWOT meeting. These persons work to communicate the good news for oppressor groups that there is still time in God's patience for us to share both the groaning and the glorious liberty of creation (Rom. 8:21). God's mercy is our opportunity for imaginative and constructive repentance.

The interesting thing about these theologians of the First World is that they can share the same method, beginning with stories of struggle, but what makes them liberation theologies is the *point of pain*. Theology becomes liberation theology when those engaged in the theology discover their own marginalization or cross as a result of their commitment to the cause of the oppressed. At this point of pain they begin to be able to theologize *in* solidarity *with* others who suffer.

The Common Task

The dialogue of the meeting focused around the common task of doing our theology at the point of pain that sets in when one acts on a commitment to solidarity. Each theology began at the point of greatest oppression and pain in that setting to search for concrete social, political, and spiritual liberation. Each was in need of comprehensive social analysis of the particular contradictions of that situation, as well as the links to wider social, economic, and political realities. Each was also in need of theological analysis that looked for the contradictions of theology and the structures of historical reality. And each had to struggle with commitment to a historical project for change in the light of a vision of justice and mended creation.

Such a method is possible in the First World context of affluence, but its corrective would require continuing linkage with those who are victims of the system in order to remain self-critical. It is possible to develop a common methodology and a common vision of God's liberating intention for all humanity and creation. But it is very costly to forge the one key link in the freedom chain: commitment to share the pain of action against the death-dealing powers of the "beast." It is that link that was being tested in Geneva, and will be tested over and over, if solidarity of First and Third World theologians and theologies is to become a reality.

NOTES

1. "The Stories of Liberation Conference," *TIA Newsletter,* 7:4 (Dec. 1982) 12–15.

2. Gustavo Gutiérrez, "Reflections from a Latin American Perspective," in Virginia Fabella and Sergio Torres, eds., *Irruption of the Third World* (Maryknoll, N.Y.: Orbis, 1983), pp. 227–28.

3. Amba Oduyoye, "Reflections from a Third World Woman's Perspective: Women's Experience and Liberation Theologies," ibid., p. 249.

4. Letty M. Russell, "Pedagogy for Oppressors," *Growth in Partnership* (Philadelphia: Westminster, 1981), pp. 110–34.

26

Ion Bria

An East European, Orthodox Perspective

I attended the EATWOT conference in Geneva as a representative of Orthodox theology and I shall make several specific remarks from the perspective of this particular tradition and experience. I immediately recognized that I felt a methodological difficulty in entering into the flow of the debate as such, which had various difficult moments. I cannot, therefore, claim to express a definitive evaluation. I was, however, impressed by the courage of the consultation in trying to articulate a new theology for and with those social categories that historically were neglected by the institutional church due to political factors. In the past, theology did not associate with "Samaritans." A new domain is open for theological reflection; it is not to be reduced simply to social analysis.

I hope that I understood the consultation to say that there is a need for a solid *theology* for those Christians who are involved in political ethics. Need for theology goes together with the need for social commitment and solidarity: both are rooted in the one evangelical faith.

A MISSING DIMENSION

In the Orthodox tradition *theologia* has several meanings, and I do not intend to mention all of them here. There are at least three *interrelated* major experiences in doing theology: the personal discipline of prayer, the ecclesial experience, and presence in the world through witness and commitment. It seems to me that the contemplative element—personal reception of the word of God through prayer—does not play an essential role in the theological method of Third World scholars. Of course my criticism is subject to correction; I know about this methodology in a very fragmentary way.

In my tradition personal dialogue with the living word of God is conceived

212

as a source of theology. Theology does not address itself to an abstract, deductive confrontation between the eternal power of salvation in Jesus Christ and a specific human context in order to determine the style of Christian life and the form of the church in a given moment. Theology presupposes an intense spiritual colloquium with the living God, a deep penetration into the mystery of communion with God through personal prayer and contemplation. The secret and public prayer of Jesus Christ, his intimate conversation with his eternal Father, were essential moments in his life. In his prayer he discovered the mystery of salvation through the cross. He became the obedient servant and he went to the cross in the context of prayer and intercession.

Prayer is for theologians a moment of profound repentance, silence before the mystery of the word of God. The spirit of prayer implants true freedom and dynamism into the mind and heart of theologians in order to receive the revelation of the Spirit. Theologians need a profound experience of intense conversation with the living God as the Lord of Life. I understood very well the irritation at any dogmatic theology that simply justifies the doctrinal decisions of an ecclesiastical magisterium. But I think that the prayerful attitude of the theologian in receiving the word of truth is fundamental in this respect.

Theology and Ideology

The use of ideological categories common to the secular interpretations of society is a critical element in the theological method of Third World scholars. The use of ideology in theology is itself a delicate issue. It is true that the traditional theology is helpless in this area. In speaking, for instance, about solidarity with the poor and oppressed today, Third World theology was obliged to adopt secular ideological vocabulary because there is no appropriate Christian terminology. Theology must keep the upper hand in respect to ideology, not only because there is a destructive element in all ideologies, which can only be rejected, but also because the church has to be free from any ideological oppression. Political and ideological freedom is absolutely necessary for a theology in view of a Christian critique of society. Theology has to be on its guard to see whether an ideology is demanding support for a particular social class, for instance.

This conceptual caution does not imply agreement with the negative attitude of fundamentalist and pietistic opponent groups, who are against solidarity with the poor and oppressed. Concern for political life as a Christian responsibility is a valid one. One cannot eliminate this dimension of the gospel just because of the ideological terminology used to express it. Social justice is not merely a secular concern but a biblical concern.

Plurality of Theologies

Another difficult area is the relationship between the plurality of theologies and the unity of Christian faith. In its content it is a common received faith. I fully agree with the insistence to respect cultural particularities in preaching the gospel and to acknowledge the plurality of struggles in different situations. The universal church is no longer a European church of the Holy Roman Empire.

But theology deals not only with the context and situations in which Christians—historically receivers and witnesses of the good news—are living. Theology should mediate the faith as a *common tradition* of the revelation of God in history. The concern for the unity of faith is not simply related to the preservation of an external universality. It springs out of an ecclesial reception of the normative tradition, which constitutes the common ground of an apostolic church. Theology has to respect this ecclesial possession of a common faith.

A Missing Partner

Could the experience of the churches living in socialist countries be meaningful for Third World theologians? In spite of the absence of Second World theologians, which was deliberately decided upon, I ask this question because these churches have a substantial contribution to bring to a Christian theology of liberation. Unfortunately, east Europe theologians are unprepared to offer a valuable working synthesis of their understanding of liberation. They cannot, therefore, immediately become partners in such a dialogue. It is a great pity not to have this experience, which might sharpen the Christian vision of social life.

SOCIAL ANALYSIS

Social analysis is a theological task not only because the *world* is present in the New Testament situation, both as place of incarnation and grace of God, and as a reality to be judged, but also because the poor and oppressed are subjects of the kingdom of God. A theological reflection and a Christian critique of socialism is, for example, not simply an intellectual exercise, but a way to struggle against new forms of poverty and oppression.

In the history of the church there is a rich tradition of social struggle, which has been forgotten or neglected. Different social movements of Christian inspiration have tried to infuse gospel values into the ethos of society. The popular character of the church in Orthodox history was preserved by a transfer of values to the social context. But it was limited to so-called social ethics. The problem now is to enable persons to express their convictions and to determine themselves what kind of a church is a popular church, and to be able to function in freedom.

It should be recognized that the theology of today has to work on a new cultural material, radically different from Christian culture. Hence the serious cultural challenge to theological articulation, catechetical instruction, and missionary proclamation. There is a methodological need to enter into a real dialogue with the new culture.

Third World theologians have to be aware of the most significant criticisms offered to their theology. At a time when European theologians are manifesting various hesitations about their theological methodology, Third World theologians have to be assured that social issues are values open for all and are not marginal in the search for unity and solidarity among all Christians.

Contributors

Appiah-Kubi, Kofi: project research director, Centre for Applied Religion and Education, Ibadan, Nigeria.

Arbour, Frances: director, Inter-Church Committee on Human Rights in Latin America, Toronto, Ontario, Canada.

Balasuriya, Tissa: director, Centre for Society and Religion, Colombo, Sri Lanka.

Blezer van de Walle, Wil: feminist theologian and pastor in the Valkenswaard deanery, Holland.

Bria, Ion: Secretary for Orthodox Studies and Relations, World Council of Churches, Geneva, Switzerland.

Carvalho, Emílio J.M. de: Methodist bishop, Luanda, Angola, and president of EATWOT.

Casalis, Georges: theologian, now retired in Noyon, France.

Cone, James H.: Charles A. Briggs Professor of Systematic Theology, Union Theological Seminary, New York City.

Fabella, Virginia: Maryknoll sister from the Philippines, currently executive secretary of EATWOT.

Fischer, Nicole: conference interpreter and president of the Ecumenical Forum of European Christian Women.

Frostin, Per: assistant professor and a member of Christians for Socialism.

Goba, Bonganjalo: minister of the United Congregational Church of Southern Africa and lecturer of systematic theology at the University of South Africa, Pretoria.

Metz, Johann Baptist: professor of theology at the University of Münster, West Germany.

Mveng, Engelbert: Jesuit priest and executive secretary of the Ecumenical Association of African Theologians.

Oduyoye, Mercy Amba: lecturer at the University of Ibadan, Nigeria.

Park, Sun Ai: minister of the Disciples of Christ, editor of *Korea Scope,* and researcher in Asian women's theology.

Potter, Philip: former secretary general of the World Council of Churches, Geneva, Switzerland.

Prange, Don: community educator/developer working in Appalachia with the Church of the People, Nora, Virginia.

Rayan, Samuel: Jesuit priest and professor of theology at the Vidyajyoti Institute of Religious Studies, Delhi, India.

Ruether, Rosemary Radford: Georgia Harkness Professor of Theology, Garrett Evangelical Theological Seminary, Evanston, Illinois, and Northwestern University Joint Graduate Program.

Richard, Pablo: Chilean theologian and professor on the staff of the Departmento Ecuménico de Investigaciones, San José, Costa Rica.

Russell, Letty M.: associate professor of theology, Yale University Divinity School, New Haven, Connecticut.

Santa Ana, Julio de: director, Centro Ecuménico de Serviços à Evangelização e Educação Popular, São Paulo, Brazil.

Sölle, Dorothee: writer and professor at Union Theological Seminary, New York City.

Tamez, Elsa: professor of Old Testament at the Seminario Bíblico Latinoamericano, San José, Costa Rica.

Torres, Sergio: Chilean priest and pastor and vice-president of EATWOT.

Wallis, Jim: editor of *Sojourners* and pastor, Sojourners community, Washington, D.C.

Wickremesinghe, Lakshman: Anglican bishop of Kurunegala, Sri Lanka, died October 23, 1983.

Other Orbis Titles . . .

WE DRINK FROM OUR OWN WELLS
The Spiritual Journey of a People
by Gustavo Gutiérrez
Preface by Henri Nouwen

"The publication of this book is an extremely significant event in the development of liberation theology. It is the fulfillment of a promise that was implicit in Gutiérrez's *A Theology of Liberation* which appeared in 1971 and soon became the charter for many Latin American theologians and pastoral workers. Gutiérrez realized from the beginning that a theology which is not coming forth from an authentic encounter with the Lord can never be fruitful. It took more than ten years before he had the occasion to fully develop this spirituality, but it was worth waiting for." *Henri J. M. Nouwen*

"Gutiérrez has introduced a new spirituality, viz., the spirituality of solidarity with the poor." *Edward Schillebeeckx*

ISBN 0-88344-707-X   *176pp. Paper $7.95*

THE POWER OF THE POOR IN HISTORY
by Gustavo Gutiérrez

"The essence of Gutiérrez's theology of liberation is evangelical militant compassion, a truly theological project based on the very core of the Gospel. He is the first person in modern history to re-actualize the great Christian themes of theology, starting from a fundamental option for the poor. . . . He conceptualizes not only the pastoral and institutional aspects of Christian ecclesial life but also its dogmatic and ethical aspects, in a way long-forgotten in Europe." *Edward Schillebeeckx*

ISBN 0-88344-388-0   *256pp. Paper $10.95*

CORRECT IDEAS DON'T FALL FROM THE SKIES
Elements for an Inductive Theology
by Georges Casalis

This is an introduction to theological method in which Casalis advocates a militant theology rooted in a commitment to social justice. Says Casalis, "A long time ago I admitted that it is not possible for me to distance myself from politics. Like any other discipline, theology cannot be neutral; the more it claims to be, the less it actually is. In this work I have chosen to be partisan and to say so frankly at the start. The only objectivity to which I lay claim is the objectivity of being committed, of being militant. The ideas that theology conveys do not, contrary to its claims, 'fall from the skies,' but come from a partial and partisan reading of biblical and traditional texts with an eye to promoting the interests of the entities to which the theology gives practical service." Georges Casalis is a French Protestant theologian widely known for his advocacy of "the wretched of the earth."

ISBN 0-88344-023-7   *240pp. Paper $8.95*

COMPASSIONATE AND FREE
An Asian Woman's Theology
by Marianne Katoppo
Illustrations by Vincent Liyanage

"This is a most compelling book. Marianne Katoppo, a prize-winning novelist, theologian, and journalist, speaks at times angrily and personally. She explains why Asian Christian women seek the right to be different, to be 'the other' rather than being satisfied to accept identities from other cultures and from men. Katoppo writes from her own Indonesian perspective." *Mission Focus*

"This is a short, easily readable, and important book. It is valuable from the point of view of what the Asian churches can hope for in the future from women in terms of their theological contributions." *International Bulletin of Missionary Research*
ISBN 0-88344-085-7   *96pp. Paper $4.95*

THE IDOLS OF DEATH AND THE GOD OF LIFE
A Theology
by Pablo Richard et al.

"There is a seismic shift taking place in the foundations of theology, and its epicenter is Latin America. . . . Even where their way is not our way, we need to listen to what they have learned. These essays make an excellent listening-post." *Walter Wink*

Authors: Richard, Croatto, Pixley, Sobrino, Araya, Casañas, Limón, Betto, Hinke-lammert, and Assmann.
ISBN 0-88344-048-2   *256pp. Paper $12.95*

PLANETARY THEOLOGY
by Tissa Balasuriya

Written by one of Asia's foremost Christian theologians, this book takes in the whole world. Says Balasuriya, "Many of the concerns that preoccupied Western theologians over the centuries were irrelevant to Third World peoples or even detrimental. Reflection on the Asian context seems especially recommendable in the search for a global theology inasmuch as Asia's population is more than half of the world population. By extension, the whole planet Earth, as an entirety, must also be seen as a context for theology."
ISBN 0-88344-400-3   *288pp. Paper $10.95*

RELIGION AND SOCIAL CONFLICTS
by Otto Maduro

"A provocative and insightful sociological analysis of religion that provides a theoretical and practical base for the struggle for social justice. The four-part book reads like a manifesto, concisely and lucidly presented. His explicit emphasis on sociology of religion and class struggle sets this book rather apart in the growing body of Latin American political theology. The four-page bibliography offers a selective but useful collection of works on these issues." *Choice*
ISBN 0-88344-428-3   *192pp. Paper $8.95*